AMERICA'S FAVORITE MOVIES

RUDY BEHLMER

With photographs

AMERICA'S FAVORITE MOVIES

BEHIND THE SCENES

FREDERICK UNGAR
PUBLISHING CO.
New York

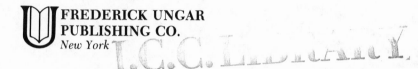

Copyright © 1982 by Rudy Behlmer
Printed in the United States of America
Designed by Irving Perkins

Library of Congress Cataloging in Publication Data

Behlmer, Rudy.
    America's favorite movies.

    Bibliography: p.
    Includes index.
    1. Moving-pictures—United States—History.
I. Title.
        PN1993.5.U6B36   791.43'0973   81-70117
        ISBN 0-8044-2036-X   AACR2
        ISBN 0-8044-6034-5 (pbk.)

*For Joanne
and
for Curt*

UNGAR FILM LIBRARY

STANLEY HOCHMAN, General Editor

OTHER FILM BOOKS

CONTENTS

ACKNOWLEDGMENTS

In addition to the people involved directly with the films discussed in this book, who are listed in the bibliography, the following individuals and organizations were extremely helpful and cooperative in various ways and over several years helped to make this project possible. My thanks and appreciation to all of them.

Academy of Motion Pictures Arts and Sciences Library, Forrest J. Ackerman, Leith Adams, The American Film Institute, Jerry Bernstein, Eddie Brandt's Saturday Matinee, Vera Culwell, Collectors Bookstore, Edward S. Comstock, Pat Corletto, Mary Corliss, Robert Cornfield, Mrs. Merian C. Cooper, James Curtis, Susan Dalton, Joanne D'Antonio, Directors Guild of America, Walt Disney Archives, George Eastman House, Larry Edmunds Bookstore, Selise Eiseman, Maxine Fleckner, George Geltzer, Joy Genese, Sam Gill, Robert Gitt, Vernon Harbin, Ronald Haver, Mike Hawks, Charles Higham, Gladys Hill, Joel Hochberg, Stanley Hochman, Sally Hope, Rick Jewell, Mary Julian, Ken Kenyon, Richard M. Kerns, Paula Klaw, Robert Knutson, George Korngold, Elaine Krause, Miles Kreuger, Max Lamb, Bill La Vallee, Janet Lorenz, Betty Ludden, Audree Malkin, Clifford McCarty, Kenneth N. McClure, Roy Moseley, Movie Star News, John Munro-Hall, Frank Murphy, Museum of Modern Art, Gunnard Nelson, Herbert S. Nusbaum, Ben Presser, James Powers, Gerald Pratley, George Pratt, Phil Raskin, Lee Reem, Dave Riback, Edana Romney, William H. Rosar, Ellis St. Joseph, Anne G. Schlosser, David Shepard, Paula Sigman, James Silke, David R. Smith, Elaine Steinbeck, John Stephens, Carl Stucke, Gay Studlar, Tom

Tarr, the Theatre Collection at the Lincoln Center Library for the Performing Arts, Tony Thomas, Mel Tormé, UCLA Film Archives, UCLA Theatre Arts Library, USC Special Collections, Berni Valentine, John Veitch, Eldridge Walker, Alan D. Williams, Wisconsin Center for Film and Theater Research, Jack Yaeger, and Joanne Yeck.

ILLUSTRATION CREDITS

Academy of Motion Picture Arts and Sciences

Forrest J. Ackerman

The American Film Institute

Eddie Brandt's Saturday Matinee

Collectors Bookstore

Walt Disney Archives

George Eastman House

Larry Edmunds Bookstore

Mary Julian

Movie Star News

Museum of Modern Art/Film Stills Archive

Gunnard Nelson

James Silke

Theater Collection at the Lincoln Center Library for the Performing Arts

Twentieth Century-Fox

UCLA Theater Arts Library

USC Special Collections

Wisconsin Center for Film and Theater Research

THE STORY BEHIND THE BOOK
AN INTRODUCTION

For this book on the making of fifteen favorite movies from the so-called golden age, primary source materials from the studios' files and archives have been of particular importance in the approach to the jigsaw puzzles of creation and execution that form the story behind the story.

The purpose behind this work is to reveal the creative process of the collaborative methods of film making during the period of the Hollywood studio system in the 1930s, 1940s, and early 1950s. I consulted early story outlines, studio correspondence, the various drafts of the scripts, story conference transcripts, production reports, memos, editing notes, music files, and any and all papers written at the time or shortly after the productions were in the works. In many cases, these primary sources had not been available previously, so they vastly enrich and give fresh insight into the behind-the-scenes evolution of particular films.

A considerable number of interviews and correspondence with key people involved in the making of these movies and the works upon which they were based also took place. Oral histories and transcripts of seminars along with some quotes from previously published books, articles, and interviews augmented my other work. These were invaluable, since in some cases the subject had died in the interim. Counter interviews were mandatory, and during these the reliability of each source was checked.

"Ten best," or "twenty best," compilations of anything are always difficult. Everyone has his or her favorites, and most certainly various popular subjects are conspicuous by their absence here. The selections in this book are not necessarily "the best," either based on pronouncements made by a supreme arbiter of excellence or by my own reckoning, but they are some of the audience's most cherished American sound feature films released between late 1931 and 1952. These are popular and perennial selections—not necessarily historically significant films, critics' choices, or milestones of the art—although many of them happen to be all of those things. And most importantly, these pictures, being outstanding examples of the Hollywood studio system of the time, are still viewed constantly. Their charm does not fade; if anything, their appeal takes on added dimensions. They are box-office successes and the highest rated nonnetwork movies on TV, and they represent the most common inclusions in a variety of popularity polls conducted by various organizations and the media during the past decade.

Foreign films and silent classics were eliminated from consideration here because they are generally not as available and therefore are not seen and appreciated by as many people. The year 1952 was chosen as the cutoff point for this survey because it more or less marked the end of the golden age. The list ends as the studio system was undergoing a major upheaval and just before the advent of Cinerama, CinemaScope, the package deals, European coproductions, Eastmancolor, and the emergence of the contemporary film, for better or worse. Therefore, the rationale for the absence of the relatively recent blockbusters ranging from, say, *The Bridge on the River Kwai* and *The Sound of Music* to *The Godfather*, *Jaws*, and *Star Wars*, to name a few, is that their appeal is not based on a reasonable perspective or the particular and special association that the popular and continued favorites from the 1930s, 1940s, and early 1950s enjoy.

But where are *Gone with the Wind*, *The Wizard of Oz*, and *King Kong*? They have been dealt with extensively in books devoted entirely to the making of each of these extremely popular films. There is little, if anything, I could add to the wealth of material already published on those subjects. But that still leaves such glaring omissions as *Citizen Kane* (which still warrants a definitive book of its own), Hitchcock, Chaplin, Lubitsch, Astaire and Rogers, the Marx Brothers, and a representative Thalberg, Goldwyn, or Paramount film, to name but a few others. The amount and kind of accessible materials from the studios regarding the making of a subject naturally influenced my final selection of titles. And some marvelous films do not have particularly interesting stories behind their making, at least based on what and who is still available.

Each studio's vaults have preserved different kinds of materials: for example, at Twentieth Century-Fox, Darryl F. Zanuck's insightful story conference transcripts are still intact, along with correspondence pertaining to the story purchases and the various drafts of the scripts. These proved fascinating in tracing the evolution of *The Grapes of Wrath* (1940), *Laura* (1944), and *All About Eve* (1950) for this volume.

On the other hand, the profuse Warner Bros. files, now divided between the Warner Bros. Archives at the University of Southern California, the Wisconsin Center for Film and Theater Research (the pre-1950 Warner films are owned by United Artists and are a part of that collection), and Princeton University, do not include formal story conference notes, but there are, in addition to the various drafts of the screenplays, detailed memos to writers, directors and story editors—particularly during the Hal Wallis and Jerry Wald years—that deal with the development of scripts and the production of the films. This was a major asset with regard to the four Warner films in this study—*The Adventures of Robin Hood* (1938), *The Maltese Falcon* (1941), *Casablanca* (1943), and *A Streetcar Named Desire* (1951).

The Walt Disney studio in Burbank is the only company still in regular production that has an official general archive (rather than legal files or story files) with full-time archivists on the premises. Disney's story conference notes (and other creative meetings) on *Snow White and the Seven Dwarfs* (1937) were recorded and transcribed as verbatim dialogue, excerpts from which are included in this volume.

RKO Radio Pictures, no longer active in production but still alive as a company, has preserved screenplay drafts, legal files, and a general cross-section of correspondence from various departments that was gathered together by a long-time RKO employee, Vernon Harbin, during the exodus from its Hollywood studios in 1957, when RKO ceased making movies. Since then the files have been maintained in the RKO office and warehouse in Los Angeles, where I unearthed considerable background data on *Gunga Din* (1939), including the unused William Faulkner adaptations, story outlines, and sequence outlines. I found additional material in the George Stevens collection at the library of the Academy of Motion Picture Arts and Sciences.

MGM has extensive legal and script files on the premises of its Culver City studio, but the production and story correspondence files from the golden age were thrown out many years ago. In the case of *Singin' in the Rain* (1952), there were enough fragments of correspondence and all of the drafts of the screenplay, together with material found in the MGM, Arthur Freed, and Roger Edens collections at USC, to provide details of the film's evolution.

The Wisconsin Center for Film and Theater Research at the University of Wisconsin-Madison houses the invaluable pre-1951 corporate records of United Artists, who were primarily distributors, but production information pertaining to specific films is for the most part not included. These files belonged to the company's independent producers, who would come and go, taking their correspondence with them. The three films included in this text that originally were released by United Artists, *Stagecoach* (1939), *The African Queen* (1951), and *High Noon* (1952), had different independent producers. There are no complete production and script files per se available on any of these pictures—just stray papers. This meant relying to a greater degree on other sources in these cases.

With regard to *High Noon*, Carl Foreman kept his initial outline and the lengthy first-draft outlines, which he graciously allowed me to study. The final script has been published. By speaking at length (and separately) with the producer, the writer, the director, the editor, the cameraman, some of the cast, and the orchestrators (after reading various quotations from the composer, Dimitri Tiomkin), I could piece together a reasonably accurate account of the development of *High Noon*.

An early draft of *The African Queen* screenplay by John Collier and some memos relating to it were in the Warner archives at USC. There are also pertinent materials relating to Collier's adaptation of Forester's novel in the Twentieth Century-Fox story files, since after Warners decided to drop the project (for Bette Davis), it was submitted to Fox (for Rex Harrison, who at the time was under contract).

Columbia Pictures' script files yielded, among other things, the scenes that comprised the original two reels of *Lost Horizon* (1937). These had been destroyed after an early sneak preview proved to be disastrous. Neither Frank Capra nor anyone else associated with the film has referred to the form and content of these scenes. (None of the major players of the final movie, other than Ronald Colman, was involved.) Indeed, Capra told me that the experience was so traumatic that he didn't remember anything about them! The various drafts of the script also revealed the extraordinary number of added or altered scenes that were done while filming was in progress, in addition to some retakes (particularly those involving the high lama). Finally, for comparison purposes, there were the picture and dialogue continuities for the altered and shortened reissue of 1942 retitled *Lost Horizon of Shangri-La*.

Universal's central files contain all of the various drafts of *Frankenstein* (1931) on microfilm, including the not previously available John L. Balderston adaptation of Peggy Webling's play. It was thus possible to trace which of the several writers credited on the screen contributed what specific material in the development of the screenplay. But the original Peggy Webling play, never produced in the United States, proved to be exceptionally elusive. In studying references to that 1927 dramatization in previous texts dealing with *Frankenstein,* it appeared that none of the researchers actually had seen or read the play. Finally I discovered that the only known copy was included in the Lord Chamberlain's collection of licensed plays housed in the British Library on Great Russell Street in London. Since nothing of this kind circulates, and photocopying of the manuscript is forbidden because of copyright restrictions, the play had to be read and notes made on the premises. Other primary-source material was found in the Universal Collection at USC.

Although not directly related to any of the fifteen films in this book, the David O. Selznick files on which I had based a previous book—*Memo from David O. Selznick* (1972)—again proved to be of aid in peripheral ways, such as information about the participation of Ingrid Bergman, under contract to Selznick, in Warners' *Casablanca*, and about the early phases of *Stagecoach*. The extensive Selznick papers have recently been moved to the University of Texas at Austin.

Although a great deal has been written about *Casablanca*, a careful study of the materials at both the Wisconsin Center for Film and Theater Research and the Warner Bros. archives at USC yielded a massive amount of primary-source material not previously available, including the original unproduced play, *Everybody Comes to Rick's*, upon which the film was based.

It is, of course, dangerous to rely on any single approach to motion picture history. I tried to check a number of possibilities other than studio archives and interviews: trade papers of the time, newspapers, additional files, books—including those primarily self-serving autobiographies that are filled with very selective memories. The Academy of Motion Picture Arts and Sciences Library in Beverly Hills has files on films and personalities, in addition to extensive back issues of industry publications and a vast number of volumes on aspects of film, all of which were invaluable. But a wary eye is necessary. Motion picture lore is riddled with hyperbole, half-truths, and the kind of nonsense that publicity mills of the old days ground out on a steady basis. Because Hollywood was a dream factory, material for the media was packaged in dreams. Then other writers, feeding on each other's works, perpetuated the myths and apocryphal accounts.

Oral histories, such as those conducted through the auspices of the American Film Institute, the Directors Guild of America, the University of Southern California, and the University of California at Los Angeles, augmented my own interviews and correspondence. Some subjects being interviewed often emphasize and romanticize their contribution to a particular film without realizing they are doing so, or understandably exhibit faulty recall with regard to names, dates, and details of long ago. In the case of conflicting versions of what happened, I have used the version that appears to be accurate after examining the possibilities and the nature of the sources. In some cases, the reader is presented with options. To be sure, the only way to relate a 100 percent accurate account of anything is to have been an impartial, detached observer to all the events during the entire evolutionary period of a project. This would have to include having the unique ability to enter people's minds and know what they were really thinking when they said or wrote something.

Viewing again (and again) the films themselves was a relatively simple matter. In the Los Angeles area there are many revival houses, and these, the County Art Museum, and the various universities, colleges, and film societies (in addition to TV) periodically schedule all of the films. Also, various 16mm rental organizations handle the titles (to say nothing of the rapidly emerging videocassette and videodisc outlets). But tracking down and viewing earlier and later versions of the subjects, influential films in the same genre, and other related material was not always so easy. Relatively obscure films were screened at the Wisconsin Center, George Eastman House, Museum of Modern Art, and the impressively expanding UCLA Film Archives, where there is lodged approximately forty minutes of assembled footage from *Lost Horizon* (minus sound track), which includes alternate camera coverage, outtakes, and temporary miniatures, conceivably made up for a proposed promotional film while the picture was still in production.

As always, some private collections yield unusual gems. During a trip I made to Chico, California, where many of the Sherwood Forest scenes in *The Adventures of Robin Hood* were filmed, I met a gentleman who had photographed extensive 16mm color and black-and-white footage of the filming of several scenes while the company was on location for many weeks in the fall of 1937. These shots are an invaluable record of the *modus operandi*, techniques, equipment, and filmmaking ambience of the times, to say nothing of the opportunity to observe the director, cameraman, crew, and performers at work and behind the scenes.

The mechanics of film making at the Hollywood studios during the golden age were not dramatically different from those of the present. But the studio systems then had little in common with now. The majority of the executives, directors, writers, technicians, crew, cast, and musicians were under contract to the studio or full-time employees. Films were regarded as product, and major companies each produced approximately fifty or more feature films a year in order to supply their wholly owned (for the most part) theaters with a first-run attraction every week or two in the key cities, including B movies, during part of the 1930s and 1940s. Today in theatrical film production, few producers, writers, directors, or actors are under contract; many films are brought to the studio as a package from the outside. Studios provide some capital, facilities, and perhaps are involved in the release of approximately fifteen pictures a year. As a result of government antitrust proceedings, companies in the early 1950s had to break up their producing, distributing, and exhibiting strangleholds, thereby obviating the studios' need to supply their theaters with continual changeover in product. This, coupled with the dramatic post–World War II drop in movie attendance (a result of modifications in America's recreational needs and the rise of television viewing), drastically altered the studio systems. Fox's Zanuck, Warner Bros.', Jack L. Warner, the MGM staff producers such as Arthur Freed and Pandro S. Berman, who, in a more or less autonomous manner, made the story and production decisions in the previous era, became increasingly less powerful.

In the following chapters, often in their own words written or spoken at the time, it is possible to see how these people, their staffs, and each studio's variation of the system functioned. We can be privy to the genesis of a famous film, the differences between the novel, play, or short story and the script, who almost was cast in the primary roles, where the film was photographed, the trials and tribulations during production, the clash of temperaments, the last-minute juggling of footage in the editing room, the approach to the music, and some of those desperate dilemmas after the preview.

Though not all of the information included in these pages is being presented for the first time, it should be emphasized that in this study there is less reliance on that which has been available and more on previously unused primary source materials, all of which provide us with an insight into the Hollywood that produced this eclectic group of favorites reflecting the then-current themes, myths, formulas, and other surefire ingredients of which most commercial films were composed. Here are movies based on fairy tales (*Snow White,*), legends (*Robin Hood*), romantic melodramas (*Casablanca*), urbane comedy-dramas (*All About Eve*), the glory of the British Empire (*Gunga Din*), American social dramas (*The Grapes of Wrath*), African romantic-comedy-adventure (*The African Queen*), Utopian romantic adventure (*Lost Horizon*), musical comedy (*Singin' in the Rain*), Westerns (*Stagecoach* and *High Noon*), tales of the macabre (*Frankenstein*), illusion and reality (*A Streetcar Named Desire*), hard-boiled private eyes (*The Maltese Falcon*), and soft-boiled detectives (*Laura*). Perhaps these older films preserve a naive and idealistic outlook, but the cream of the pictures continue to enthrall, engross, and otherwise enchant, regardless of one's age or frame of reference.

Rudy Behlmer

IN HIS OWN IMAGE:
FRANKENSTEIN
(1931)

It all began on a stormy June night in 1816 with a nineteen-year-old woman who was lying half awake in a Swiss villa on the shores of Lake Leman. Mary Wollstonecraft Godwin was staying there with her lover—later her husband—the poet Shelley. Together with their neighbor, Lord Byron, his physician, Dr. Polidori, and Mary's step-sister, Claire, they would often gather on those chilly, wet evenings and read ghost stories aloud.

One evening Byron suggested they each try their hand at writing a story of the supernatural. On another night Mary had listened to an intense conversation between Shelley and Byron concerning "the nature of the principle of life" and whether it might ever be "discovered and communicated." According to Mary, the talk went on to include speculation that "perhaps a corpse would be reanimated . . . perhaps the component parts of a creature might be manufactured, brought together, and embued with vital warmth."

After going to bed, she later wrote:

> I did not sleep, nor could I be said to think . . . . I saw—with shut eyes, but acute mental vision—I saw the pale student of unhallowed arts kneeling beside the thing he had put together.

1

> I saw the hideous phantasm of a man stretched out, and then,
> on the working of some powerful engine, show signs of life,
> and stir with an uneasy, half vital motion . . . . His success
> would terrify the artist; he would rush away from his odious
> handiwork, horror-stricken . . . I could not so easily get rid
> of my hideous phantom; still it haunted me . . . . On the
> morrow I announced that I had thought of a story.

Shelley encouraged her to develop and expand the material. He also helped
her to edit the manuscript as it evolved. Twenty-one months later, in March
1818, *Frankenstein, or the Modern Prometheus** was published. In 1831,
Mary Shelley revised her novel for a new edition; she also added an
introduction, which tells the story of its origin and ends with Mary bidding
her "hideous progeny go forth and prosper." And indeed it did. *Frankenstein*
is one of the most often reprinted novels in the history of literature.

The adaptability of the story to the theater was recognized immediately.
In 1823 alone there were at least five stage versions, both serious and comic.
One, *Presumption; or the Fate of Frankenstein* (1823), by Richard Peake,
was to serve as a basic transcription of the novel for the stage and a source
for further elaboration. Action and melodrama were the keynotes of Peake's
play, and Frankenstein, the creator, and his creature were presented as
instant antagonists. There is a major creation sequence (not in the novel),
an assistant to Frankenstein named Fritz (not in the novel), and a nontalking
monster. (In the book, Frankenstein's creature eventually becomes verbose,
with an impressive vocabulary and masterful syntax. His monologues run
on for pages and, on occasion, entire chapters.)

Other stage adaptations followed through the nineteenth century and into
the twentieth. English theatrical producer and actor Hamilton Deane in
1927 decided to try out another subject for his company to alternate with
his version of Bram Stoker's novel *Dracula* on his tour of the English
provinces. This was to be a new adaptation of *Frankenstein* by Peggy
Webling, who was a member of Deane's troupe. The initial presentation of
this *Frankenstein* took place late in 1927 in Preston, England. It continued
to alternate in the provinces with *Dracula*, and it finally opened in London,
considerably revised, in February 1930.

Peggy Webling retained certain basic ideas from the novel and previous
plays, but she made substantial changes in time, locale, incidents, and
characters. Mary Shelley's narrative took place over a considerable period
of time. In the novel, Frankenstein vows to destroy his creation and pursues

---

* In Greek mythology Prometheus created the human race out of clay and water. He then
stole fire from the gods and gave it to humanity.

Mary Wollstonecraft Shelley, author of Frankenstein,
painted by Sir Charles L. Eastlake in the 1830s.

him to the arctic, where the scientist dies and his foe goes off into the ice
and mist, presumably to his death.

Shortly after the play opened in London, the London *Times* announced
that it would be produced on Broadway. As with Deane's *Dracula*, playwright
and newspaper correspondent John L. Balderston, who had recently written
Berkeley Square, was engaged to revise and brush up the material for
American consumption. He kept, for the most part, Peggy Webling's
modifications and structure, but he added several touches of his own. For
example, Fritz, the hunchback who assists Frankenstein in his experiments,
was added (although he is mute in Balderston's version).

With the release of *Dracula* in early 1931, Universal Pictures had a major
success. Even before the feature was in theaters there had been discussions
regarding a follow-up. *Frankenstein* was a logical choice. The film *Dracula*

was based more on the 1924 Hamilton Deane play than on the novel. This stage version had been exceptionally well received, both in England and in America.

Because Universal had bought the play version of *Dracula* from Hamilton Deane and John Balderston, they decided to do the same with *Frankenstein*. The original novel, of course, was in the public domain. In May 1931, the screen rights for the play were purchased for $20,000, with an additional one percent of the gross earnings to go to Webling and Balderston. Perhaps because of Universal's stipulation, the play was not produced in America, and never has been, contrary to the original plan.

Prior to the 1931 *Frankenstein* there were three silent film productions of the story, the first going back to 1910. The Edison Company's brief (approximately fifteen minutes long) version, which according to the surviving script was a "liberal adaptation of Mrs. Shelley's famous story," featured a hunchbacked and shaggy-chested monster—suggestive of Quasimodo—with a stark white face and a mass of matted hair. The monster was formed in a "cauldron of blazing chemical" rather than with the aid of electricity. The climax of the film introduced some aspects of the Jekyll-Hyde theme. The monster was defeated by the power of love.

Then there was the feature length *Life without Soul* (1915). In this adaptation, the monster had no bizarre trappings or unusual makeup. He was "awe inspiring but never grotesque." One of the characters was established by being shown reading the story of the film from a book. When Frankenstein died after killing the monster, the book was closed and each of the characters revealed to be alive and well.

The third filming was done in Italy in 1920 and called *Il Mostro di Frankenstein*. No known negatives or prints survive of the silent productions with the exception of the 1910 version.

Either some time before the purchase of the material by Universal or just after, Richard Schayer, Universal's story editor, asked writer-director Robert Florey to work on the screen adaptation. Florey apparently was given to understand that he might also direct the film.

Florey wrote me in 1977 that "at first Schayer thought that the . . . novel couldn't be adapted into a feature. However, I went home and typed a five- or six-page synopsis following, but taking liberties with the author's story . . . . I also learned later that John Balderston had adapted Peggy Webling's play *Frankenstein*—which I never saw nor read."

In another letter Florey said that he and Schalyer "worked with Garrett Fort [who wrote Universal's *Dracula*] on the first screenplay following the lines of my synopsis treatment . . . . Fort wrote the dialogue. . . . My contribution . . . was its continuity of action and development."

In the novel, Frankenstein is a student of science, not a doctor or the son of a baron. The scene in which the monster is given life takes place in the upstairs room of Frankenstein's house, not, as in the 1931 film, an old watchtower. There is no elaborate electrical apparatus giving forth a pyrotechnic display during the creation; no raging electrical storm outside.

In the Webling-Balderston play, Frankenstein's study "in an old house at Goldstadt" in Switzerland has been fashioned into a laboratory, and there is a storm during the creation scene. In the early versions of the screenplay, an abandoned windmill is used for the lab and a storm is raging. A description of the setting in a preliminary draft of the script in the studio files mentions "something suggestive of the laboratory in *Metropolis.*" (The 1926 German silent film had a "mad scientist" involved in a laboratory creation scene amidst considerable electrical paraphernalia.)

In Mary Shelley's book, the description of the procedures by which Frankenstein gave his creation life is vague; indeed, this major sequence of the creation, a high point in the 1931 film, is presented in one not very detailed paragraph in the book:

> It was on a dreary night of November, that I beheld the accomplishment of my toils. With an anxiety that almost amounted to agony, I collected the instruments of life around me, that I might infuse a spark of being into the lifeless thing that lay at my feet. It was already one in the morning; the rain pattered dismally against the panes, and my candle was nearly burnt out, when, by the glimmer of the half-extinguished light, I saw the dull yellow eye of the creature open; it breathed hard, and a convulsive motion agitated its limbs.

Then in another paragraph she wrote:

> I had worked hard for nearly two years, for the sole purpose of infusing life into an inanimate body. For this I had deprived myself of rest and health. I had desired it with an ardour that far exceeded moderation; but now that I had finished, the beauty of the dream vanished, and breathless horror and disgust filled my heart.*

Florey claims to have suggested the deserted mill for the locale of Frankenstein's experiments and for the spectacular conclusion of the film

* The monster has been described as a projection of Mary Shelley's feelings of isolation and hatred, which stemmed from the death of her mother when she was only ten days old. Mary was barely tolerated by her cruel, intolerant father and was driven inward, spending her childhood in solitary pastimes such as reading, writing, and daydreaming.

involving creator and monster inside the mill as the enraged villagers set fire to it. The original plan, according to Garrett Fort's early script, was to have the monster seek the mill, the only refuge it knew from the time its life began. Florey says in his letter that "living in an apartment [on Ivar Street in Hollywood] above a Van de Kamp bakery with its windmill rotating, inspired me to place the laboratory in an old mill."

Florey also takes credit for the incident in the screen version in which Frankenstein's hunchbacked assistant steals from the university the brain of an abnormal criminal to be placed in the head of the creature instead of the "normal" brain he was told to bring back. This incident is in neither the novel nor in the play versions of Webling and Balderston.

Referring to sequences of the monster frightening the villagers, Garrett Fort wrote a memo to Richard Schayer on June 15, 1931, in which he stated that "until a director is definitely assigned, Florey has definite ideas about shooting this with considerable effectiveness."

That same month Florey directed a test, shot on the castle set left from *Dracula*, with Bela (Dracula) Lugosi in the role of the monster. As early as April, Lugosi had been announced for *Frankenstein*. Florey claims he had thought of him for the role of Frankenstein, but that Universal executives insisted he play the monster. According to Florey's letter, the edited test ran for twenty minutes (which seems extraordinarily long). It was photographed by Paul Ivano, and it started in Dr. Waldman's study with a short conversation between Victor Moritz and Waldman leading to both going to the Frankenstein laboratory. Following a scene with Frankenstein and Fritz in the lab, there was the arrival of Waldman and Victor. According to Florey, the test lasted up to and including the initial awakening of the monster. The actors involved were Edward Van Sloan, Dwight Frye, Lugosi (all from the film *Dracula*), and two stock players. Florey says in his letter: "After [producer] C. Laemmle Junior gave our screenplay to James Whale—and I presume showed him the test I directed—it [the test] was never seen again . . . . I also started to prepare a final directorial script indicating all set ups, camera angles, and lenses I intended to use. It remained unfinished when I was switched to [direct *The Murders in the*] *Rue Morgue*."

Lugosi's test makeup and garb were reminiscent of Paul Wegener in *The Golem*, a 1920 German film about a legendary figure of clay brought to life by Rabbi Loew in the fifteenth century. According to Forrest J. Ackerman's interview with Edward Van Sloan, who later played the major role of Doctor Waldman in *Frankenstein*, Lugosi arrived for the test with a head "about four times normal size, with a broad wig on it. He had a polished, clay-like skin." This approach to the character was similar to Hamilton Deane's in the Peggy Webling stage version.

Advance ad for the film at the time Bela Lugosi was slated to play the Monster.

The 1920 *Golem* certainly is a strong precursor in many ways to *Frankenstein*, particularly the second half of the film when the Golem gets out of control, turns upon humanity, creates havoc, and is destroyed. In both films, the lonely creatures find temporary friends in children too innocent to fear them.

Either Lugosi or Universal executives (or both) were disenchanted with the results of his *Frankenstein* test. Lugosi claimed he did not want to play a speechless brute laden with makeup. (Mary Shelley's and Webling and Balderston's talking monster had been relieved of speech along the way. But he did speak in Universal's first sequel, *Bride of Frankenstein* (1935), for which Balderston received coadaptation credit.)

Although not followed to the letter, the general structure of the first half or so of the Webling-Balderston play was at least in evidence in the evolving film script for *Frankenstein*, but the last part of the play was not used until Universal made *Bride of Frankenstein* four years later. The final act of the play was concerned with Frankenstein's preparations—with the monster's aid—for the making of a mate for the creature (this originated in the novel). But the monster kills Frankenstein in the play, after his creator decides at the last moment not to provide him with a mate; then the monster stumbles into the electrical apparatus and dies as a result of a flash of lightning and the machine that brought him to life.*

By the end of June a director was confirmed for *Frankenstein*—Britisher James Whale. Whale was relatively new to Universal. He had just finished directing a screen adaptation of Robert Sherwood's play *Waterloo Bridge* for that studio. His previous film-directing credits were the dialogue scenes in Howard Hughes's aviation epic, *Hell's Angels* (1930) and all of *Journey's End* (1930), the screen version of the exceptionally popular R. C. Sherriff World War I play that Whale had directed on the stage in London and then in New York.

After the success of *Waterloo Bridge*, Universal offered Whale his choice of scripts. He selected *Frankenstein* because "of thirty available stories it was the strongest meat and gave me a chance to dabble in the macabre. I thought it would be amusing to try and make what everybody knows is a physical impossibility seem believable . . . . Also, it offered fine pictorial chances, had two grand characterizations, and had a subject matter that might go anywhere, and that is part of the fun of making pictures."

Among the changes made in the script by the new writer, Francis Edwards

* Between the time the play premiered in Preston, England, in 1927, and its London opening in 1930, there were considerable changes in the script. In the early version, the monster leaps from a cliff and destroys himself. Frankenstein and his fiancée (whom the monster had wanted to possess) are then happily reunited. There is no material regarding the plan to create a mate for the monster.

Faragoh (*Little Caesar*), was giving dialogue to Fritz, Frankenstein's assistant, who in the previous Universal scripts had been a mute. Also, Frankenstein's laboratory was now located in an old watchtower rather than in the deserted mill. The mill, however, was retained for the final scene.

It is a reasonable assumption that Whale and one or more contributors to the script studied at least four important films and subsequently utilized certain aspects of these films in the evolution of the script, the design of some of the sets, and the direction and photography. The influences of *Metropolis* and *The Golem* already have been mentioned. *The Cabinet of Dr. Caligari*, a 1919 German exercise in expressionism, was an influence on the somewhat stylized sets, and to a degree, on the approach to the overall visualization of the monster. Also, a scene in which the monster entered the room of Frankenstein's bride paralleled a scene in *Caligari* and *The Golem* (although it originally derived from the novel and later the Webling play). *Variety*, on July 14, 1931, reported that Whale had screened *Caligari* "to get some ideas for *Frankenstein*."

The Magician, a 1926 Rex Ingram film made in France for MGM release, was based on Somerset Maugham's novel of the same name. The climax of the story takes place in "an ancient sorcerer's tower" behind Monte Carlo. Here in a laboratory a student of the occult has found "the secret of the creation of human life by magic." The creation experiment includes life-giving bolts of lightning to be received from the top of the tower during a furious storm (however, there is no electrical apparatus). The sorcerer works with a dwarf assistant. (The "mad scientist" in *Metropolis* also had a dwarf servant.)

As Donald Glut points out in his exhaustive study, *The Frankenstein Legend* (1973): "The similarities between the towers in *The Magician* and James Whale's 1931 *Frankenstein* can hardly be coincidence. Inside and out (a miniature), the tower . . . is a close copy."

Of course, before Whale entered the scene, Robert Florey admitted that he consciously put into his approach to the adaptation Grand Guignol situations of the Théâtre de l'Épouvante and details from macabre German silent films. In addition to *The Magician*, *The Cabinet of Dr. Caligari*, *The Golem*, and *Metropolis*, a 1916 German serial called *Homunculus* may have been one of the influential films. Like the Golem and Frankenstein's monster, the homunculus was artificial and without a soul, created by a famous but mad scientist and his assistant with predictably dire consequences. The homunculus falls in love with a beautiful woman, discovers that she is repulsed by him, and then decides to try to destroy the world. Eventually he is killed by lightning.

Although Leslie Howard had been mentioned at one time for the title role in the 1931 *Frankenstein*, Whale insisted on Colin Clive, the British leading player of both the stage and screen versions of *Journey's End*. Universal went along with Whale, and Clive sailed from England. When he stepped off the ship in New York the script and a letter from the director awaited him. The letter said, in part, that Whale was planning on "Bela Lugosi or Boris Karloff as the monster . . . and I am making a test of Mae Clarke as Elizabeth* . . . . I want the picture to be a very modern, materialistic treatment of this medieval story—something of *Doctor Caligari*, something of Edgar Allan Poe, and of course a good deal of us."

In the same letter, Whale described the way he perceived the character of Frankenstein: "An intensely sane person, at times rather fanatical and in one or two scenes a little hysterical, and a little reminiscent of the breakdown in *Journey's End*. Similar to Stanhope [Clive's role in *Journey's End*], Frankenstein's nerves are all to pieces . . . . All the time I should feel that Frankenstein is normally and [sic] extremely intelligent, a sane and lovable person, never unsympathetic, even to the monster."

In the play—especially in Balderston's version—Frankenstein's relationship to the monster is decreed, in Frankenstein's words, as "only command. Blind obedience, no discussion." He treats the creature cruelly, and in Balderston's adaptation makes considerable use of a whip and hot iron. He also finds satisfaction in having the monster perform "tricks like a puppy," literally commanding him to "lie down, roll over," and he refers to him as a "slave." Frankenstein announces that the creature "must be afraid of me. He must obey me." This cruelty is transferred in the final screen version to the character of Fritz, the hunchback, who continually provokes Frankenstein's creation with whip and torch, thereby making Frankenstein more sympathetic. (Incidentally, many people refer to the monster by the name of Frankenstein. In fact, in Peggy Webling's 1927 play, the revised 1930 presentation, and Balderston's version of the play, the monster *is* called Frankenstein, after its creator, on numerous occasions by some of the characters.)

Shortly after taking over the project, James Whale met fellow Britisher Boris Karloff, who was on the Universal lot playing the role of the murderer in *Graft*, and decided to test him for the part of the monster. Whale said later that "Karloff's face has always fascinated me . . . . His physique was weaker than I could wish, but that queer, penetrating personality of his, I felt, was more important than his shape, which could easily be altered."

Although Karloff had been in American films since 1919, he was hardly a well-known performer. Most of his parts in silent films were small or not

* Earlier, Bette Davis had been mentioned as a possibility for the role. She was under contract at Universal for six months.

particularly notable or memorable. But after a good role in both the stage and screen versions of *The Criminal Code* (1930), his stock started to rise and he was offered more interesting characterizations in better pictures.

For three hours every evening over a three-week period, after studio shooting hours, Universal makeup artist Jack Pierce worked with Karloff devising the makeup to be used for the test. Pierce later described his approach for *The New York Times:*

> I didn't depend on imagination . . . . My anatomical studies taught me that there are six ways a surgeon can cut the skull in order to take out or put in a brain. I figured that Frankenstein, who was a scientist but no practicing surgeon, would take the simplest surgical way. He would cut the top of the skull off straight across like a pot-lid, hinge it, pop the brain in, and then clamp it on tight. That is the reason I decided to make the Monster's head square and flat like a shoe box and dig that big scar across his forehead with the metal clamps holding it together.
>
> I read that the Egyptians used to bind some criminals hand and foot and bury them alive. When their blood turned to water after death, it flowed to their extremities, stretched their arms to gorilla length, and swelled their hands, feet and faces to abnormal proportions. I thought this might make a nice touch for the Monster, since he was supposed to be made from the corpses of executed felons. So I fixed Karloff up that way.

Part of this effect was accomplished by ordering an ill-fitting black suit made up with shortened sleeves to make the arms appear longer. To give the monster a primitive, Neanderthal appearance, Pierce shaped a protruding brow from tin and blended it with the actor's own features with layers of putty. Several of Karloff's teeth on the right side of his mouth were false. They were removed, allowing the side of his face to become indented. Karloff, according to some accounts, suggested that his eyelids be heavily caked, giving the creature a look of only partial awareness. Pierce accomplished this with mortician's wax. The two metal studs that protruded from the sides of the monster's neck were "inlets for electricity." Significantly, the creative makeup always allowed Karloff's features and expressions full play, and this accounts to a considerable degree for the effectiveness of his characterization.

A five-pound brace was prepared for the actor's spine to keep his movements impaired and relatively rigid. His legs were stiffened by steel

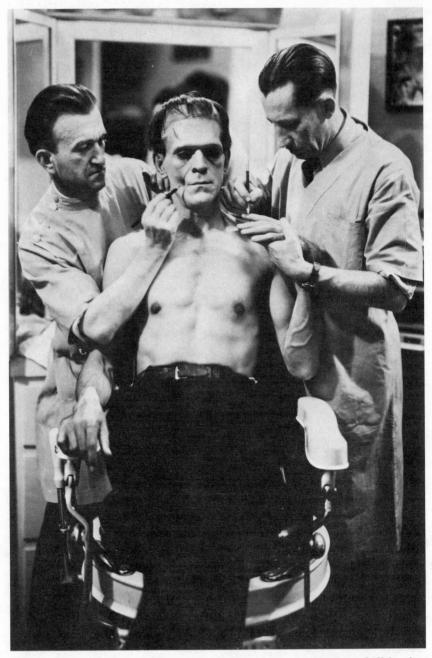

Makeup artist Jack Pierce (left) and his assistant preparing Boris Karloff for the role of the Monster in Frankenstein.

struts. To add to the bulk, he wore a double-quilted suit and raised boots—each weighing twelve-and-one-half pounds—to further hamper his walking. All of the embellishments weighed forty-eight pounds. Years later Pierce stated that the monster's final visage was "a compromise" between his own ideas and those of Whale. The overall look of the monster in all of the subsequent Universal sequels was never as effective as it was in the original production.

Karloff's test convinced Whale and Universal executives that he was perfect for the part. Then in August the picture started filming. Mae Clarke, Whale's leading lady in the recently completed *Waterloo Bridge*, whom he liked, was a natural choice for Frankenstein's fiancée. She had been in films since 1929, and before that was a dancer-actress-singer appearing primarily in nightclubs, Broadway musicals, and vaudeville. In 1974 author Anita Loos revealed that Clarke was the inspiration for her Lorelei Lee in *Gentlemen Prefer Blondes* (1926). "I patterned her on a cute little blonde H. L. Mencken was escorting at the time. Her name was Mae Clarke . . . . Mencken was a beau of mine." In *The Public Enemy*, also made in 1931, Clarke was the memorable recipient of a half-grapefruit slapped and twisted on her face by James Cagney.

As to the rest of the casting, Edward Van Sloan as Dr. Waldman (doing a virtual repeat of his Professor Van Helsing in the stage and screen *Dracula*) and Dwight Frye as Frankenstein's hunchbacked assistant (Renfield in *Dracula*) had been penciled in all along. Actor-singer John Boles, another contract player, was agreed to for the role of Frankenstein's friend and rival for Elizabeth, Victor Moritz. In the play, for unknown reasons, Peggy Webling changed the name of the novel's Victor Frankenstein to Henry Frankenstein. Henry Clerval, in the book Frankenstein's best friend, was transposed to Victor Moritz. The film kept the changes.

Budgeted at $262,000 and given a thirty-day shooting schedule, *Frankenstein* was laid out to be filmed in continuity, for the most part, starting on August 24, according to the studio's breakdown and estimate sheet. Most of the picture was filmed on Universal's sound stages, including the exterior opening scenes in the graveyard and at the anachronistic gibbett, and the later sequence where Frankenstein and the villagers comb the mountains with torches to find the monster. Whale and company did go outside to the exterior European village on the back lot, which was originally built for *All Quiet on the Western Front* (1930). The village also was used in the many *Frankenstein* sequels and in any number of other films over the years.

Apparently there were no major problems and no drastic changes were made during the filming period. (The schedule ran over by five days, and shooting was completed on October 3.) But one crucial scene, which was

In both The Golem *(1920) and* Frankenstein, *the lonely creatures find a temporary friend in a child too innocent to fear them.*

suggested by an incident in Peggy Webling's play, brought about strong disagreement between Whale and Karloff, who apparently otherwise got along quite well. At one point, while wandering the countryside, the monster for the first and only time finds a human being who is unafraid of him—an innocent peasant child, who, attempting to play with the creature, shows him how flower petals float like boats on the lake. Touched and excited with his first encounter with beauty, the monster tries to float the little girl like the petals, and feels intense pain and confusion when she sinks. Similarly, in the Webling play the monster accidentally crushes a dove in his hands and throws it into the lake, where, much to his delight, it floats. Then he takes Frankenstein's little crippled sister (a character not in the novel or film) out in a boat and tries to make her float like the dove, but she drowns. His remorse at this act is one of the motivations that leads to his flinging himself off the cliff in the 1927 play version.

Karloff was upset because of the manner in which Whale wanted the scene staged. In general, according to the actor: "Whale and I both saw the character [of the monster] as an innocent one . . . . This was a pathetic creature who, like us all, had neither wish nor say in his creation and certainly did not wish upon itself the hideous image which automatically terrified humans whom it tried to befriend . . . . What astonished us was the fantastic number of ordinary people that got this general air of sympathy. I found all my letters heavy with it." In another interview Karloff said: "My conception of the scene [mentioned above] was that he should look up at the little girl in bewilderment, and, in his mind, she would become a flower. Without moving, he would pick her up gently and put her in the water exactly as he had done to the flower—and to his horror, she would sink. Well, Jimmy [Whale] made me pick her up and do *that* [motioning violently] over my head, which became a brutal and deliberate act. By no stretch of the imagination could you make that innocent. The whole pathos of the scene, to my mind, should have been—and I'm sure that's the way it was written—completely innocent and unaware."

Forrest Ackerman recalls seeing the deleted sequence in a print shown in the late 1930s. He told me that there was nothing violent, brutal, or deliberate about the motivation or interpretation of the scene in the least; it was a completely innocent act.

In any case, there apparently was adverse reaction to the scene as filmed at a nearby lake, and it was modified in a manner that paradoxically compounded the problem. The action played as photographed up to the point where the monster had thrown his last daisy into the water; he watched it, then looked at his empty hands and held them out toward the child. The rest of the scene was deleted shortly before or shortly after the film's release. The next time the girl was seen she was a corpse carried by her father through the streets of the village.

Although Mae Clarke remembers tea breaks every midafternoon during filming, she never had an opportunity to get to know Karloff very well:

> He would arrive at four A.M. and spend four hours in make-up. He didn't have lunch with us in the studio commissary because it was easier for him, due to the make-up, to eat alone in his dressing room bungalow where he could remove some of his body padding. Then a couple of hours would be spent in removing his make-up at the end of the day and he would require a rub-down after stomping around all day with those weights in his shoes, which gave him that stilted walk and allowed him to lean forward.

The Universal executives were not quite certain how to handle their most unusual film. According to *Variety*, there was a large percentage of audience walkouts during previews. It should be recalled that "horror" films were not a staple commodity in those days—they were few and far between and not referred to as horror pictures. These occasional tales of the macabre, mostly drawn from Gothic themes, did not constitute a cycle. Universal had produced the biggest and most successful of the genre during the 1920s— *The Phantom of the Opera* (1925), with Lon Chaney. *Dracula*, of course, was the current catalyst, but the completed *Frankenstein* contained even stronger elements of horror, causing Carl Laemmle Sr. and Carl Laemmle Jr., who ran Universal on the West Coast, considerable apprehension. Finally, following previews and discussions, they decided to play up rather than tone down the horror aspects in advertising, promotion, and publicity. For example, registered nurses were stationed in theater lobbies in case patrons should need their services. A prologue was photographed, in which Edward Van Sloan steps from behind a theatrical curtain to prepare the audience and tell them of the nature of the strange story to follow:

VAN SLOAN

> How do you do. Mr. Carl Laemmle feels that it would be a little unkind to present this picture without just a word of friendly warning. We are about to unfold the story of Frankenstein—a man of science, who sought to create a man after his own image without reckoning upon God. It is one of the strangest stories ever told. It deals with the two great mysteries of creation—life and death. I think it will thrill you. It may

shock you. It might even—horrify you! So then, if you feel
that you do not care to subject your nerves to such a strain,
now is your chance to—well, we've warned you!

The ending of the film was changed at the last moment before the film's
opening dates. Up to this time it was intended that both Frankenstein and
his creation would die at the conclusion of the film, as in the Webling-
Balderston play. Apparently, negative reaction at the previews caused
Universal executives to decide on a new ending, which necessitated the
filming of a short epilogue depicting Henry Frankenstein recovering from
his injuries and reunited with Elizabeth while his father, the baron, and the
maids drink a toast to "a son of the house of Frankenstein." Fade out and
then fade in to the closing titles accompanied by a short mood-music cue
written in the 1920s by Giuseppe Becce for motion pictures and called
"Grand Appassionato." The only other music in the entire film is heard
during the opening titles. This was an original "mysterioso" composition
written for the picture by film composer Bernard Kaun.

The enormously successful *Frankenstein*, produced at a final cost of
$291,000, spawned an incredible number of sequels, imitations, variations,
and remakes over the years, the best of which is probably *Bride of
Frankenstein*, the first sequel, made in 1935 by Universal with Karloff and
Colin Clive repeating their original roles and James Whale again directing.

In 1938, encouraged by a few test engagements, Universal reissued
nationally the original *Frankenstein* and *Dracula* films as a "Double Horror
Show." At this time, another cut was made at the climax of the creation
scene to appease the Production Code office: Frankenstein exclaims excit-
edly, "It's alive—it's alive—it's alive!" His friend Victor tries to restrain
him: "Henry, in the name of God!" And Frankenstein replies, "Oh, in the
name of God. Now I know what it feels like to be God!" The scene was
reedited to conclude before the references to God. Mae Clarke said in 1971:
"Oh, how I remember that voice. Jim Whale would say about Colin, 'his
voice is like a pipe organ. You just arrange him and pull out all the stops
and his voice comes out like music.' " In 1937, at the age of 37, Colin Clive
died as a result of alcoholism.

The reissue package of *Frankenstein* and *Dracula* did incredibly good
business, prompting Universal to put *Son of Frankenstein* (1939) into
production with an A picture budget, cast, and physical mounting. Boris
Karloff declined to participate after this third film, so in succeeding Universal
features Lon Chaney, Jr. (*The Ghost of Frankenstein*, 1942), Bela Lugosi
(*Frankenstein Meets the Wolf Man*, 1943), and Glenn Strange (*The House
of Frankenstein*, 1944; *The House of Dracula*, 1945; *Abbott and Costello*

Meet Frankenstein, 1948) played the monster. Following the Abbott and Costello mixture of horror and slapstick, the monster and the Frankenstein family went into suspended animation. It appeared as though the theme had been played out.

Nine years later the relatively small Hammer Films of England produced a new version of the original tale called *The Curse of Frankenstein* (1957). Although the novel was in public domain, the Webling-Balderston play and the concepts and executions of the various Universal films, including the visualization of the monster, had to be avoided, because they were copyrighted. Hammer chose to emphasize Baron Frankenstein (Peter Cushing) instead of the monster (Christopher Lee). Here was a decadent late Victorian interpretation with the accent on explicit blood and gore, sadism, necrophilia, and an occasional dash of the erotic. As counterpoint to the horror, there were scenes amidst elegant Victorian decor in which the baron moved with the assurance and manner of an imperious and unscrupulous Byronic hero. For the first time a Frankenstein film was photographed in color. The success of *The Curse of Frankenstein* all over the world exceeded anyone's wildest expectations and prompted a number of follow-ups.

Mae Clarke, John Boles, and unidentified player in a scene cut from Frankenstein.

Boris Karloff and director James Whale on the set of Bride of Frankenstein
(1935).

Andy Warhol's Frankenstein (1974), also in color, was a spoof of the
Hammer style, while Mel Brooks's *Young Frankenstein*, made the same
year in black and white, was an affectionate homage to Universal's approach
in the 1930s. Taking characters, situations, and other elements from the
first three Universal films, *Young Frankenstein* is a mixture of satire,
burlesque, parody, and pastiche that works very well, even for those who
have only a nodding acquaintance with Universal's Frankenstein canon.
Gene Wilder is Frankenstein's grandson and Peter Boyle the monster.

There seems to be no question about the durability of the Frankenstein
theme with its innumerable interpretations: the cosmic theme of the limits
of man and the power of God, which extends to man emulating God; the
disturbing idea that science could create life, possibly even eternal life; the
fascination with dolls, mechanical puppets, and robots that effectively
simulate life; the Faustian concept of the overreacher who momentarily

commands divine power only to be destroyed because of it; the father/ creator who abandons his child (Frankenstein's crime was that he abandoned his creature); the theme of the divided self (in this instance, creator and creature) that is part of the human psyche and derives from ancient legend; the dumb innocent craving love and understanding but forced to become violent and exercise hatred because of the lack of compassion and the fear of others (frustration and overwhelming rejection were the cause of the monster's brutality).

Frankenstein, then, is a mixture of fascination and horror, dream and nightmare. Mary Shelley succeeded in creating a tale that would, she said, "speak to the mysterious fears of our nature, and awaken thrilling horror." There is no doubt about that.

A DREAM AND A VISION:
LOST HORIZON
(1937)

In December 1934, Harry Cohn, head of Columbia Pictures, invited a studio group to go to a Stanford–USC football game in Palo Alto. Browsing in Union Station's newsstand for something to read on the train, producer-director Frank Capra, whose recent *It Happened One Night* had been a big success, saw a book that critic Alexander Woollcott had praised on the radio and that Capra's friend, screenwriter Jo Swerling, had told him about: James Hilton's *Lost Horizon*. "I read it," recounts Capra, "not only read it, but dreamed about it all night."

The next morning, as Capra tells it, during breakfast in the dining car, Capra expressed his enthusiasm for the book and asked Cohn to buy it for him immediately. He also told him that there was only one actor in the world to play the lead in the movie—Ronald Colman.

After the property was purchased (for $17,500), Capra and his long-time collaborator, Robert Riskin, went to a desert retreat called La Quinta, about twenty miles from Palm Springs, to work on the adaptation. Hilton's novel had been published in England and America in the autumn of 1933, but sales were slow. Then the same author's *Goodbye, Mr. Chips* appeared in April 1934 and was immensely popular. As a result, a new edition of *Lost Horizon* came out just a year after the first one, and the next week Alexander

FRANK CAPRA'S
GREATEST PRODUCTION
RONALD COLMAN
in

LOST HORIZON

with
JANE WYATT · JOHN HOWARD
MARGO · THOMAS MITCHELL
Edward Everett HORTON · ISABEL JEWELL
H. B. WARNER · SAM JAFFE
From the novel by JAMES HILTON
Screen Play by ROBERT RISKIN
A COLUMBIA PICTURE

COLUMBIA

Copyrighted by Columbia Pictures Corp., New York, N. Y., 1937   PRINTED IN U.S.A.

Woollcott announced on his *Town Crier* radio program that he had "gone quietly mad" about it. With this impetus sales rose sharply until the book was selling six thousand copies a week by Christmas of 1934.

Hilton's novel told a strangely compelling story of the forced adventure of a small group of assorted people mysteriously carried away by airplane from Baskul in Afghanistan to a high plateau called Shangri-La in the mountains of Tibet. Here they find a utopia of great peace and beauty ruled by a high lama who is said to be three hundred years old. The inhabitants live a life devoid of fear, hatred, or greed. "Be kind" is the prevailing philosophy. Music, art, great literature, and the wisdom of the world are their treasures. It is the thought by the high lama that Shangri-La will rule the world when the world's mad people have destroyed civilization by their lust for war. Men and women of sixty appear young, and time is of little consequence in Shangri-La. It is possible that Hunzaland, a remote valley high in the Himalayas with an amazingly high proportion of very old people, figured in Hilton's original thinking about his story.

Also, Hilton had many times been to Lauterbrunnen, a resort in the Swiss Alps at the foot of the snow-clad Jungfrau mountain. This lush valley with its meadows, brooks, extremely pleasant climate, and spectacular setting figured in his visualization of Shangri-La, according to Jane Wyatt's

James Hilton, author of Lost Horizon, *in 1936.*

husband, Edgar Ward, who knew Hilton. In 1133, Augustinian monks came to this lovely region and built a monastery that flourished and soon became the center of life in the Bernese Oberland. Mountaineering attracted Hilton, and he set his utopia among the peaks of the unexplored Kuen-Luns, drawing on his own climbing experiences in the Alps to lend authenticity to the setting. And he made Conway, the protagonist, a trained mountaineer.

Lost Horizon took six years to form in Hilton's mind, six months to think about consciously, and just six weeks to put down on paper. Hilton said in 1936 that "the idea for the book was germinated out of anxiety over the European situation at that time and a desire to stage a conception of a world as far removed from this sort of thing as possible." Most of his Tibetan material was cribbed from the British Museum library, particularly from the *Travels of the Abbé Huc*, an early French work. Hilton never had been to Tibet. He said that "I always had a feeling that imagination will get you further than knowledge, or first-hand experience, and economic circumstances." As for the name "Shangri-La," Hilton explained at the time:

> La means "mountain pass" in the language of Tibet, but the "Shangri" was my own idea. Made it up out of whole cloth because it *sounded* so Tibetan, you see. Later on, a Far Eastern scholar wrote and told me "Shangri" means "secret" in Tibetan, so there you have it—"secret mountain pass," which is exactly what it was, you know.

Lost Horizon in general is outside the mainstream of Frank Capra's work, which during his golden years dealt with the common man—Mr. Deeds, Mr. Smith, John Doe—a man of the people rising to be leader of the people by the vote of the people. The pursuit of happiness underlined all of these films, and this idea was expressed in abstract, idealistic terms in *Lost*

Horizon. The film's foreword supplied the guide line. It tells us that everyone is searching for something: Some call it Utopia, others the Fountain of Youth, and others "that little chicken farm." Capra has also admitted that "My whole philosophy is in my films. People are basically good or can be made good."

While Robert Riskin worked on the script, Capra began to do prodigious research on Tibet, the locale of the story. Capra acquired the services of Harrison Forman, an American explorer and authority on Tibet, as technical adviser. Forman had taken hundreds of photographs of Tibet, its people, manners, customs, animals, lamaseries, and so on. These were studied carefully and used as reference.

The first draft of the script was completed in May 1935, and the picture was budgeted at $1,200,000. Some character changes had been made from the novel. The hero's name, Hugh "Glory" Conway, was modified to Robert Conway (Ronald Colman), the British consul at Baskul. The vice-consul, Mallinson, became Conway's younger brother George (John Howard). A lady missionary was transformed into a tubercular prostitute (Isabel Jewell), and the role of a fussy paleontologist was written especially for character comedian Edward Everett Horton in order to provide comic relief. Another passenger, an American businessman who is later found to be an absconding embezzler (Thomas Mitchell), remained intact from the book.

In the novel, one of the principal characters at Shangri-La is an apparently young Manchu woman (in reality she is 65 years old) called Lo-Tsen, with whom Conway quietly fell in love. Romantic passion as such held no appeal for the Conway of the book. He had been injured while fighting in World War I, and having spent his passions during that time now wanted nothing more than a life of quiet contemplation. The delicate little Manchu knew no English and never spoke to Conway. Her sensitive playing of Western music on the harpsichord enchanted him. Then the great illusion of Conway's perfect love for Lo-Tsen was shattered when he learns that she and Mallinson, the vice-consul, have been lovers. He immediately decides to leave Shangri-La with Mallinson, Lo-Tsen, and the porters.

In the film, Lo-Tsen is divided into two women. Sondra (Jane Wyatt) is a lovely young woman of thirty who, having learned to know Conway through his books, prevailed upon the high lama to bring him to Shangri-La. (Interestingly, references to this were cut after the initial reserved-seat release.) Conway is presented as a world-famous British foreign secretary (England's "Man of the East"), author, and adventurer, whereas in the novel he served in the consul service at small outposts by his own choice and was hardly a world celebrity. In contrast to the Conway of the book, the Conway of the film develops a romantic, passionate attachment for Sondra. The second half of the original female character is Maria (Margo), a Russian who appears to be a young woman at Shangri-La. She falls in love with Conway's brother, and after leaving Shangri-La, she reverts to the old woman she is in actuality, as Lo-Tsen does in the novel.

Author Hilton spent six months in the Los Angeles area during the time the film was being prepared. He wrote at the time:

> I first met Capra at [screenwriter] Frances Marion's house a few days after I arrived in Hollywood. We then talked for two hours about *Lost Horizon;* he explained and described his ideas about making a screenplay of it, and the changes (most of them slight) that seemed advisable to him and to Robert Riskin, who was writing the script. I found him in complete sympathy with the mood and spirit of the story; actually I was inclined for more changes than he was . . . .
>
> Later I met both Capra and Riskin many times.

Hilton, by all accounts, seemed pleased with the alterations; indeed, he was quoted as saying that the changes were actually improvements, and that he wished he had thought of them while writing his book. This attitude is rare among adapted novelists, to say the least.

Capra showed the script to Ronald Colman, who reacted positively to it, but was less than enthusiastic about the prospect of filming at little Columbia Pictures, a "poverty row" lot, considerably beneath the dignity and prestige of MGM, Paramount, Warners or Fox. Colman also equated Capra with comedy and wasn't convinced at first that the director was right for this kind of idyllic romantic adventure. Negotiations stalled, and at one point, feeling that he would not get Colman, Capra decided to go ahead with Brian Aherne, but just before he was going to tell Aherne, Capra found out that at last Colman had signed the contract (according to Aherne). The director still had to wait almost a year before Colman would be free from his previous commitments. While preproduction work on *Lost Horizon* continued, Capra and Harry Cohn decided to do *Mr. Deeds Goes to Town* while they were waiting for Colman.

Colman was then at the peak of a long and illustrious career. Born in England, he had appeared on the stage and screen there and later came to America, eventually to emerge as a major star in silent films (*Beau Geste, The Dark Angel, Stella Dallas*). He became even more popular after the introduction of sound, thanks to his charming voice and accent and his ability to deliver dialogue in a debonair, intelligent manner. Colman epitomized the cultured and dignified Britisher—reticent, unobtrusive, and self-confident. His roles usually emphasized melancholy fatalism, escape from his past, noble and unselfish acts, sophisticated humor, humanistic touches, courage, resourcefulness, and sacrifices—elaborate and otherwise—including his life. Shortly before doing *Lost Horizon*, which drew from many of the above attributes in addition to projecting aspects of a visionary idealist, Colman had made one of his most popular films, *A Tale of Two Cities* (1935), in which he deliberately dies on the guillotine in place of the husband of the woman he loves. Immediately after *Lost Horizon*, he starred in another of his most popular films, *The Prisoner of Zenda* (1937), in which he and the queen unselfishly renounce their great love for the ultimate good of a kingdom. Colman was perfect for the role of Conway in *Lost Horizon*.

Most of the remainder of the casting was done in early 1936 after Capra had finished *Mr. Deeds*. Jane Wyatt had done a considerable amount of stage work, including taking over Margaret Sullavan's role in the New York presentation of *Dinner at Eight* and starring in the 1934 Broadway production of *Lost Horizons*, a dramatic fantasy which had nothing to do with Hilton's story. In this she played a suicide compelled to learn in the beyond how the life she cut off would have benefitted unknown others. Wyatt had made a few films while under contract to Universal from 1934 to 1936, but they were relatively inconsequential, so she was considered a newcomer when, following a test, Capra selected her for Colman's romantic interest a few days before shooting began on March 23, 1936.

The distinguished British actor H. B. Warner, who had been on the stage since 1883 and in Hollywood as a film actor since 1917 (he played Jesus in the silent version of *The King of Kings*), was cast in the important role of the well-educated, English-speaking Chinese lama, Chang, who is the epitome of formal courtesy sprinkled with subtle humor.

The high lama proved to be the most difficult role to cast. Capra felt that if the actor chosen did not come across just right, the mood and effect of the whole picture would be shattered. The film went into production without a high lama. After seventy-five days of shooting, the role still had not been cast. An emaciated stage actor, A. E. Anson, who had appeared in only two films several years earlier, was tested and found to be right, but he died shortly after being told he had the role. Another strong possibility was veteran Henry B. Walthall, in films since 1909, but he died before a test could be made. Finally, in late June, following a test, thirty-eight-year-old Sam Jaffe was signed. He had impressed Capra in the Broadway productions of *The Jazz Singer* and *Grand Hotel* and had also played with the Ben Greet Shakespearean Company.

The problem of getting Tibetan villagers for the Valley of the Blue Moon was solved by using Pala Indians from the San Diego Mountains as well as

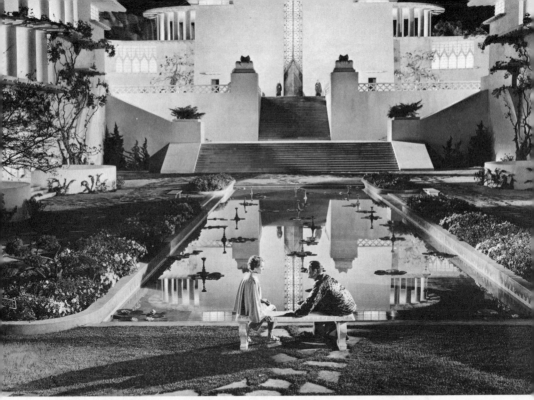

The Lamasery for Lost Horizon *(built on the Columbia ranch backlot in Burbank).*

other Indians from Arizona and New Mexico who closely resembled the Tibetans.

The biggest set was the huge exterior of the lamasery built on the Columbia Ranch in Burbank. In early sketches and models the lamasery was of a more modest conception—and very Oriental in character—than the controversial architectural design eventually realized by art director Stephen Goosson. Complete with delicate pavilions reached by flights of marble stairways, rambling gardens of luxuriant foliage, lily-covered pools, fountains, and flowered terraces, the lamasery was dominated by a huge edifice that moviegoers were to find either awe-inspiring in its symmetry and uncluttered lines or a cross between a deco/modern Southern California movie palace and a particularly ambitious WPA post office. After viewing the set, James Hilton wrote that the "stylized architecture of the lamasery background caught the exact paradox of something permanent enough to exist forever and too ethereal to exist at all."

In Sherwood Forest—just beyond the San Fernando Valley, forty miles from Hollywood—a complete Tibetan village was built to represent the Valley of the Blue Moon situated at the base of the lamasery. The old Metropolitan Airport, commercially unused for several years, with its background of the towering San Bernardino Mountains, was the setting for the opening evacuation of Baskul during a military uprising. The brilliant

The Lamasery for the 1973 remake of Lost Horizon *was a modification of the four-acre* Camelot *(1967) castle set on the back lot of Warner Bros. and Columbia's Burbank Studio.*

sequence showing the refueling of the aircraft on the Tibetan border by Mongolian tribesmen was shot 150 miles away, at Lucerne Dry Lake. The waterfall interlude at Shangri-La brought the filming company briefly to Palm Springs. The High Sierras near Lone Pine served as the snowy Tibetan mountains for aerial shots photographed by specialist Elmer Dyer. All of the interiors at the lamasery were shot on Columbia's sound stages on Gower Street in Hollywood.

Capra insisted that the ice, snow, mountains, storms, and in particular, the cold, not look phony. It was important, he said, that the actors' breath show. That meant shooting scenes in below-twenty-degree weather: a difficult requirement. Capra had an idea. He and his assistant searched for an insulated cold-storage warehouse large enough to shoot in, and they found one in the industrial section of Los Angeles. It was complete with artificial snow machines that were used to grind up ice blocks into fine snow and blow the particles out over the frozen swordfish that were stacked throughout the insulated building. Capra says in his autobiography:

> It cost us plenty, but we rented the ice house and converted it into a working studio. For six weeks we shot all our "cold" scenes (about twenty percent of the picture) in sub-freezing temperatures, while outside it was a broiling ninety degrees

> or higher. But we ran into a nightmare of technical hang-ups. Cold film rolling through the cameras developed static electricity that fogged the film. We had to cover film magazines with electrically heated "overcoats." New cold-resisting lubricants had to be found for cameras and motors. The extreme range of temperatures from "on" to "off" cracked light sockets and shattered bulbs. . . . Actors feared pneumonia going in and out of temperatures between 90 and 15.

In the refrigerating plant most of the plane's interior sequences, the exterior scenes of the plane following its crackup, the close shots of the trek, blizzards, and the avalanche that engulfed the porters, Maria suddenly turning into an old woman, and the close shots of Conway's return to Shangri-La were shot. Large painted backdrops, wind machines, snow machines, and back projection were set up in the ice house and used to conjure up the rigors of the Himalayas.

Interspersed with all of the ice-house footage were long shots of the windswept mountains, the porters, the avalanche, and Conway making his way alone in the snowy wilderness. These pieces came from two German feature films, *Stürme über dem Montblanc* (*Storm Over Mont Blanc* [1930], also known as *Avalanche*) and *Der Dämon des Himalaya* (*The Demon of the Himalayas*, 1934). The first was one of Arnold Fanck's numerous mountain films made throughout the 1920s and early 1930s. These fictional stories, photographed in the Alps, usually extolled the beauties of the high mountains and included majestic cloud displays over glaciers, diverse meteorological catastrophes, and the inevitable rescue party. *The Demon of the Himalayas* was made during an international Himalaya expedition in 1934. Its director, Andrew Marton, told me that because he was familiar with the footage in both films he tracked down the material and arranged for Capra to view the sequences applicable to his needs. The selected footage worked well. The only instance of a giveaway is the match from a long shot, which purports to be Conway collapsing upon arrival at a remote village in China (actually Gustav Diessl in *The Demon*), and the next close-up of Conway (Colman). Colman's hair and beard are relatively close-cropped; Diessl's are obviously bushier and longer.*

Filming continued for a hundred and ten days. Cameraman Joseph Walker said that "Frank Capra sometimes used three or four cameras on the dramatic scenes . . . . Lighting and camera angles had to be compromised, but I am sure that this 'one take' method resulted in better performances by the actors."

---

* Long shots from *Storm over Mont Blanc*, featuring mountaineer Sepp Rist battling the elements, were used for intercuts purporting to be Colman.

Months of editing followed. During this period, it was decided to shoot the two sequences involving the high lama again, this time with Columbia contract player Walter Connolly, who had just finished playing a Chinese man in *The Good Earth*. This is a controversial issue. Capra denies that Connolly was considered or photographed as the high lama, but various accounts at the time refer to this. Capra claims that the confusion stems from his original intent to cast Connolly as the fugitive industrialist, but Connolly's unavailability opened up the role to Thomas Mitchell. When I asked Jaffe about Connolly, he preferred not to comment, knowing Capra's current position on the matter.

Various other sequences were being revised, rewritten, reshot, and dropped. Capra finally came up with a version of the film that ran approximately three hours.

Meanwhile, composer Dimitri Tiomkin had spent a considerable time working on the score. He was hired by Capra before the film went into production and was often on the set during the shooting, and thus was able to absorb atmosphere and evolve themes slowly. The standard procedure was for the composer to start on salary after the film had been edited and have only a few weeks in which to create and record the music. Even the three-hour sneak preview version was partially scored. Usually original background music is not recorded until after the final cut.

This sequence and others for Lost Horizon *were photographed in an insulated cold storage warehouse in Los Angeles.*

This was the score that really launched Tiomkin's career. He had been a close friend of Capra's for many years, but *Lost Horizon* was the first time they had worked together. The assignment was a formidable one, calling for music depicting high adventure, arduous treks, mystical chants, romantic interludes, and the high lama's spectacular funeral procession. The latter makes use of the primary Shangri-La theme, with its extremely effective long melodic line suggestive of Oriental or medieval monody. According to musicologist William H. Rosar, Tiomkin had considerable aid, following his actual composition phase, from the no fewer than nine orchestrators involved in various sections of the score (George Parrish, Charles Maxwell, William Grant Still, Hugo Friedhofer, Bernard Kaun, Robert Russell Bennett, Max Reese, Peter Brunelli, and Herman Hand).

Max Steiner was borrowed from Selznick International to serve as music director and conductor of the large orchestra, which was augmented on several occasions by the usually wordless chanting of the Hall Johnson Choir, a popular group of black singers. According to Tiomkin, the "Tibetan" words sung by the chorus when Conway and the rest of the party arrive at Shangri-La were neologisms concocted out of thin air.

A sneak preview at a Santa Barbara theater was arranged on or about November 20, 1936. The three-hour version did not go well. Apparently there was restless laughter early on and some walkouts. Capra was stunned:

> For the next two days I walked and walked and walked in a dark trance. Over and over I mentally reconstructed the

Director Frank Capra and Ronald Colman take a coffee break in the subfreezing temperature of the refrigerated industrial plant turned sound stage for Lost Horizon.

film—scene by scene, look by look, word by word—seeking
the elusive psychological key that made *Lost Horizon* appealing
when seen by a few [at studio screenings], ridiculous when
seen by many.

On the third morning I drove fast to the studio, rushed to
the cutting rooms, ordered Gene Havlick, my film editor, to
take the main title from the beginning of the *first* reel of the
picture and splice it onto the beginning of the *third* reel.

Capra has said that he wasn't sure this would work, but it was the only
solution he could think of in three days without sleep.

What exactly was cut? According to the final draft screenplay, dated
March 23, 1936, the picture originally began near the conclusion of the
story as we know it, in London where members of the Foreign Office are
elated over the news that Conway has been found by Lord Gainsford (Hugh
Buckler) in a small Chinese mission after having been missing for a year. A
newspaper headline montage follows, which points up Conway's return to
London aboard the S.S. *Manchuria*, then a dissolve to Lord Gainsford
dictating to the radio operator on the *Manchuria* a message regarding
Conway's suffering from a complete loss of memory; dissolve to a table in
the ship's bar where Gainsford joins a group of men, who are in turn joined
by Conway. He indeed recalls nothing at all prior to being found in the
mission.

Next door in the salon the eminent pianist Sieveking, played by concert
pianist and studio musician Max Rabinowitz, is giving a concert. Conway is
drawn to the music. After the concert is over, he sits at the piano and starts
to play.* Sieveking is most interested, and asks Conway what he is playing.
Conway begins to remember: a Chopin study. This surprises Sieveking,
who knows all of Chopin's works, but not this one. Conway recalls that it
was never printed; he learned it from a pupil of Chopin's. Sieveking is
startled; he tells Conway that if a pupil of Chopin were alive today, he
would have to be over a hundred and twenty years old.

As Conway continues to play (what is actually an arrangement of Tiomkin's
love theme for the film), his face seems encased in an expression of profound
disturbance. Suddenly he begins to remember the past and insists on getting
off the ship at the next stop. (All of the above was originally in the novel.)
While waiting on deck, Conway starts to tell Gainsford and the others his
story. On the middle of page fifteen in the script a dissolve is indicated to
the exterior of the flying field at Baskul, where the picture actually begins
as a flashback.

* James Hilton was a relatively accomplished nonprofessional pianist and had a great love for
music.

Left to right: Frank Capra, Margo, Ronald Colman, Jane Wyatt, and John Howard in the Hollywood Columbia Studio between scenes of Lost Horizon.

Not mentioned by Capra is another scene near the end of the film that out of necessity was cut. This was actually a continuation of the prologue in which Conway concludes his story to the group on deck. By now the ship is in dock. Conway rushes to pack. Gainsford locks him in his stateroom, but he gets through a small window and escapes down the gangplank. This episode then dissolves to the sequence in the film as we know it, where Lord Gainsford enters a fashionable London club and recounts his adventures of ten months of trying to track down Conway.

More footage was reshuffled. Dropped along the way (but not mentioned by Capra) were such scenes as Sondra and Maria playing violin and piano, and material dealing with the other white lamas, including the student of Chopin's. Three possible endings had been contemplated and photographed. In one, Conway is toasted by his friends in London, who wish him luck on his plan to return to Shangri-La (used at the first preview); in another, Conway is seen trudging through the snowy mountains until he suddenly sees the entrance to the lamasery; a third shows him reaching the lamasery and reunited with Sondra. The last scene was dropped in the released version, but the other two were both used. In the novel, as in the first preview version, Conway's fate is not resolved.

The high lama's two scences were rewritten, considerably condensed,

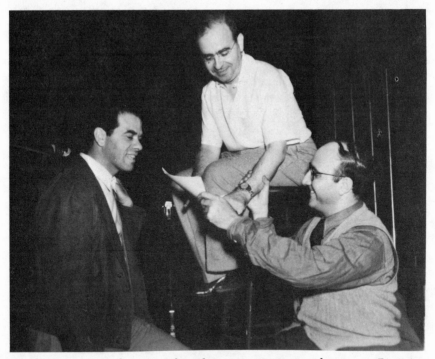

Frank Capra, music director and conductor Max Steiner, and composer Dimitri Tiomkin on Columbia's scoring stage in Hollywood at the time the music for Lost Horizon *was being recorded.*

and photographed again with Sam Jaffe during this period, according to various sources and confirmed by Jaffe in an interview. In the novel and in the final shooting script (distributed when the picture began shooting), and in the initial preview version,* the high lama's soliloquies were of marathon length. James Hilton, in an article published in late 1936, stated that he "wanted to shorten rather drastically some of the high lama's speeches, whereas Capra believed he could keep more of them intact." Obviously, they did not sustain attention at their original length.

According to *The Hollywood Reporter*, Jack Dawn was borrowed from MGM in October to redesign Sam Jaffe's makeup and so give the high lama even greater age in the retakes. Jaffe recalls that in order to achieve the effect of extreme old age in his face, cigarette paper, dry oatmeal, and then fish skin were tried. Finally, a cast was taken of his face at MGM and a built-in piece for either side of his face—complete with furrows—was used. "Concerning my voice, Mr. Capra and I felt that since Shangri-La possessed

* Based on an examination of music materials pertaining to the score, which are preserved.

such health-preserving miracles . . . rather than the halting, hesitating, feeble quality associated with age, the lama's voice should reflect a sort of benign simplicity."

The next preview, with all the modifications and with approximately forty-five minutes of running time pruned, apparently went well, and the picture went on to open in its new form, starting with the burning of Baskul. The reserved-seat, twice-daily showings in the major cities (the so-called road show presentations) began in early March 1937. At that time, the film ran for two hours and twelve minutes. When it went into general release on September 1, it was cut by about fourteen minutes.

In order to capitalize on President Roosevelt's facetious claim in April 1942 that the planes that took part in the famous Doolittle first bombing raid on Tokyo during World War II had come from Shangri-La, Columbia in the fall of 1942 reissued the film and retitled it *Lost Horizon of Shangri-La*. Additional cuts were made, and the local Baskul revolution of 1936 (1931 in the novel) was attributed via a revised prefatory title to aggression by the Japanese!

A few years later the film was reissued again with a bit more footage deleted, reducing the length to one hour and forty-eight minutes. Material from the original road show version that was dropped along the way includes a scene on the airplane between Conway and his brother in which Conway disclaims any credit for saving a handful of whites while leaving thousands of natives to die. Then Conway discusses his unique ideas on how to do away with war altogether. In addition to making for an abrupt transition,

Deleted sequence from Lost Horizon: *Conway (Ronald Colman), on board ship, plays a Chopin study while suffering from amnesia.*

Deleted sequence from Lost
Horizon: *recovering his memory on
board ship, Conway (Colman) wants
to go back to Shangri-La.*

this cut denies audiences a key insight into Conway's character. Also deleted
was smoother and fuller development of the romantic relationship between
Conway and Sondra; considerable footage involving the consumptive girl
played by Isabel Jewell; a discussion of religion between Chang and Conway;
the paleontologist's descent into the Valley of the Blue Moon (and other
scenes with Edward Everett Horton); the porters firing on Conway, his
brother, and Maria, thus precipitating an avalanche, which now seems only
a chance occurrence; and various other relatively important bits.

The elaborate production had cost about $2,000,000. This would have
been an exceptionally expensive film in 1936–1937 even for opulent MGM,
but for the relatively modest Columbia it was an incredible sum. Few
Columbia features up to that time had cost one-fourth of that amount.
Although *Lost Horizon* was a popular picture, its cost worked against it, as
reflected in Columbia Pictures' financial statement. The company's gross
receipts had doubled to $20,000,000 between 1933 and 1938, but profits,
which had reached a high of $1,815,267 in 1935, following the release of
Capra's *It Happened One Night*, fell to a perilous $183,393 in 1938, after
the release of *Lost Horizon. It Happened One Night* cost approximately
$325,000 and only occupied Capra for a few months, whereas *Lost Horizon*
at $2,000,000 had taken up almost two years of the director's time.

An elaborate stage musical version of *Lost Horizon*, called *Shangri-La*,
ran on Broadway for only twenty-one performances in 1956. The music was

by Harry Warren with the book and lyrics by James Hilton, Jerome Lawrence, and Robert E. Lee. Dennis King, replacing Lew Ayres, who dropped out in Boston just before the show opened on Broadway, played Conway, and Shirley Yamaguchi, brought from Japan at the last minute, played Lo-Tsen. The relationship of Conway, Lo-Tsen, and Conway's brother (Jack Cassidy) was closer to the novel than the 1937 film. Alice Ghostley as the lady missionary of the novel replaced the tubercular prostitute played by Isabel Jewell, and a pair of USO dancers (Harold Lang and Joan Holloway) took the place of the characters portrayed by Thomas Mitchell and Edward Everett Horton. Martyn Green was Chang and Berry Kroeger was the high lama.

Columbia's $8,000,000 screen musical remake was released in 1973 and featured Peter Finch and Liv Ullmann. The remake followed the construction of the 1937 film closely. The consumptive prostitute (Sally Kellerman) became a suicidal, pill-popping *Newsweek* photographer-correspondent; the embezzling businessman (George Kennedy), Chang (John Gielgud), the high lama (Charles Boyer), Maria (Olivia Hussey), and Conway's brother (Michael York) stayed more or less intact, except that some of the latter's excessive abrasiveness was toned down. Edward Everett Horton's paleontologist was changed to a down-at-heels USO performer (Bobby Van). The exterior lamasery was a modification of the four-acre *Camelot* castle set on the back lot of Warner Bros. and Columbia's Burbank Studio.

Although the picture starts promisingly, once Conway and his group arrive in Shangri-La the entire concept and execution turn into a disaster. The new score by Burt Bacharach and Hal David, along with Hermes Pan's dance direction, are embarrassing and unintentionally funny. All in all the film was a major miscalculation that did not fare at all well with the public or the critics. It certainly has not and will not diminish the charm and quality of the original production.

The road-show negative and the subsequent general-release negative of the first production of *Lost Horizon* are believed to have been lost or destroyed. *Lost Horizon of Shangri-La* was the only version intact until 1969, when Columbia Pictures turned their nitrate studio print of the general release version over to the American Film Institute, but fourteen minutes of road-show bits and pieces were still missing (to say nothing of the footage that made up the original three-hour preview edition, which probably was destroyed years ago). The American Film Institute has been continually searching for any additional material to fill in the missing sections. As of this writing, a version incorporating material from the Columbia Studio print, several variant versions, in addition to the complete road-show soundtrack from the National Film Archive in London, and a

16mm worn television print, dubbed into French, from Canada have yielded what the AFI calls a "restoration in progress" version that runs the full 132 minutes and has the complete dialogue but is missing six minutes of picture in five different places. A title appears on the screen during those segments stating "Scene Missing." And the search goes on: Rumors have it that a complete print has been located in Czechoslovakia, and the AFI has been negotiating for two years with a private collector in Europe who claims to have a copy.

Meanwhile the film continues to have a magical effect on many—specifically those who can relate to the abstract search for a personal Shangri-La, or the Fountain of Youth, Utopia, Nirvana, the Garden of Eden, or vaguely similar concepts. In the novel, written in 1933, the high lama says:

> We have a dream and a vision. It is a vision that first appeared to old Perrault [the high lama] . . . . It seemed to him that all the loveliest things were transient and perishable, and that war, lust, and brutality might some day crush them until there were no more left in the world. He . . . saw the nations strengthening, not in wisdom, but in vulgar passions and the will to destroy; he saw their machine power multiplying . . . . He foresaw a time when men, exultant in the technique of homicide, would rage so hotly over the world that every precious thing would be in danger, every book and picture and harmony, every treasure garnered through two milenniums, the small, the delicate, the defenseless—all would be lost . . . .
>
> Here [in Shangri-La] we shall stay with our books and our music and our meditations, conserving the frail elegancies of a dying age, and seeking such wisdom as men will need when their passions are all spent. We have a heritage to cherish and bequeath . . . .
>
> Then, my son, when the strong have devoured each other, the Christian ethic may at last be fulfilled, and the meek shall inherit the earth.

In 1936 Hilton said, "The theme, of course, was not new, nor the character either. It was almost a Christ theme; just the story of a simple, naive goodness and wisdom. Writers have written that over and over again . . . .

"No, you're right—it doesn't seem to have done much good."

3

THEY CALLED IT "DISNEY'S FOLLY": SNOW WHITE AND THE SEVEN DWARFS (1937)

By 1933, Walt Disney's Mickey Mouse and Silly Symphony cartoon short subjects had been audience favorites since they were introduced in the late 1920s. Mickey's star power was remarkable. His name meant more on a theater marquee than many a Hollywood flesh-and-blood luminary. In order to experiment and not concentrate solely on the antics of continuing characters, Disney had developed his Silly Symphony cartoons shortly after the initial success of Mickey. The scope broadened. Music became an important ingredient at the conceptual stage of the Symphonies. Three-color Technicolor was introduced for the first time with a 1932 Silly Symphony, *Flowers and Trees,* and thereafter all Symphonies were done in Technicolor—Mickey following with color in 1935.

Hamilton Luske, an animator who joined the Disney Studio in 1931, says that in the early 1930s Disney "began to see animation as not merely the cartooning of broad caricatures, gags and comic situations, but as a means of bringing life and motion to fine illustration. The Silly Symphony short subjects were the proving ground." Animator Ward Kimball, who went to Disney in 1934, says that "if you were a top animator at Disney, you would work on the Silly Symphonies because they were the artistic cartoons. Mickey Mouse was the potboiler."

Gradually fairy tales, fables, Mother Goose stories, and nursery tales formed the basis of many of the Silly Symphonies. In 1933 Disney scored his most spectacular success up to that time with *Three Little Pigs*, which perfectly integrated a beloved story, well-developed characters—straight, comedic, and villainous—with advanced color rendering and an original song that became a major hit: "Who's Afraid of the Big Bad Wolf?"

Disney took stock. *Three Little Pigs* had required considerably more time and money to make than the cartoons of his competitors, but since it was merely a short subject there was only so much revenue potential, regardless of its phenomenal success. *Three Little Pigs* cost $15,719 to produce and netted the studio $4,000 profit. Disney was not interested in making cheap products or in repeating himself again and again. He constantly sought new areas to explore, better quality, and fresh techniques.

A feature-length cartoon was in the back of his mind at least as early as 1933. After all, Charlie Chaplin, Harold Lloyd, Buster Keaton, and other famous stars of popular short subjects discovered in the early 1920s that the only way to derive sufficient profits from their labors was to switch from the limitations of the shorts field to the feature. The considerable acclaim of *Three Little Pigs* gave impetus to Disney's random thoughts about a feature. Some time earlier, Mary Pickford wanted him to produce a feature-length *Alice In Wonderland* with herself as Alice but all the other characters hand-drawn. Disney recalled in 1937 that "she was going to put up the money . . . . It wouldn't have been too difficult in black and white—just a lot of intricate process shots. I worked out a plan. Then Paramount came along with a production of *Alice* [in late 1933], and that knocked out our idea."

Another time in the early 1930s, Disney revealed, he and Will Rogers conferred on a feature-length version of *Rip Van Winkle*, with the little men to be done by animation and Rogers portraying Rip. But Paramount wouldn't release its rights to the famous play that was based on the novel.

In the spring of 1933, there were talks between Disney and producer Merian C. Cooper about doing a feature-length animated version of *Babes in Toyland*, which RKO Radio Pictures owned, in the new three-color Technicolor. According to Cooper, he recommended that RKO put up the money for and release the feature, but RKO executives in New York turned down the proposal.

Also, sometime in 1933, after the success of *Three Little Pigs*, the fairy tale *Snow White* was discussed at the studio as one of the future Silly

Symphonies. As time went on, Disney started to realize the potential of this material for his first feature. The plan for *Snow White* to be a short subject was shelved, but Disney kept the story in the back of his mind.

A rather primitive precursor to *Snow White* was produced in 1932 by Disney as a Silly Symphony called *Babes in the Woods*, which is actually a variation on "Hansel and Gretel." Elements that had a vague similarity to those in *Snow White* included the frightened children going into the woods and imagining the threats of trees turning into ogres and the like; the children discovering a lair of singing dwarfs deep in the forest; a wicked witch who lures the children to her candy-covered house, where inside, by using a magic potion, she has changed children into animals, reptiles, and insects; the dwarfs going after the witch and liberating the children, and so on.

By the summer of 1934 ideas were being formulated for a feature version of *Snow White* to cost about $250,000. An exploratory outline in the studio's archives dated August 9 includes a discussion of the dwarfs with fifty possible names that "will immediately identify the character in the minds of the audience." Five of the eventual seven were on the list—all but Doc and Dopey. Some of the other names include Hoppy, Weepy, Dirty, Hungry, Thrifty, Nifty, Shifty, Woeful, Doleful, Soulful, Awful, Snoopy, Gabby, Blabby, Neurtsy, Gloomy, Daffy, Gaspy, Hotsy, Jaunty, Biggy, Biggy-Wiggy, and Biggo-Ego. Character comedian Sterling Holloway was suggested for the voice and some visual characteristics of Sleepy, while Awful was described as "the most lovable and interesting of the dwarf characters. He steals and drinks and is very dirty,"

The early outline also lists a number of song possibilities, among them "Some Day My Prince Will Come," which became one of the big hits in the eventually realized film three-and-one-half years later.

The outline at this time differs in various ways from the original tale and from the final draft of the script. For example, in the early outline Snow White, before arriving at the dwarfs' house, travels through a series of strange, enchanted sites such as Sleepy Valley with its vast poppy fields, the Morass of Monsters, and the Valley of the Dragons, in addition to Upside-down or Backward Lane.

By October 1934, the dwarfs' names were almost resolved: Happy, Sleepy, Doc, Bashful, Jumpy, Grumpy, and an unnamed seventh described as "deaf—always listening intently—happy, quick movements, spry." Jumpy ("like a chap in constant fear of being goosed") was later replaced by Sneezy, and Dopey evolved slowly and was not named until quite late in the proceedings. The October Cast of Characters describes Snow White as a "Janet Gaynor type—14 years old"; the Prince, "Doug Fairbanks type—18 years old"; the Queen, "A mixture of Lady Macbeth and The Big Bad Wolf."

Snow White (© WALT DISNEY PRODUCTIONS)

Disney's basic story outline was derived from one of the tales the Brothers Grimm collected in the early nineteenth century from oral tradition in Cassel, Germany. It has subsequently been found with little variation over a wide area from Ireland to Asia Minor, and in several parts of Africa. The tale contains elements that have their origins in European folk tradition, but it is not necessarily an old story, and has probably come under literary influence. For example, the theme of the glass coffin containing the body of a beautiful young girl who is not really dead was a feature of *Pentamerone*, a collection of fairy tales by Giambattista Basile, published in 1634.

The Grimm *Snow White* was embellished by Disney in many ways, modified in some, and pruned in others. Disney added a Cinderella touch at the opening of the film by showing Snow White forced to wear rags and work as a scullery maid despite her royal blood, because of the jealousy of her wicked stepmother, the Queen. Disney even referred to her at the time as "A Cinderella type."

He also introduced the Prince at the opening, whereas in the old story he appears only at the end. In the early drafts of the Disney version the Prince has a great deal to do. He is taken prisoner by the wicked Queen. She enters the dungeon where the gagged Prince dangles from chains suspended from the ceiling. Confronting him are several skeletons, also chained and gagged. "This is a sequence of gruesome comedy—of dancing skeletons—fantastic shadows—witchcraft and deviltry."

The Queen torments the Prince by telling him of her scheme to murder Snow White with the poisoned comb. She works the skeletons like marionettes so that they bow, shake hands, and dance. She starts a tiny trickle of water into his cell. As the water seeps in faster and faster, the Queen, disguised this time as an ugly, witchlike crone, leaves by the river tunnel.

Now the water is waist-deep. The Prince's struggles are futile. Birds looking in the cell window register understanding of his plight. They pick the keys off the guard's belt, insert a key into the lock and put a stick through the key. The weight of their bodies working on this makeshift lever turns the key. The force of the water pushes the door open and the wall of water sweeps down the corridor, tumbling the guard along as the birds fly to the Prince with the keys and free him.

The early continuity continues: "The guard sounds the alarm and rushes for the Prince's open cell; but the Prince is waiting for him—socks him—takes his sword, and springs into the corridor. Both ends of the passageway are blocked by soldiers closing in on him. With the technique of Doug Fairbanks, he hacks his way to freedom. He whistles, and his horse leaps from the palace stables and charges to his side. The Prince springs on his horse and battles his way into the woods and to safety . . . . They must track the wicked Queen and rescue Snow White . . . . They're off in a cloud of dust!"

None of the above was used in the later script, and none of it was animated. Years later, however, the Prince in Disney's *Sleeping Beauty* (1959) was given a good deal to do. Indeed, he was a prisoner in the evil witch's (Maleficent) castle dungeon, from which he makes a swashbuckling escape with the help of three good fairies, who reduce themselves to miniature size and perform functions similar to those of the birds described above.

The Prince was also involved in an elaborate fantasy sequence in the clouds in earlier *Snow White* scripts. He and Snow White dance a waltz to "Some Day My Prince Will Come," after which little stars lead them to a

Animators' early model sheet for the dwarfs in Snow White and the Seven Dwarfs. (© WALT DISNEY PRODUCTIONS)

Early model sheet for the Queen, Snow White, and the Prince in Snow White. (© WALT DISNEY PRODUCTIONS)

Adviana Caselotti, Snow White's speaking and singing voice.

swanlike ship. The stars push the ship over the Milky Way, and the wind, with chorus accompaniment, carries it into a castle in the clouds. This sequence was later dropped before it was animated, and Snow White, in the final film, merely sings the song to the dwarfs in the cottage.

The Prince's role kept diminishing in subsequent drafts because of animation difficulties. The realistically rendered Prince, Snow White, Queen, and Huntsman were extraordinarily difficult to animate properly—they appeared stiff and cumbersome in tests—whereas the dwarfs and animal characters were relatively easy, because of the cartoon styling. The Prince and Snow White posed the most problems, because they were straight juvenile leads. Disney, recognizing the difficulties in animating the human form, wanted to give his animators experience in this area. They were already taking art classes set up at the studio, and in late 1934, as improvements were noted, several animators were assigned to work on a Silly Symphony called *The Goddess of Spring*, based on the Greek myth of Persephone. Drawing Persephone was a trial run for the later drawing of

Snow White. The results were relatively crude, but Disney kept the art classes going, expanded his staff from six in 1928 to 187 in 1934, and continued to experiment with rendering human beings.

In 1935, Disney instructed Don Graham, the head of his art school, to find 300 artists! A major talent search began. Graham signed up artists from all over the country. Primarily they were young men who had graduated from universities and colleges with degrees in architecture, painting, and illustration. Because of the Depression, they were unable to find work in their fields. Graham recalled years later:

> Disney's educational program went into high gear. From eight in the morning till nine at night what was probably the most unique art school in the world was conducted. As *Snow White* began to take shape, various experts from all branches of the studio were called upon to contribute to the program. Intensive lectures on character construction, animation, layout, background, mechanics and direction extended studio knowledge to the youngest neophyte.

Animator Marc Davis remembers the enthusiasm at the studio during that period:

> Whatever we were doing hadn't been done before . . . . There was excitement and there was competition; everyone was young and everyone was doing something.
>
> We saw every ballet, we saw every film. If a film was good we would go and see it five times. At one time Walt rented a studio up in North Hollywood and every Wednesday night we would see a selection of films—anything from Chaplin to unusual subjects. Anything that might produce growth, that might be stimulating—the cutting of scenes, the staging, how a group of scenes was put together. Everybody was studying constantly . . . . We weren't making much because the Studio didn't have much, but it was a perfect time of many things coming together in one orbit. Walt was that lodestone.

Disney veteran Ken Anderson reports:

> I kept a notebook in those days of camera angles and camera moves from live-action pictures. Walt took a look at the notebooks and had others start keeping them too. He was always trying to overcome the limitations of the cartoon medium, though he never expressed it in so many words.

But animation director Ben Sharpsteen, who joined Disney in 1929, says:

> *Snow White* required talent galore that was not possessed by
> many of the old-guard artists. And the newer people that
> possessed the artistic talents or finesse were usually sadly
> lacking in showmanship and entertainment. This condition led
> to many personnel problems as it divided artists up into two
> groups. One, that was dedicated to getting laughs—even
> slapstick—anything for entertainment. The other one, known
> as the arty group . . . .

For *Snow White* Disney had actors and models photographed on motion-picture film for the animators to study frame by frame. These players were actually acting out individual scenes from the film with appropriate movements and gestures. Marjorie Belcher, a young dancer—later known as Marge Champion, the wife and dance partner of Gower Champion—was Snow White's model for the entire film.

The little birds and animals in the forest who became Snow White's friends were strictly a Disney touch, having been a proven and popular ingredient from the shorts. The dwarfs had no names or individual characteristics in the original fairy tale, and they did not participate to any degree in the kind of inventive and comic incidents evolved at the Disney studio. Out of the Disney-expanded treatment of the dwarfs and their relationship with Snow White grew a variation on what was regarded as an always effective formula: thrusting a sweet, trusting child among grouchy, elderly guardians (*Little Lord Fauntleroy, Three Wise Fools, Daddies, Grumpy,* and so forth).

In the Grimm version of the tale, the Queen disguised herself on three separate occasions to visit Snow White at the dwarfs' cottage in order to kill her. The last attempt was with the poisoned apple. Disney reduced the three attempts to only the apple episode (although early drafts contained the poisoned comb visit as well). But what originally was described in the Grimm text as "then she [the Queen] dressed herself up as a peasant's wife and traveled over the hills to the dwarfs' cottage [with the poisoned apple]" became an embellished, macabre metamorphosis, as described by Disney when he personally told the entire story of *Snow White* at his old Hyperion Studio on the evening of December 22, 1936. Present were twenty-nine members of his staff. The telling, which was taken down by a stenographer, is a tour de force that runs eleven typewritten legal-size pages. Here is the excerpt:

> She puts various poisons in these retorts, and these different
> mixtures bubble, sob, and make weird sounds . . . . She will

have a cackle of an old hag. Then she mixes the various liquids from all these retorts, and it foams . . . . She then drinks this mixture to the success of Snow White's death . . . .

When the Queen is making her transformation, you see a lot of shadows, and from the shadows the Queen emerges— like Dr. Jekyll and Mr. Hyde. You don't see her face change, you see her shape change. You see the raven watching . . . . Her voice becomes changed and her shape is changed . . . . She may be a terrible old hag, but she is happy—not even her pet [raven] would recognize her.

Some film aficionados believe that the title character from RKO's 1935 version of H. Rider Haggard's fantastic adventure tale, *She*, served as a major influence for Disney's visual and vocal approach to the Queen. There are certainly some parallels with Helen Gahagan's look and portrayal, but whether this was conscious or coincidental cannot be verified.

Disney adapted an element from *Sleeping Beauty*. In the Grimm *Snow White*, the Prince discovers Snow White, ostensibly dead, in a glass coffin, but when the coffin is lifted to be taken away, the piece of poisoned apple falls from between Snow White's lips and she awakens. Disney had the Prince awaken Snow White with a kiss, in the manner of *Sleeping Beauty*, with no evidence of the apple remaining.

Disney believed that *Snow White* was the ideal vehicle containing all the necessary ingredients for his first feature. Furthermore, the foreign market was highly important, and the story of *Snow White* was a beloved tale in almost every country in the world. From a personal standpoint, it was a nostalgic favorite of Disney's:

> When I was a child, every evening after supper, my grand-
> mother would take down from the shelf the well-worn volumes
> of Grimms' Fairy Tales and Hans Christian Andersen. It was
> the best time of day for me, and the stories and characters in
> them seemed quite as real as my schoolmates and our games.
> Of all the characters in the fairy tales, I loved Snow White the
> best.

When Disney went back to his home in Kansas City in 1932, he found the book of Grimms' fairy tales that he had not seen since his childhood. It is possible that this was the catalyst for his desire to film *Snow White*.

When Disney was a newsboy in Kansas City, he had been invited to attend the silent 1916 feature-film version of *Snow White*, starring Marguerite Clark, at the Convention Hall. The film was projected on four screens simultaneously in the huge auditorium, and he was able to watch two of

The wicked Queen in Snow White. (© WALT DISNEY PRODUCTIONS)

them from where he was sitting. It had been his most vivid early memory of going to the movies.

The lavish Marguerite Clark version, in which the dwarfs were played by dwarfs, was the fourth time the story had been adapted for the screen. The first was a 1910 French production called *Little Snowdrop*, which ran only about fifteen minutes; next was a forty-minute 1913 film called simply *Snow White*, in which the dwarfs were played by children ("The Powers Kids"). As in the Sleeping Beauty story and the later Disney *Snow White*, the Prince awakens Snow White from her deathlike sleep with a kiss. Another *Snow White*, released by Educational Films at about the same time as the Marguerite Clark entry and running a little under an hour, had a cast composed entirely of children. None of these versions contained any animation.

The actual animation phase of Disney's *Snow White* did not begin until 1936. During 1934 and 1935 the work on the adaptation had been done, together with the attendant incident and character development. Then voices for the characters were definitely decided on in 1936. All of this was going on in conjunction with the regular Disney Studio program of approximately sixteen or seventeen Mickey Mouse and Silly Symphony short subjects each year.

As late as December 1935, in a letter to director Sidney Franklin, Disney said:

> Our feature, *Snow White*, is beginning to roll along now, although it has been one terrible job getting the thing started—

Helen Gahagan playing the title role in She *(1935)—a major influence for Disney's visual and vocal approach to the Queen in* Snow White?

I've had continuity all wrapped around my neck like a bunch of spaghetti. While my story is not yet completely worked out, I believe we have something that is going to be good.

I have at least a full year's work ahead of me, but during this time I am sure I shall gain a great deal of valuable experience that we can put to good use when we start on *Bambi.*

Preserved in the archives at the Disney Studio are stenographers' transcripts of the many story conferences held during the preparation of *Snow White.* They are invaluable insights into the creative process of Disney and his staff at the time. A major sequence, in which Snow White and her animal friends clean up the dwarfs' cottage, was discussed in a conference on October 31, 1935, and is typical of the inventive and imaginative developments that took place. The following is a brief condensation of what was probably a two-hour meeting among Disney and staff members Hamilton Luske, Charles Thorson, and Harry Reeves:

It was agreed to incorporate the housecleaning sequence with finding the [dwarfs'] house, instead of breaking away to the dwarfs and then back to the housecleaning.

HAM: Find something for every animal accompanying Snow White to do—something adapted to the animal. Deer could lick plates—dust with short tail—use squirrel's long bushy tail, etc . . . .

The Prince about to awaken the Princess from her death-like sleep in Snow White.
(© WALT DISNEY PRODUCTIONS)

The Prince, in Disney's Sleeping Beauty *(1959), about to awaken the Princess from her death-like sleep.* (© WALT DISNEY PRODUCTIONS)

HARRY: Raccoon would make a good duster.

WALT: Have some birds up in the rafters getting cobwebs around their tails . . . . I think Snow White should impress birds and animals with "we've got to clean it up and surprise them when they come home and maybe they'll let me stay and keep house for them . . . ."

HAM: Different tails could work like different kinds of mops—washing windows—one long tail would slap the water on, another animal would squeegee the water off.

HARRY: As she picks up sock, nuts fall out and squirrels make a scramble . . . .

HAM: These are all such little animals that most of the work has to be done in teams—two or four to carry things.

CHARLES: Would a long shot of the outside of the house work well there—with dust coming out of the window, etc.?

HAM: Are there any gags on the animals themselves—like bird trying to clean gourd; gets head stuck . . . .

WALT: Yes, that is what we ought to do, but not bring in gags that have nothing to do with cleaning . . . . Have rabbits dusting vigorously; dust gets the best of them—they sneeze and keep on dusting . . . . At that point she would catch the squirrels sweeping stuff under the floor. They sweep dust to hole in baseboard to get rid of it; stuff comes flying out and rat comes out . . . .

HAM: Clothes are washed and birds hang them up . . . .

WALT: Change words of song so they fit in more with Snow White's handing the animals brushes, etc. . . . Snow White: "If you just hum a merry tune"—and they start humming. . . . Then Snow White would start to tell them to "whistle while you work." She would start giving the animals things to do. By that time she has sung, of course . . . . Birds could come marching in. Try to arrange to stay with the birds for a section of the whistling. Orchestra would play with a whistling effect . . . . Get it in the woodwinds—like playing something instrumentally to sound like whistling . . . . Get a way to finish the song that isn't just an end. Work in a shot trucking [moving] out of the house. Truck back and show animals shaking rugs out of the windows—little characters outside beating things out in the yard. Truck out and the melody of "Whistle While You Work" gets quieter and quieter. Leave them all working—birds scrubbing clothes. The last thing you see as you truck away is little birds hanging up clothes. Fade out on that and music would fade out—At the end all you would hear is the flute—before fading into the Dig, Dig song [Heigh-Ho] and the hammering rhythm.

Voices were auditioned over a long period of time, Snow White's being the most difficult to find. The auditions at the studio were wired through Disney's office, and each day or so he heard at least two or three, deliberately choosing not to see the face and body that went with the voice. None possessed the proper quality Disney had in his imagination. When he finally heard one high-pitched, youthful soprano voice, there was no question in his mind. She was eighteen-year-old Adriana Caselotti, who had been family trained in Italian opera.

The voices of the other characters came from various sources. They were radio-artists, character actors from films, vaudeville performers. One of the reliable in-house people Disney had used for the short subjects—Pinto Colvig, the voice of Goofy and The Big Bad Wolf—became the voice for both Grumpy and Sleepy. Screen comedian Billy Gilbert, whose specialty was a sneeze that developed in the form of a mighty crescendo, read in *Variety* that one dwarf was to be called Sneezy and immediately called Disney, who agreed to an audition. After Disney caught his act in the office there was no contest—he had the part. Lucille La Verne, whose specialty was playing old hags in films (*Orphans of the Storm, A Tale of Two Cities*), provided the voice for the wicked Queen and her metamorphosed old peddler woman.*

From the beginning, music was to play a strong role in the evolution of Snow White. The Silly Symphonies were as important musically as they were visually, and since *Snow White* was referred to at the studio as the "Feature Symphony," great care was taken in developing the musical aspects. Staff composer Frank Churchill, who had written "Who's Afraid of the Big Bad Wolf" for *Three Little Pigs*, was assigned the task of creating the music for the songs, which were to be an integral part of the picture's continuity. Larry Morey, another staff man, was responsible for the lyrics.

---

* Radio actor Roy Atwell supplied the voice for Doc, film actor Otis Harlan was Happy, Scotty Mattraw played Bashful, singer Harry Stockwell's voice was used for the Prince, and although Dopey did not speak, his facial expressions were modeled on burlesque comic Eddie Collins. Stage and film actor Moroni Olsen was the voice of the Magic Mirror, and Stuart Buchanan played the Queen's Huntsman.

Innumerable song possibilities were discussed, developed, and eventually discarded because they did not come up to Disney's expectations. Disney was always on hand to dictate the content of each song, to say what had to be expressed at each point, to listen and then have things modified or redone when needed, and to correct lyrics and put in new words. Since the musical sequences, which constituted a large percentage of the film, could not be animated until the tunes were recorded, most of the numbers were recorded in 1936. The background score was done after the picture was finished and edited.

It was Disney's objective that the songs would either offer exposition, develop characters and situations, or advance the plot, rather than be mere musical interludes inserted here and there. He wanted a fusion of story, character, and music. During one of his *Snow White* conferences he said to members of his staff: "It can still be good music and not follow the same pattern everybody in the country has followed. We still haven't hit it in any of these songs . . . . It's still that influence from the musicals they have been doing for years. Really, we should set a new pattern—a new way to use music—weave it into the story so somebody doesn't just burst into song." Although this approach later became more or less standard, it was not at the time. In films, *The Wizard of Oz*, which appeared a year and a half after *Snow White* and indeed was inspired by it, has often been given credit for its marvelous innovative fusion of story and music.

Three of *Snow White's* eight songs—"Heigh-Ho," "Whistle While You Work," and "Some Day My Prince Will Come"—were major hits, played incessantly on the radio, frequently recorded, and popular with dance bands of the day. Two other melodies—"One Song" and "With a Smile and a Song"—were not too far behind in public enthusiasm, while the remainder of the tunes—"I'm Wishing," "The Washing Song," and "The Silly Song" (Dwarfs' Yodel Song)—were special-situation material that did not work particularly well out of context. The underscoring, by Leigh Harline, Frank Churchill, and Paul J. Smith, based in part on the songs, was complete with leitmotifs and standard nineteenth-century symphonic orchestral coloring, textures, and effects. It was done lushly, with a large orchestra and mixed chorus.

Following the development of the script, character design, and song composition, Disney started assigning his sequence directors, supervising animators, animators, layout teams, and background designers. Individual artists were cast because of their particular areas of talent and strength. An artist who would be marvelously inventive with regard to the dwarfs would not necessarily be suitable to animate the Queen or the animals, for example.

Grim Natwick, one of the finest animators of the female form and character, was assigned (along with others) the animation of Snow White herself:

> They didn't want her to look like a princess, really. They wanted her to look like a cute little girl who could be a princess. So instead of a little crown, it ended with a little bow . . . . They allowed me two months of experimental animation before they ever asked me to animate one scene in the picture . . . . Disney had only one rule: whatever we did had to be better than anybody else could do it, even if you had to animate it nine times, as I once did.

Ward Kimball recalls that as work progressed on *Snow White*, Disney would imitate all the dwarfs whenever he or one of the animators wanted to make them behave in a certain way. "He was as good a pantomimist as Chaplin."

Color was a major consideration. During a meeting with some of his key people on December 1, 1936, Disney emphasized:

> I think we are trying to achieve something different here. We are not going after the comic supplement coloring. We have to strive for a certain depth and realism . . . . We have to get a lot of depth through the use of colors—the subduing of the colors at the right time and for the right effect . . . . Inside the [dwarfs'] house I see a very rich effect gotten by throwing the distance in shadows and subduing a lot of the background colors . . . . There is going to be an hour and thirty minutes of this. If you have seen Technicolor features you perhaps felt there was a lot of color splashed through it . . . . There will be a tendency on our part to look at individual scenes, then individual sequences. We have to go further and look at the picture as a whole, and not try to get every color trick effect in every sequence, but rely on the number of different effects we have in the picture as a whole—not try to cram everything in every sequence.

Because of the demands of the first feature, Disney's special effects department was enlarged and became more and more involved in finding methods of creating realistic effects, such as rain and lightning. During the final months of production, a multiplane camera was developed at the studio—one that could shoot simultaneously several layers of action and background, layers that were separated in such a way as to produce an accurate sense of depth. Although the multiplane was developed too late for extensive use on *Snow White*, some special scenes were either saved or redone to take advantage of this dimensional technique.

While much of the production work was telescoped into the final ten or twelve months, *Snow White* was the result of more than three years of concentrated effort. And, of course, there were innumerable problems. The increasing delays and mounting costs were due mostly to discoveries of possibilities for improvement. Then Disney would order his staff to go back and make changes.

Although technically perhaps it was not the first full-length feature cartoon, *Snow White* was the first American film of its kind, and the first anywhere to be done in sound and color and with music.* The original 1934 budget of $250,000 was soon adjusted to $500,000 and then climbed steadily upward. Finally, over $1,000,000 was tied up in the film, but it was still not finished when the money ran out. United Artists, Disney's distributor before he started releasing through RKO in 1937, apparently had exhibited little enthusiasm for the project, and key industry figures doubted the wisdom of Disney's experiment—labeled "Disney's Folly" around the film community. Before the Bank of America would loan more money to finish *Snow White*, a special screening of incomplete material augmented with filmed pencil sketches and rough layouts to provide the connective tissue was arranged for the bank executive who supervised loans to Walt Disney Productions. Disney was apprehensive. He disliked showing work in progress to outsiders, but in this instance he had no choice. Completion money was desperately needed. Joseph Rosenberg, the bank executive, sat in silence while Disney showed him the fragmentary and patched *Snow White*. As he left after the screening Rosenberg supposedly said, "That thing is going to make a hatful of money." Thus financing was assured and work resumed. The eventual negative cost was $1,488,423.

Animator Ward Kimball says that:

> Walt was . . . the world's best salesman because he believed
> in his product. You know, it wasn't a con routine with him.
> I used to sit in awe watching this guy when he'd sell a banker
> or a group of private backers on an idea. He'd get up and act

---

* There have been references to *The Apostle* (1917) and *Peludopolis* (1931), feature-length cartoon political satires made in Argentina, but no longer available, and an Italian animated feature version of *The Adventures of Pinocchio* (circa 1936). Other features have been erroneously labeled "animated," in the drawn sense, but in reality they were produced with puppets, silhouette cutouts, or object stop-motion. Two Max Fleischer films, *Einstein's Theory of Relativity* (1923) and *Darwin's Theory of Evolution* (1923), although almost feature-length, contained only some animation.

out all the parts. He could see the whole thing. After he finished, so could everyone he was talking to . . . .

He felt that if you put your heart into a project and if you were a perfectionist, people would automatically like it. They would appreciate the quality . . . . He would take a little more time, spend a little more money. And he made sure there was a good story blocked out from the beginning.

As work on *Snow White* neared completion in late 1937, Disney decided to eliminate two sequences on which considerable work already had been done. Both sequences were described by Disney at the staff meeting on the night of December 22, 1936:

> Just as they are finishing the Washing Sequence, we come to Snow White and the Soup Sequence. The Soup Sequence is a musical sequence, and it is working out very funny. There are all soup sounds, and the different ways they [the dwarfs] guzzle soup. Snow White . . . stops them. They are all making this noise to music . . . when she says, "That isn't the way gentlemen eat soup." She starts them out with "spoon in the hand, bend in the wrist," etc., and the little guys all repeat after her, and Snow White tells them that it is perfect. Then they all make a terrific noise. They start in sucking the soup off the spoon six inches away from their mouths. The very thing she is trying to correct, they have not corrected. She finally gives up in disgust.

The musical sequence, with the song "Music in Your Soup," continues with a great many physical gags, mostly involving Dopey swallowing a soup spoon.

The second sequence that was eliminated followed the scene in which Snow White kisses the dwarfs goodbye as they are leaving for work:

> We then come along to the dwarfs having a meeting in the woods. Doc is conducting the meeting, and the dwarfs are discussing how much they all like Snow White . . . . Doc raps in on the muddle and says, "Quiet!" and says that he wants to do something for the Princess to gladden her heart. One of the dwarfs makes the suggestion that they give her a present . . . . [Doc] gets them thinking, and it ends up that they all decide to make her a bed, which is Sleepy's suggestion. Each one tells what part he will play in making the bed. There are various gags of them building the bed. We fade out . . . and come to Snow White, who is busy making pies.

Disney eliminated these sequences because of his ruthless sense of editing. As sequences—taken by themselves—they were excellent, but in the final analysis, in the words of the animator of both episodes, Ward Kimball, "when Walt started seeing the whole picture, he thought that [these were] places that we ought to get on with the story."

There was never any material written or drawn and photographed for the film showing Snow White's real mother, who dies in childbirth, although references or drawings of this and other embellishments were made up for authorized book versions and comic strips.

During the last months of production, the entire studio felt the pressure. Everyone was working nights and weekends. Disney never let up in his striving for perfection. He kept wanting to redo parts of the film. But time was running out for the Christmas 1937 release date. Disney said at the time, "I've seen so much of *Snow White* that I am conscious only of the places where it could be improved. You see, we've learned such a lot since we started this thing! I wish I could yank it back and do it all over again." Finally, Roy Disney, the business head of the studio, told his brother that not only was there no more time, but that the money had run out again and this time no more could be borrowed. But there was one more thing to fix. When the Prince leaned over to kiss Snow White in her glass coffin, the animation had a shimmying effect. Walt Disney insisted that this be redone. Roy Disney insisted that it not. The Prince has continued to shimmy through the years.

Finally, on December 21, 1937, *Snow White and the Seven Dwarfs* was premiered at the Carthay Circle Theater in Los Angeles. It seems inconceivable today that there was great concern at the Disney Studio over the possibility of the movie being a failure. As the budget grew it was feared that the feature would not be able to recover its astronomical cost. It was, of course, an overwhelming success.

As Christopher Finch says in *The Art of Walt Disney* (1973), "*Snow White* is distinguished by two seemingly opposed characteristics: economy of construction and extravagance of invention . . . . Above all, the entire movie manages to sustain the ambiance of timelessness which is so essential to the fairy tale genre." It is also nineteenth-century story-book illustration merged with a distinct cartoon style and transferred to motion pictures using a panorama of live-action film techniques that go back to Griffith and Eisenstein. Within the film are a multitude of examples of cranelike shots, montage, cross-cutting, parallel editing, "mood" lighting, zoom shots, "dutch" angles, and much more. These were a direct influence of Disney's policy of screening every kind of film for his staff.

Snow White is the only film discussed in this book that has yet to be sold to or shown on television. The Disney policy carefully allows for full-scale theatrical reissue of most of their features approximately every seven years. *Snow White* was reissued in 1944, 1952, 1958, 1967, and 1975. Presumably it will continue to be seen by children everywhere and by the child within the adult in perpetuity.

Walt Disney said:

> I do not make films primarily for children. I make them for the child in all of us, whether we be six or sixty. Call the child innocence. The worst of us is not without innocence.

And Ward Kimball comments:

> If you want to know the real secret of Walt's success, it's that he never tried to make money. He was always trying to make something that he could have fun with or be proud of.

"WELCOME TO SHERWOOD!":
THE ADVENTURES OF ROBIN HOOD
(1938)

While working as a costume and set consultant on Warner Bros.' *Captain Blood* in 1935, period authority Dwight Franklin sent this memo on July 19 to studio head Jack L. Warner:

> Don't you think Cagney would make a swell Robin Hood? Maybe as a follow up to the [*Midsummer Night's*] *Dream*. With the gang as his Merry Men. McHugh, Jenkins, Alexander, Herbert, etc.
>
> Entirely different from the [Douglas] Fairbanks picture.
>
> I have a lot of ideas on this if you are interested.

The "gang" to which Franklin referred consisted of Warner contract players Frank McHugh, Allen Jenkins, Ross Alexander, and Hugh Herbert. Franklin's suggestion came at an opportune time. *Captain Blood*, a swash-

This material appeared in a somewhat altered form in *The Adventures of Robin Hood*, published by the University of Wisconsin Press, © 1979.

buckling romance of the type so popular during the 1920s, was being prepared with two young newcomers in the leading roles—Errol Flynn and Olivia de Havilland. The costume adventure film was once again in vogue after years of decline. Two non-Warner films, *The Count of Monte Cristo* (Reliance-United Artists) and *Treasure Island* (MGM), both released in 1934, had done particularly well critically and commercially and served as catalysts for the period adventure film renaissance. Also the "literary" or historical film was a convenient refuge from the new strength manifested in the Production Code Administration (the Breen office). The film industry had been under considerable fire during the early 1930s for presenting, in contemporary settings, excessive sex and violence on the screen. Pressure groups forced a new and tougher censorship.

One of Warner Bros.' biggest draws in 1935 was James Cagney. As box-office insurance and for a change of pace, he and other popular Warner players were cast in *A Midsummer Night's Dream*, the initial example of the studio's renewed interest in "prestige." Cagney was continually trying to convince Warners to give him different kinds of roles. The idea of *Robin Hood* for Cagney intrigued the executives and was immediately pursued.

It was discovered that Warners, through one of their music-publishing firms, had a controlling interest in the popular Reginald de Koven–Harry B. Smith light opera version of *Robin Hood*, originally presented in 1890. It also was discovered that MGM was planning an operetta version of *Robin Hood* for Jeanette MacDonald and Nelson Eddy, whose initial teaming in *Naughty Marietta* (1935) had proven extraordinarily successful. Naturally the studio was scrambling for follow-ups. In line with this, MGM already had concluded a deal with Reliance Pictures, a relatively modest independent production company that released its films through United Artists, to purchase two treatments of Reliance's proposed nonmusical version of *Robin Hood and His Merry Men* by Bernard McConville. The deal included a working outline and an incomplete first-draft continuity of two other approaches by Philip Dunne that had been commissioned by Reliance Pictures. These were for possible use in adapting the light opera at MGM. Producer Edward Small of Reliance originally had planned to make *Robin Hood* Following the success of his *The Count of Monte Cristo* in 1934, but for reasons unknown he abandoned the idea after considerable research and writing had been done. These script drafts are dated March and April 1935.

Meanwhile, in August, after working on the screenplay of Warners' *The Charge of the Light Brigade* for several months, Rowland Leigh, a writer from England (not to be confused with director Rowland V. Lee), was assigned by executive producer Hal Wallis at Warners to prepare a script dealing with the legendary outlaw, and *Robin Hood* was officially listed as an upcoming Warner attraction with James Cagney to star and contract player Guy Kibbee to play Friar Tuck. Leigh worked with executive story editor Walter MacEwen in evolving an approach to the subject while Herman Lissauer and members of his research department at the studio were engaged in gathering background data on the legend and the period.

It has been impossible for scholars or historians to trace the beginnings of the Robin Hood legend, or to place Robin Hood within a specific historical period. The concept of an English outlaw who robbed the rich to give to the poor apparently was well developed by the first half of the fourteenth century, and wandering minstrels, singing of his exploits, elaborated through the years what originally was probably a simple tale. By the close of the fifteenth century or the beginning of the sixteenth, ballads dealing with Robin and his merry men began to be printed.

As to reliable evidence that Robin existed and participated in events involving King Richard the Lion Heart and his brother, Prince John, there is none. In fact, few modern historians have favored a twelfth-century date for the outlaw.

The earliest motion picture use of the character was in the American *Robin Hood* (Kalem, 1908), a one-reel production about which little is known, and *Robin Hood and His Merry Men* (Clarendon, 1908), a British one-reel film dealing with the outlawed Earl of Huntingdon (Robin Hood) going to Sherwood Forest with Maid Marian and gathering his band to fight injustice. There followed various British and American films on the subject, including two 1913 versions of *Ivanhoe*, in which the redoubtable Robin (or "Locksley") is present. Sir Walter Scott's 1819 novel, *Ivanhoe*, utilized Robin Hood as a key character along with actual historical figures and fictional creations.

In 1922, flush with the success of his *The Mark of Zorro* (1920) and *The Three Musketeers* (1921), Douglas Fairbanks began a grandiose *Robin Hood*, which physically was the biggest film undertaking since D. W. Griffith's *Intolerance* (1916). Almost nothing of the legend appears in this version. Little John, Will Scarlet, Friar Tuck, and other familiar figures are present, but in relatively unimportant roles. The accent is on sweep, romance, chivalrous deeds, and acrobatics.

As historian Jeffrey Richards has said: "Visually the film is pure nineteenth-century Romanticism . . . . Similarly the pure and noble concept of chivalry is a product of Scott [*Ivanhoe*] and Tennyson [*The Foresters*] rather than of the actual Middle Ages. Textually the film comes close to Munday." Anthony Munday was an Elizabethan dramatist who wrote unquestionably the most influential of all pieces of dramatic writing about Robin Hood and was responsible for changing the ideal yeoman of the ballads into the unjustly dispossessed noble—the Earl of Huntingdon.

Maid Marian was not included in the early Robin Hood ballads. In his early notes on the approach to the 1938 Warner screen version, writer Rowland Leigh went so far as to say: "I would strenuously put forth the suggestion in this case either that Maid Marian be omitted completely, in that she is a later . . . addition to the story of Robin Hood, or that she be brought in as little as possible, because women had no place in the scheme of life of Robin Hood and his band of merry men."

In November of 1935, three months after Rowland Leigh had commenced work on the *Robin Hood* script, James Cagney, in a contractual dispute with Warners, walked out and didn't return to the studio for two years. *Robin Hood* was put on the back burner, although research continued, along with Leigh's work on a treatment. In April of 1936, Walter MacEwen sent Hal Wallis the first forty pages of Leigh's *Robin Hood* script. In an accompanying memo, MacEwen stated, "The great difficulty is to use as much of the traditional Robin Hood stuff as possible, without having it appear episodic and disjointed, but I think Leigh is on the right track now. The language to be used was another problem; Leigh has evolved a good modification of the actual language of the period, but it may be possible to modify it still further if you feel the need." MacEwen added that the script made liberal use of period ballads and that the music that goes with them "should help the feeling of the picture."

Also in April, the studio announced that *Robin Hood*, previously planned for Cagney, would now star Errol Flynn. Flynn had scored strongly as *Captain Blood*, released only a few months earlier. Before that he had been a relatively obscure Australian actor who had some stage experience in English repertory, the lead in a minor British film, and had played the role of Fletcher Christian in an Australian film production of 1933, *In the Wake of the Bounty*, which had launched his acting career.

In May an agreement with MGM, long discussed, was concluded whereby MGM gave Warners the Bernard McConville and Philip Dunne script materials acquired from Reliance Pictures and the right to make a straight dramatic picture without singing to be called *The Adventures of Robin Hood*, which had to be released prior to February 14, 1938. In turn, MGM acquired from Warners all their right, title, and interest in the de Koven–Smith operetta version of *Robin Hood* (intended for MacDonald and Eddy), with the provision that its film release be withheld until at least the end of 1939.

In November 1936, Rowland Leigh finished his first-draft continuity for the Warner Bros. film. In this version, Robin (Robert of Locksley) is the yeoman described in the earliest ballads, not the Saxon knight (Sir Robin of Locksley) presented in later drafts of the script. Lady Marian Fitzwalter (Maid Marian) is the ward of Sir Guy of Gisbourne (a character in one of the

On location for The Adventures of Robin Hood *in Chico, California. Director William Keighley with his hand on cameraman Tony Gaudio's shoulder; Olivia de Havilland and Errol Flynn at right.*

old ballads), who is a rival for Marian's affection. This triangle was not a part of the legend but was introduced in a considerably different manner in the de Koven–Smith light opera. A variation had been used in a 1912 Eclair motion-picture version of the Robin Hood legend and in Douglas Fairbanks's elaborate 1922 film.

Many of the characters and incidents used by Leigh were included consciously or unconsciously in the earlier outlines and treatments and in the later drafts of the script by other writers, although the connective tissue and dialogue are considerably different in the Leigh versions. There is the basic enmity of the Normans and the Saxons, drawn mostly from Sir Walter Scott's interpretation in his novel *Ivanhoe*, which many historians say did not exist as late as the end of the twelfth century. The Norman conquerors and the conquered Anglo-Saxons of 1066 were supposedly well assimilated by the time of Richard the Lion Heart's reign.

Other aspects of the Leigh draft include Robin's meeting with Little John and their bout with quarterstaves on a log spanning a stream (derived from the ballads); Robin and his men attacking the royal ransom caravan and subsequently feasting in the forest (suggested in part by the ballads); the archery tournament, during which Robin splits an opponent's arrow (from one of the earliest recorded ballads); Robin being captured and then rescued from hanging by his band; King Richard coming to Sherwood Forest in disguise (also from one of the earliest recorded ballads); and a duel-to-the-death between Robin and Sir Guy at Nottingham Castle (suggested by an old ballad). The spectacular climactic siege of Nottingham Castle by King Richard and his army and Robin and his men in Leigh's version takes place for the most part outside of the castle with catapults, hurling javelins, and stone throwers covering the advance while archers on the battlements unleash showers of arrows at the oncoming foe and then pour molten lead and oil as a huge movable tower approaches the castle. The sequence suggests nothing from the Robin Hood ballads, but could have been inspired by the battle of Torquilstone Castle from Scott's *Ivanhoe*, which is a vivid depiction of a massive medieval siege. Robin Hood—or Locksley—participated with his band, along with King Richard, in the assault on the castle. At least one of the prose versions of *Robin Hood*, Edith Heal's 1928 volume, featured a siege of Nottingham Castle more or less as outlined in the Leigh draft. Much of what has been incorporated into the various retellings and filmings of the Robin Hood tradition in the nineteenth and twentieth centuries derives from Sir Walter Scott's interpretation of the material and period in *Ivanhoe*.

In a memo to Henry Blanke, who had been assigned as the project's associate producer (or "supervisor," as the function was called then) in June 1936, Wallis said:

> I read the [Leigh] script of *Robin Hood* and I am frankly not too enthusiastic about it . . . . The position of Sir Guy and his connection with the Regent, Prince John, is not made clear in the early sequences. The development of the romance between Marian and Robin is too quick . . . . The episodes leading up to Robin becoming an outlaw do not seem important enough . . . . It seems to me that in this story they will expect to see Robin in action—robbing the rich, giving to the poor, and doing things for which the character was famous . . . . The most important matter is that of the dialogue. This is too poetical and too much like *Midsummer Night's Dream* . . . . You cannot have the maid or anyone else reading lines such as, "Oh M'Lord, tarry not too long for, I fear, in her remorse, she may fling herself from the window—some harm will befall her, I know!" . . . . This may be all right if we were doing the picture as an operetta, but as a straight movie it won't do.

Errol Flynn's original wig for The Adventures of Robin Hood *(director William Keighley at right).*

In April of 1937 contract writer Norman Reilly Raine, who had recently collaborated on the screenplay for Warners' prestigious *The Life of Emile Zola* (1937), was assigned to rewrite the script. Raine was given the story material acquired from MGM as well as the Leigh continuity and the studio research data for reference and possible use. On May 18, MacEwen, in behalf of Jack L. Warner, requested that Raine "keep color in mind when rewriting the script. When we originally started on *Robin Hood* it was not contemplated as a Technicolor production. But now . . . Mr. Warner wants to be sure that every advantage is taken of the color medium."

Raine's first draft is dated July 7, 1937. Although for the most part it embodies his own approach and dialogue, he did read and assimilate ideas from Leigh, Dunne, and McConville (and naturally other writers of Robin Hood books, plays, and screenplays), with certain aspects from each being

The Adventures of Robin Hood: *Flynn's revised wig, per his suggestion (with Olivia de Havilland).*

reflected in his draft. Bernard McConville's two treatments had portrayed Robert, Earl of Locksley and Huntingdon, as a Saxon noble described by McConville in his notes as, "*not* a highway robber, but an *emancipator*." Marian, a Saxon rather than a Norman lady, is the ward of Sir Guy of Gisbourne, who is in love with her. The Norman–Saxon enmity is present, as are several of the incidents used by Leigh.

Philip Dunne's working outline contained many of the same elements and the familiar incidents but excluded Sir Guy completely. In his version, there is an emphasis on Prince John's plan to collect Richard's ransom and use the money to seize the realm. This and the idea of a tax-gathering montage were consciously or unconsciously appropriated into much later versions of the script, along with Robin appearing at the Nottingham Castle banquet and accusing Prince John of attempting to usurp the throne.

Now we come to Norman Reilly Raine's first draft: In the opening, Robert of Locksley is a Saxon freeman who has been proclaimed an outlaw by Sir Guy. Robin is already in Sherwood as this approach begins. Marian is a Norman lady who was the ward of King Richard before he left on the Third Crusade. Robin is not present at the banquet at the castle—called Hagthorn Castle rather than Nottingham Castle in this draft—but Sir Will of Gamwell (later Will Scarlet), a Norman knight, performs the same function, as he dares to challenge Prince John with such lines as (some familiar to enthusiasts of the film) "I've a stomach for honest meat—but none for traitors! . . . You've used your brother's misfortune to seize his power—and for that you're a traitor, and so is every man here who gives you allegiance! . . . Of course, you may talk of paying the King's ransom . . . but it's the serfs who will pay; the Saxon hinds, eh?" Prince John bellows "Take him!" but Sir Will escapes from the castle and later joins Robin's band in Sherwood.

Some of the scenes in Robin Hood's camp were designated in this draft to take place at night, with bonfires supplying illumination. They were changed to day scenes following a budget meeting, thereby saving about $50,000. The biggest night scene was to be the climax of the picture, which in this version was the attack on the tax-gathering caravan in Sherwood, following which a knight in Robin's camp reveals himself to be King Richard. The King knights Robin, and the last scene is the marriage of Robin and Marian in the forest.

On June 25 Norman Reilly Raine sent a memo to Henry Blanke saying that he "was not satisfied with the present ending [in the forest]; and it is not the one I first intended to use; but due to the rush of getting the script finished . . . there was not time to give to the intended ending that care which it justified, so will have to delay it . . . . If the present one is satisfactory it will have the added merit of being less expensive to produce, as the original ending entailed the storming, capture, and burning of Hagthorn Castle."

On July 6 Hal Wallis wrote to Blanke, "The budget on Robin Hood according to the last script [the Rowland Leigh version] is $1,185,000 . . . . Of course, we cannot have a budget of this kind on the picture and in our rewrite let us bear this in mind and work towards the elimination of the huge mob scenes that were called for in the original script."

After story conferences with Wallis, Blanke, and William Keighley, a Warner Bros. staff director assigned to the picture, Raine worked on a revision of his first script. This time the hero is introduced as a Saxon noble, Sir Robin of Locksley. Will of Gamwell is his squire. Marian is a Saxon lady who is already in love with Robin at the beginning of the story. As in the final film, Sir Robin attends the banquet at Nottingham Castle (changed from Hagthorn Castle) and escapes after defying Prince John.

Then Seton I. Miller, who recently had done the screenplay for the popular *Kid Galahad* (1937), among many others, for Warners, was assigned to collaborate with Raine on another revision, starting some time in August. On August 31, Wallis wrote to them: "I know that you are both working very hard on the *Robin Hood* script . . . . As you know, we are up against a serious problem with our Technicolor commitment which we have already postponed from the end of August to the middle of September, and it will be very costly if we are forced to postpone this again. I have been in close touch with Keighley and Blanke and I feel that the story is now properly blocked out, and if you will . . . try to get us a complete script, or at least two-thirds of it, before September 10th, it will be of great help."

It is difficult to ascertain who contributed what in the collaboration of Raine and Miller, to say nothing of the ideas that stemmed from the suggestions of the producers and the director (and the previous writers). Apparently director Keighley put forth the idea of opening the film with a large-scale jousting tournament, which was incorporated into the first Raine–Miller version. This tournament served to introduce Sir Robin, Lady Marian (back to being a Norman and King Richard's ward), Prince John, and Sir Guy. Robin and Sir Guy jousted on horseback with lances. A good deal of the expository dialogue that earlier had been included in the banquet at Nottingham Castle was now inserted at the joust. Raine, for one, was anything but pleased about this sequence, particularly since there were severe budgetary problems. In a memo to Hal Wallis, Raine stated that it was his understanding that Keighley wanted the sequence because people who remembered the Douglas Fairbanks silent feature would expect a spectacular opening sequence (the 1922 Fairbanks film began with a jousting tournament); also, it would set up and advance the story as well as illustrate the pageantry of the period. Raine felt that people would not remember the details of the Fairbanks picture; therefore, the pageantry and color and chivalry inherent in the background itself, if the revised final was followed, would satisfy them, especially since the film was to be in color:

> The jousting tournament never can be anything but a prologue which, if done with the magnificence Mr. Keighley sees, will have the disastrous effect of putting the climax of the picture at the beginning—and I'll be god-damned if that is good construction dramatically in fiction, stage or screen, because the only way you could ever top it would be to have a slam-bang hell of a battle or something equally spectacular— and expensive—at the end. Maybe I'm crazy—but what we set out to tell was the story of Robin Hood—the swashbuckling, reckless, rake-hell type of character who, *by his personal adventures*, has endeared himself to generations. It is not by thoughts of knights and castles and tournaments that this character has lived . . . . The archery tournament will certainly suffer pictorially if we stick a jousting tournament in the beginning. Christ's second coming in a cloud of glory would seem tame if we showed the creation of the world first . . . .
> The Fairbanks picture, *in order to* live up to its tournament fade-in, had to ring in the whole goddamned Crusades; and a light taste of the real Robin Hood story was dragged in as a tag at the end to justify the use of the name.

But despite Raine's plea, the jousting tournament remained in the script, at least for the time being.

Most of the cast members were set by the middle of September, as the picture had a revised starting date of September 27, 1937. There had been some vacillation regarding the casting of Maid Marian. Originally Olivia de Havilland had been strongly considered, she and Flynn having played together effectively in *Captain Blood* and *The Charge of the Light Brigade*. Then, in the middle of June, Jack L. Warner wrote Hal Wallis that he was thinking seriously of putting Anita Louise in *The Adventures of Robin Hood* to play the part of Maid Marian. "At the salary she is now receiving she will have to do something or get off the pot. She will especially be marvelous in color and we won't have Olivia de Havilland in every other picture."

In early September Wallis noted to director William Keighley that "we have decided definitely to use Anita Louise." On September 16 Wallis wrote that "Olivia de Havilland will definitely play the part of Maid Marian."

Born in Tokyo of British parents, Olivia de Havilland was discovered by famed Austrian producer-director Max Reinhardt, who cast her as Hermia in his production of *A Midsummer Night's Dream* at the Hollywood Bowl and subsequently in the film version he did at Warner Bros. She then signed a seven-year contract with Warners and appeared in two inconsequential films before being selected to play opposite Flynn in *Captain Blood*.

Arch villain Basil Rathbone was set to play Sir Guy. He and Flynn had worked together previously in *Captain Blood*. Rathbone had made his stage debut in England in 1911. For many years he alternated varied stage and screen roles in England and America, but his performance in MGM's *David Copperfield* (1935) resulted in his being type cast more often than not as the bad guy. (This was before his portrayal of Sherlock Holmes.)

David Niven was wanted for the part of Will Scarlet, but he was on vacation in England as shooting on *Robin Hood* was about to begin. Patric Knowles replaced him. The traditional Sheriff of Nottingham from the early ballads was written by Raine and Miller as a blustering, cowardly comic villain, and Melville Cooper was chosen to interpret the role. Contract players Claude Rains and Ian Hunter were agreed upon for the roles of Prince John and King Richard.

For several weeks prior to the start of production, twenty-four hand-picked men rehearsed with broadswords and quarterstaves on Stage One at Warners under the tutelage of Belgian fencing master Fred Cavens and his son, Albert, who instructed and set up the sword and quarterstaff routines for the principal players as well.

On August 9, studio production manager T. C. [Tenny] Wright wrote Jack L. Warner:

> Errol Flynn's four week vacation will be up August 12th . . . . Kindly have a talk with Mr. Flynn and tell him to be on time for his call . . . . Also, he is not to be dissipating around and come in to the studio with bags under his eyes, as this is a very expensive picture . . . . Get him straightened out before we go into production.

More script revisions were being made as the company was getting ready to leave for the start of production on location. On September 13, Wallis wrote Blanke and Keighley about Robin's entrance into Nottingham Castle during the banquet sequence. In the script then current, Robin enters the Great Hall on horseback with a dead villager, who had been killed by the Sheriff of Nottingham, across his saddle. Riding straight for Prince John, Robin halts at his table, slips from the saddle, lifts the body and dumps it

Filming The Adventures of Robin Hood *at Warners' Burbank studio (note the old Technicolor camera). Left to right: Olivia de Havilland, Errol Flynn, director William Keighley, cameraman Tony Gaudio (with cap).*

on the table in front of Prince John. In an earlier version of the script, Robin had entered with two members of his band, one of whom was carrying a dead deer. The deer was then dropped on the table. Wallis said that he did not like the new approach with the dead villager as much as the earlier version where Robin, after entering, sat and fenced verbally with Prince John in an exchange which led to the break between them. He regarded this as "a suspenseful scene, and there is always the suggestion of an explosion to come during the entire scene . . . . On the other hand, if he rides in and drops a corpse in front of Prince John it is a momentary kick and your scene is over."

The big dilemma with regard to the script was what to do about the climax. The earlier versions' exterior storming of the castle with King Richard and his army and Robin and his men against Prince John and Guy of Gisbourne's forces had been abandoned because of the excessive cost, and the alternate plan, with the final confrontation taking place in Sherwood, was never satisfactory. What was needed was an exciting and elaborate finish with a fresh dramatic device that would not cost a fortune. Someone or some combination of people came up with a sound solution, as delineated in the September 17 addition to the script: When King Richard and his retinue, who had come to Sherwood disguised as monks after returning to England, reveal themselves to Robin and his band, it is discovered that Prince John, having arranged for Richard to be murdered, is going to be crowned king in a ceremony to be performed by the Bishop of the Black Canons the following day in Nottingham Castle. It is also discovered that Marian has been imprisoned in the castle and is to be executed for treason. Realizing that it would be useless to storm the castle, Robin decides to visit the bishop that evening to persuade him to suggest a way to rescue Marian and stop the coronation. Fade out and fade in to the next day. Robin's entire band and Richard, all disguised as monks, enter the castle as part of the ceremony, disrupt the proceedings, and, after an exciting battle royal, Gisbourne is killed, Marian is freed, John is ousted, and Richard reigns again.

The new continuity solved various problems and was dramatically effective. A coronation ceremony had been the climax of Warners' recently released *The Prince and the Pauper* (1937) as well as an important ingredient in David O. Selznick's production of *The Prisoner of Zenda* (1937). Both were inspired by the much-heralded coronation of George VI following the abdication of Edward VIII. Now, for the first time, the pomp and circumstance would be in color. Since the Great Hall at Nottingham Castle was already a key set for other sequences, most importantly the elaborate banquet and Robin's lengthy escape near the beginning of the film, it was a natural locale for the coronation, the battle, and the concluding scenes. Thus an entire exterior castle set could be eliminated. Richard's army was also not required, and his retinue was reduced to five men.

The new climax meant the building up of what previously had been a small role—the Bishop of the Black Canons, played by Montagu Love (Donald Crisp turned down the part)—who becomes involved in the evil machinations of Prince John. This bishop does not derive from the Robin Hood tradition. Rowland Leigh's early notes regarding the approach to *Robin Hood* pointed out that the handling of the religious aspects of the legend could be difficult. "There is no doubt about it that Robin Hood's chief antagonists were the bishops, abbots, and friars who bled the poor in order to enrich themselves. This point is insisted upon again and again by every reliable expert on Robin Hood lore. Undoubtedly in medieval times the church took unwarranted liberties with its power and influence. Equally undoubtedly we have no desire to offend either the Catholic or Protestant church of today, and I feel that a tactful compromise will have to be arrived at. This may possibly eliminate the Bishop of Hereford [a character in the old ballads] as the villainous character he actually is." Joseph Ritson stated in his still indispensable 1795 handbook of the legend that "notwithstanding, however, the aversion in which he [Robin] appears to have held the clergy of every denomination, he was a man of exemplary piety, according to the notions of that age." Robin Hood is the product of a period when the state was relatively weak and when great local power was held by the sheriff and the abbot. In all the previous drafts of the script there were no clergymen included (other than Friar Tuck and "the Black Bishop" who had a small part in Raine's original draft).

The attempted coronation of Prince John with Richard and Robin and his men disguised as monks had not been used before and was not drawn from any legendary or historical source. In reality, at the time of Richard's return to England, Prince John was in France. Also, Richard came back to England in March 1194 and made a state entry into London complete with a great procession and celebration. All of England was aware of his return. However, at that time it was decreed that John, having violated his oath of fealty, should be deprived of all his land in England and that his castles should be seized, by force if necessary. The last castle to hold out, Nottingham Castle, was taken by King Richard himself while John was still in France. Historical records state that while in Nottingham, Richard visited Sherwood Forest, which he had never seen.

Warner Bros.' Sherwood Forest location was 2400-acre Bidwell Park, which was filled with giant oaks and sycamores, in the town of Chico, California, about 350 miles northeast of Los Angeles. The park runs nine miles up into the rugged and picturesque Chico Canyon along Big Chico Creek (the creek being the site for the filming of Robin's first meeting with Little John and, later, Friar Tuck). The main location in the park was Robin Hood's camp, a mile or so from the park entrance. This was the scene of the outdoor feast following the outlaw's capture of the treasure caravan. Throughout the area, art director Carl Jules Weyl augmented nature by building prop trees and a number of imitation rocks to lend variety to the scenery. Hundreds of bushes, ferns, and flowers were planted temporarily and then removed when the work was completed.

Production manager Tenny Wright was concerned about the location junket and sent a memo to Hal Wallis on September 7, three weeks before filming was to begin:

> I wonder if we are wrong in allowing *Robin Hood* to be shot at Chico . . . . *Robin Hood* will not start until the later part of this month . . . and the rains generally set in around the first of October . . . .
>
> Do you think that the locations there are so vastly superior to the ones we can secure down here at [Lake] Sherwood?
>
> I mean by this, is it worth gambling on the weather?

Tenny Wright's concern notwithstanding, shooting commenced in Bidwell Park on September 27, 1937, with the meeting of Robin and Little John. The ballad version of this first encounter with quarterstaves, as well as Robin's meeting with Friar Tuck, was depicted for the first time on the screen in the Warner version. Alan Hale had played Little John in the 1922 Fairbanks picture, and was signed by Warners for the same part. Although Guy Kibbee had been announced for the Friar Tuck role in 1935, he was no longer a contract player in 1937, and Eugene Pallette, a free-lance performer, was chosen instead. Apparently Friar Tuck is a fusion of two different friars: an actual renegade English outlaw who assumed the name "Frere Tuk" and the almost always anonymous and buffoonlike "frere" of the morris dances. Little John, one of the first and best known of Robin's companions, was mentioned in conjunction with the outlaw as early as 1341.

Norman Reilly Raine was at the Chico location from late September until October 13, working on revisions, adding comedy material for Herbert Mundin, who played Much the Miller's Son (one of the earliest recorded members of Robin's band), and shortening the forest banquet sequence. Things went slowly on location, because of weather and other factors. Tenny Wright's apprehension was valid. Wallis wired Keighley on October 6 about his concern that it had taken three days to film the meeting between Robin and Little John and it was not yet complete. "Don't know what you can do about it except to cut down angles and not spend so much time." The next day, Wallis insisted that the jousting tournament and a christening scene of the merry men be deleted from the script to save time and money. The christening sequence was to follow immediately Robin's meeting with Friar Tuck and consisted of the friar and Robin ducking the members of the band's heads into a cask of ale ("Name?" "Will of Gamwell." They duck him and pull him out. "Rise—Will Scarlet"). To speed up things a second unit director, B. Reeves ("Breezy") Eason, was dispatched to Chico toward the end of October to film some of the shots of the treasure caravan, the merry men swinging and dropping on Sir Guy's party, and other material involving horse action without the principal players.

Olivia de Havilland did not arrive in Chico until October 22, almost a month after the rest of the company. She had been finishing work on *Gold Is Where You Find It.*

On October 24th, Errol Flynn wrote to Hal Wallis from Chico:

> Now one other minor, but to me very important squawk. My wig—I loathe the bloody thing. With the hat on it's fine, and the alteration I want to suggest does not affect any of the stuff we've shot so far—the part that's wrong is hidden by the hat. The centre part in the wig is my chief complaint. I would like an almost unnoticeable part on either side so that one side or the other could sweep back like this [rough sketch] off the forehead. The fringes would then, when the hat is removed, not look like fringes but just a few locks of loose hair carelessly falling over the brow . . . . I haven't had my hat off yet and when I do the new wig would match . . . . I've had nothing but comments from people, when they see it with the hat off, about the stupid looking fringe [bangs] and centre part.

Wallis agreed and a new wig was made per Flynn's suggestions. The next day, however, Wallis wired Flynn:

> HAVE HAD REPORTS ABOUT YOUR JOYRIDING IN
> [PRIVATE] PLANES UP THERE AND REQUESTED
> [UNIT MANAGER AL] ALLEBORN TO ASK YOU TO
> PLEASE DISCONTINUE DOING SO. IN SPITE OF
> THIS UNDERSTAND YOU ARE CONTINUING
> FLYING. HAVE ALWAYS TRIED TO BE
> COOPERATIVE AND ACCEDE TO VARIOUS
> REQUESTS FROM YOU FROM TIME TO TIME. AM
> ASKING YOU NOW TO PLEASE CUT OUT THE
> FLYING AT LEAST UNTIL THE PICTURE IS
> FINISHED.

Fragmentary Nottingham Castle exterior for The Advantures of Robin Hood *at* Warners' Calabasas Ranch.

Nine days behind schedule, the company finished shooting in Chico on November 8 and returned to begin filming at Warners' Burbank studio on sets representing Marian's apartment in the castle, Kent Road Tavern, and the Saracen's Head Inn. In the middle of November work began on the archery tournament sequence at the old Busch Gardens in Pasadena (long since gone). The jousting tournament, now dropped, was to have been shot there as well. The archery tournament had been used in a 1913 Thanhouser *Robin Hood* film, but not in the two motion picture versions of Scott's *Ivanhoe,* also released in 1913 (or, for that matter, in the MGM 1952 *Ivanhoe* production). In his novel, Scott has Robin ("Locksley") appear before Prince John as an entrant in an archery competition, during which the outlaw splits another's arrow. As previously mentioned, the famous incident derives from one of the earliest of the extant ballads.

By November 30, 1937, *The Adventures of Robin Hood* was fifteen days behind schedule and over its revised September 28 budget of $1,440,000. It was decided to replace Keighley with Michael Curtiz. Keighley, an American, was a relatively soft-spoken gentleman who, before coming to Warners in 1932, had been an actor and later director in the theater,

A composite matte painting and live action scene taken from the actual film of The Adventures of Robin Hood.

working with such luminaries as John Barrymore in *Richard III* (1920) and Ethel Barrymore in *Romeo and Juliet* (1922). Keighley had directed *The Prince and the Pauper* with Flynn shortly before *Robin Hood,* and Warner, Wallis, and Blanke had felt that he had the requisite feel for the subject and period. Undoubtedly another important factor in the decision to use Keighley and cameraman Tony Guadio was that they had done Warners' first three-color Technicolor feature, *God's Country and the Woman* (1937), a considerable amount of which was shot on location.

Curtiz, who had directed films in his native Hungary and in Vienna as early as 1913 before coming to America and Warners in 1926, was the antithesis of Keighley. He was rough-hewn, tough, and indefatigable. Curtiz had directed Flynn's first screen appearance in this country (a bit part in *The Case of the Curious Bride,* 1935) and the first two films in which he was starred: *Captain Blood* and *The Charge of the Light Brigade.* According to various sources, Flynn disliked Curtiz and his working methods intensely but was fond of the urbane Keighley.

Curtiz and the replacement director of photography for Tony Gaudio, Sol Polito, who was Curtiz's favorite cameraman at that time, were expected to show a burst of speed and also to produce a high standard of quality. (They had recently completed Warners' second three-color Technicolor feature, *Gold Is Where You Find It.*) All of the big scenes in Nottingham Castle, including the banquet and Robin's subsequent escape, the coronation, final battle and duel-to-the-death, were scheduled with Curtiz on Stage One at the studio during the month of December. The director was certainly in his element. As Wallis stated in a memo to Blanke at the time Curtiz took over the picture: "In his enthusiasm to make great shots and composition and utilize the great production values on this picture, he is, of course, more likely to go overboard than anyone else, because he just naturally loves to work with mobs and props of this kind."

Wallis was concerned about Robin's early escape from the castle being overdone and appearing ridiculous. "The quicker he [Robin] gets out of the room and up on the balcony the better, and don't let him [Curtiz] have Robin holding off a hundred men with a bow and arrow, or the audience will scream, and from that point on you won't ever get them back into the story again. This must be handled very carefully and worked out very carefully."

Some of the bits of business shot for the escape were deleted much later by Wallis. At one point, Robin begins to fight his way out of the Great Hall after narrowly averting a spear that had been hurled through the back of his chair. Wallis told Ralph Dawson, the editor, to "lose the cut when he [Robin] knocks the man down and climbs up on the table and drinks the

Filming the conclusion of The Adventures of Robin Hood: *director Michael Curtiz left foreground with back to the camera; cameraman Sol Polito far right.*

toast, and the cut of [Prince] John drinking the toast . . . . When Flynn runs across the banquet room, let him run right up the stairs and climb up over the balcony. Take out the business of grabbing the shield and catching the arrows on it and throwing the torch at the men."

By December 4, Al Alleborn, the unit manager, mentioned in his daily report that "this company with a new crew is moving along 100% better than the other crew . . . . The balance of the work that is left to do in the castle has been walked through and explained to . . . Mr. Wallis and Blanke who have approved of the way Mike [Curtiz] is to play it and the number of [camera] set-ups necessary for the action."

The film was a boon to the stuntmen. In addition to the fights with weapons, there was dropping from trees, vine swinging, high falls (Fred Graham, doubling for Basil Rathbone as Sir Guy, took a spectacular fall in the final duel and broke his ankle), arrows plunging into padded chests and backs (the studio paid $150 per shot to stuntmen and bit players for letting famed bowman Howard Hill hit them with arrows). Although Flynn did most of his own dueling (as did Rathbone), quarterstaff fighting, and other action stunts, he was doubled on his leap with his hands tied behind his back from the gallows onto a horse (as well as on an earlier leap onto a horse), his swinging ride up the cut rope to the top of the Nottingham Gate, and his drop to the ground on the other side. The emphasis on the stunts was in part a homage paid to the Doug Fairbanks heritage.

On December 8, Alleborn reported that "Mr. Blanke is going to discuss with Mr. Wallis and the writers necessary scenes that have to be retaken and added scenes as well to build up sequences that were shot by Mr. Keighley." By now it was considered necessary to go all out in an attempt to make *Robin Hood* a super attraction. The costs had soared, but in order to guarantee a profit, perfection was the objective and every scene was carefully studied to determine what improvements or embellishments were deemed necessary. This was definitely not the usual *modus operandi* of the efficiently run, cost-conscious Warner studio.

The attack on the treasure caravan in Sherwood was enriched by Curtiz with footage of Robin's men preparing for the attack by rigging and climbing the vines and a few more shots of the men dropping from high in the trees, in addition to further details of the fight on the ground. These were photographed in the nearby Lake Sherwood and Sherwood Forest area, so named after being used for the forest location in Fairbanks's *Robin Hood*. The 1912 Eclair *Robin Hood* film contained a sequence in which Robin and his men fall upon Sir Guy's party from the treetops. In Fairbanks's 1922 production the merry men drop on the Sheriff of Nottingham's troopers in Sherwood. In Edith Heal's 1928 book version of the legend, she describes

Robin's capture of Sir Guy in the forest. This incident stems from remotely similar ideas derived from the old ballads.

Additional shots and some retakes for the archery tournament in the Warner production were photographed later at the Midwick Country Club (Busch Gardens being too expensive and not necessary at this point), and material that took place in the streets of Nottingham was photographed on the so-called Dijon Street on the Warner back lot. The exterior portcullis of Nottingham Castle was on the top of a hill at the Warner ranch in Calabasas. Only small portions of the exterior castle were built. The remainder of the castle views were paintings matted with the full-scale fragments.

Finally, on January 14, according to Al Alleborn's report, "Curtiz company called 8:30 A.M. . . . finished shooting at 3:10 A.M. this morning, 1/15." The company had worked for over eighteen continuous hours. The picture had an additional shooting day of bits and pieces one week later, which put it thirty-eight days behind schedule and considerably over budget. The negative cost, including editing and scoring, came to about $1,900,000—the most expensive picture, by a considerable margin, to be made at Warners up to that time.

MGM had consented in October 1937 to an extension of the Warner release date of *The Adventures of Robin Hood* from the originally agreed-upon February 14, 1938, to before June 1. MGM officially announced in 1939 that they were going to produce an adaptation of the de Koven–Smith operetta with Jeanette MacDonald and Nelson Eddy, but the film never was made.

Although the Warner production had been assembled and edited while filming was in progress, final shaping and tightening was being done immediately after shooting was completed. Then Hal Wallis ran the edited version and made more cuts and trims throughout, in line with the Warner practice of moving things along in a swift, staccato manner without any excess footage. Wallis's editorial notes on *Robin Hood* abound with such instructions as:

> Cut quicker to Rathbone . . . . Take out the stall before the line . . . . Trim the beginning of the long shot . . . . After Prince John announces that he is regent of England, make the reaction cuts all exactly the same footage . . . You stay too long on the man that falls . . . . Cut right to the girl; lose all the panning around . . . . Take about three feet off the end of that scene . . . . Dissolve quicker to the trumpeters after the first flight of arrows . . . . Cut out that business [of Flynn]

looking over the arrow at the girl . . . . Don't have him
hesitate . . . . Trim just a little—a few frames, a half a foot,
a foot, or whatever is necessary on all the cuts from the
shooting of the first arrow in the gallows sequence . . . . We'll
shoot an insert of a sign "Kent Road Tavern" . . . . Let the
scene run as long as possible where he [Flynn] says, "And
persuade him to find a way" . . . . Take out the dialogue with
Hale and Pallette [during the final battle]. Just put cuts of
them fighting . . . . After the jump over the table [in the
duel], go back to about two more cuts upstairs, then pick
Flynn and Rathbone up . . . . Take out Rathbone's closeup
where his face twitches in the last part of the duel . . . . Take
out the line "I only pray that I have a son to succeed my
throne."

Although Warner staff composer Max Steiner was tentatively set to score
the film, Erich Wolfgang Korngold (*Captain Blood, The Prince and the
Pauper*) was preferred for the assignment. Korngold, an esteemed composer
of operas and concert works, had an agreement with Warners, but at this
time he was in Vienna completing and arranging for the premiere of his new
opera, *Die Kathrin*. Then, in mid-January 1938, when it was thought that
the premiere would be delayed until fall, Wallis and Blanke cabled him to
come back immediately for *Robin Hood*. Upon his return, the edited print
was screened for him at Warners. A day or two later, on February 11,
Korngold wrote Wallis turning down the assignment. He said in part:

> *Robin Hood* is no picture for me. I have no relation to it and
> therefore cannot produce any music for it. I am a musician of
> the heart, of passions and psychology; I am not a musical
> illustrator for a 90% action picture. Being a conscientious
> person, I cannot take the responsibility for a job which, as I
> already know, would leave me artistically completely dissat-
> isfied and which, therefore, I would have to drop even after
> several weeks of work on it . . . . Please do not try to make
> me change my mind; my resolve is unshakeable.

The next day Leo Forbstein, head of Warners' music department, arrived
at the Korngold residence at the urging of Warner, Wallis, and Blanke and
implored him to take the film. When Forbstein said that Korngold could
work on a weekly basis and could leave the project at the end of any given
week, in which case someone else might finish the score, Korngold agreed.
What prompted him to change his mind was hearing that Chancellor
Schuschnigg of Austria had had his ill-fated meeting with Hitler at Ber-

chtesgaden. Shortly afterwards Korngold's property in Vienna was confiscated by the invading Nazis.

Korngold had seven weeks to compose and record a score that was to be wedded to the picture in time for its new release date of May 14. His style for the Flynn swashbucklers resembled that of the creators of late nineteenth-century and early twentieth-century German symphonic tone poems. It incorporated chromatic harmonies, lush instrumental effects, passionate climaxes, all performed in a generally romantic manner. Korngold's original and distinctive style was influenced by the Wagnerian leitmotif, the orchestral virtuosity of Richard Strauss, the delicacy and broad melodic sweep of Puccini, and the long-line development of Gustav Mahler.

The "Robin of Locksley" theme and its expansion and development is the only material in the *Robin Hood* score Korngold did not compose specifically for it. Originally conceived as a symphonic overture, *Sursum Corda*, Korngold had composed in 1919, it proved effective underneath the lengthy sequence of Robin's escape from Nottingham Castle.

Meanwhile, the Technicolor people, working from the approved final cut, were busy preparing their three-color dye transfer prints, a considerably more complex and time-consuming process than black-and-white printing or the color processes used subsequently.

In early April *The Adventures of Robin Hood* was sneak previewed—with Korngold's music—in Pomona, near Los Angeles. Jack L. Warner sent a telegram to executives in Warners' New York Office saying that "In history of our company never have we had picture that scored in front of audience like this did." On April 11, Hal Wallis wired New York: "Had second sneak preview Warner Bros. Downtown Theater [in Los Angeles] and went even better than Pomona, which is hard to believe." Two weeks later there was a preview at Warners' Hollywood Theater. Wallis cabled that the screening was "absolutely sensational. Spontaneous applause throughout picture. Terrific hand at finish. Review sensational. Important people throughout business phoning congratulations this morning . . . . Its success is without question." There were little or no changes made in the film after the

Composer-conducter Erich Wolfgang Korngold and Basil Rathbone at the NBC radio broadcast of excerpts from The Adventures of Robin Hood *music score (May 11, 1938). Rathbone narrated.*

previews, and the picture opened to outstanding critical and audience applause.

An important element in this unique mesh—besides the Technicolor process and the Warner syle—was the excellent casting, including Errol Flynn, who, at 29, was at his peak and perfect for the role. He was the personification of a hero, and Olivia de Havilland was by now his ideal screen lover. Their romantic scenes in this picture, especially, were played with believable ardor, grace, and more than a touch of humor.

The Adventures of Robin Hood did not fall prey to the pitfalls of so many other films in the historical romance genre. The subject had been extraordinarily popular for over six hundred years, and Warner Bros. had the good sense not to alter the material drastically or to make it seem more substantial than it was. All the elements were handled in a relatively simple and straighforward manner. The dialogue was not too flowery and archaic in an attempt to be faithful to the period; there was always vigor and pace to offset the pomp and ceremony, and nothing tedious marred the proceedings. Rather than lasting two hours or longer, as so many costume adventure films do and did, *Robin Hood* runs its course in a brisk one hour and forty-two minutes. During that time, the film is literally crammed with incident and action.

The characters, costumes, castle, and forest are idealized, but then the film is not a document of medieval life; rather it is a fairy tale illustrated by Technicolor. The love interest, usually clumsy and arbitrary in costume adventure films, is here properly motivated and nicely woven into the plot fabric. And the rich score serves as marvelous connective tissue, literally sweeping the film along.

In 1948, ten years after its first release, Warners reissued the film everywhere with new Technicolor prints, treating it in the manner of one of their big, fresh attractions. Following the Warner production of the Robin Hood legend, there have been many others; some, like Disney's live-action feature of 1952, *The Story of Robin Hood*, presented a different in detail but substantially similar story. Several films offered further adventures of the outlaw that were but figments in the minds of screenwriters; finally, there were various tales relating to a son and even a daughter of Robin Hood, none of which had any basis in the evolution of the legend.

The Fairbanks production was everybody's favorite in the 1920s, but the definitive Robin Hood for most people since 1938 is the Warner version, wherein many elements of popular entertainment are beautifully fused: fairy tale romance, spectacle, color, action, pageantry, humor, the triumph of right over might, the exultation of the Free Spirit, the charm of the greenwood, and a vague nostalgia for a partly mythical age of chivalry.

5

THE ROVER BOYS IN INDIA:
GUNGA DIN
(1939)

During the 1930s, Hollywood seemed intent on waving the British flag and romanticizing honor, duty and self-sacrifice where the sun never sets rather than glorifying England herself. The Anglo-Egyptian Sudan and India's north-west frontier were perennial reminders on film of the splendor of remote and exotic terrain being held in check by stalwart officers, rollicking enlisted men, and humble, loyal natives attached to the regiment somewhere in the middle of nowhere.

Rudyard Kipling, grand interpreter of Anglo-Indian themes, the army, and British imperialism, came into his own in motion pictures in the mid-1930s as part of this wave of nostalgic celebration of the Empire. He died just about the time his works began to be translated to the screen in large quantities. *Elephant Boy*, based somewhat remotely on "Toomai of the Elephants," *Captains Courageous*, and *Wee Willie Winkie* were released in early 1937, followed by *The Light That Failed* (1939), *Jungle Book* (1942), and one of the most popular adventure films to come out of Hollywood—*Gunga Din* (1939).

Kipling's poem "Gunga Din," published in 1892, dealt with a native water carrier (*bhisti*) attached to a British regiment in India during the Victorian years, when the campaign against the fierce fighters of India's northern boundary seemed always to be a constant threat or an actuality. Hardly able

87

to speak at all with the British soldiers, often abused by them, the faithful *bhisti* trudged along giving water to those who called. In battles they risked their lives to help the wounded, and they sometimes even gave their lives in service. In his famous poem, Kipling tells of a private's appreciation of a particular *bhisti*. With deepest admiration of the water carrier's loyalty, heroism, and self-sacrifice, the soldier cries out, "You're a better man than I am, Gunga Din!"*

MGM had considered doing a feature film based on Kipling's poem in late 1928 (the only previous version was a fifteen-minute 1911 silent visualization of the poem with interiors and exteriors photographed in and around the New York Powers Studio). Irving Thalberg assigned John Neville and Norman Houston to develop an adaptation. Their scripts were put aside, and then, in January 1929, Sarah Y. Mason and John Howard Lawson did a sketch for a treatment at MGM. This was followed by a new adaptation by C. Gardner Sullivan in 1931. These approaches were purely exploratory, since no agreement had been made between Kipling and MGM. Then Thalberg dropped the project.

Independent film producer Edward Small planned to produce a film based on Kipling's poem in the early 1930s. Director Alf Goulding submitted a dramatic composition (copyrighted by Goulding in 1931) to Small in 1933 purely on speculation. Nothing happened with that particular approach, but in October 1934, Small took an option to purchase "Gunga Din" from Kipling. Still nothing happened. In February 1935 he officially dropped his plans because, he stated, of the prevalence of films with a similar background being released—specifically, *The Lives of a Bengal Lancer* and *Clive of India.*

But a year later he became interested again, and rights to the title "Gunga Din" were finally sold by Kipling's widow to Edward Small's Reliance Pictures in March 1936 for £5000. The producer assigned novelist (and future Nobel Prize winner) William Faulkner to develop an original approach to the adaptation. "Adaptation" is not really the appropriate word. There was hardly enough narrative in the poem for a full-fledged commercial feature film, so perhaps the often-used phrase "inspired by" is more accurate with regard to Faulkner's and the other screenwriters' work.

Faulkner spent several weeks on the project, starting in April 1936, and left notes for two original stories, a partial treatment, an incomplete story outline, and various sequence outlines. The narrative lines are rather complex and have little to do with the plot of the film as we know it. In general, the drafts involve variations on a theme of two (in some cases three)

* "Gunga" is the Hindu name for the Ganges River; "Din" is the Arabic word for faith.

officers arriving in India to join the regimental staff of a garrison. One of the officers wins the total devotion of a native water boy, Gunga Din, by saving him from a beating. The development involves hostile tribes, one officer's weakness for liquor, his falling victim to sunstroke, and the villainous Afghan Khan's seductive woman spy, who gets the drunken officer to betray army secrets. Even the Battle of Lucknow—after which Disraeli gave Queen Victoria the title "Empress of India"—is included. In one early Faulkner outline, Din is depicted as a liar, braggart, and petty thief who had been captured in the hills and still has a wife and a child there. He always manages to lose his money by getting drunk or by gambling.

Faulkner devised several endings: One has Din faking orders from the colonel and giving them to his master so that the officer can leave a battle to rejoin his wife, who is in serious condition following the birth of their child. Upon returning to the battalion, the officer is arrested for desertion. Din admits the truth to the colonel and is ordered to be executed. To save Din from dishonor, his master gives him a loaded revolver and Din shoots himself. Another ending has Din arranging to go to the Afghans as a hostage—although he knows this means torture and death—so that the British can escape from the surrounding Afghan troops. At the fade out, two officers stand beside Din's grave and offer a toast to the brave water boy: "You're a better man than I am, Gunga Din!"

In June, RKO Radio Pictures acquired the rights to Gunga Din along with other literary properties as part of an arrangement with Edward Small, who joined RKO as a producer at that time. That same month, writer Lester Cohen was hired for about two months, and he contributed another approach via research notes, an outline, and a rough treatment totally different from the Faulkner version. In these, Din is a Calcutta guide and tonga driver at the beginning of the story. Then John Colton contributed a treatment, resembling none of the others, in September 1936. All of these had little or nothing to do with the characters or events as they evolved in the later scripts.

During that same month, producer-director Howard Hawks signed a long-term contract with RKO (which was terminated eighteen months later). Hawks now became involved with Gunga Din, although King Vidor had been mentioned for the project in August. Hawks began working in New York with his friends and collaborators Ben Hecht and Charles MacArthur on a completely different approach to the story. Hecht had written the screenplay of Hawks's Scarface (1932) and Viva Villa! (1934). (On the latter, Hawks was replaced during filming.) Hecht and his frequent collaborator, playwright and screenwriter MacArthur, had worked with Hawks on Twentieth Century (1934) and Barbary Coast (1935).

From New York on October 27, 1936, the three sent a wire to Sam Briskin, at the time production head of RKO:

> HAVE FINALLY FIGURED OUT TALE INVOLVING
> TWO SACRIFICES, ONE FOR LOVE, THE OTHER
> FOR ENGLAND, WHICH NEITHER RESEMBLES
> "BENGAL LANCERS" NOR "CHARGE OF THE LIGHT
> BRIGADE," AND CONTAINS SOMETHING LIKE TWO
> THOUSAND DEATHS, THIRTY ELEPHANTS AND A
> PECK OF MAHARAJAHS STOP WE HAVE THIS NOW
> IN A COCKTAIL SHAKER AND HAVE POURED OUT
> SOME THIRTY-FIVE PAGES OF GLITTERING PROSE
> WHICH LOOK GOOD. BEST REGARDS.

Shortly thereafter thoughts were given to casting Ronald Colman, Victor McLaglen, and Madeleine Carroll in starring roles. A little later, Hawks suggested Robert Donat.

By December the basic characters and story line as we know them from the finished film were all there—the narrative of the water carrier interspersed with the adventures of the three comrades,* a religious fanatic on the warpath, the attack at the village, the elephant medicine sequence at the ball, the elephant knocking down the jail to rescue Cutter, the events at the gold temple, and so on. This outline, together with the previous and subsequent versions of the script, are in the RKO or MGM files.

It was a clever fusion. First there was Kipling's poem, "Gunga Din." A short time before he conceived "Gunga Din," Kipling published *Soldiers Three* (1888); a collection of stories about the humorous adventures of three privates in the British forces in India—a reckless Irishman of long service, a fighting Yorkshireman, and a London Cockney. These comrades were transferred to the *Gunga Din* narrative, but in spirit only. None of the incidents from the various stories was even suggested in the script. In the 1928 MGM treatments, the adventures of three soldiers (Irish, Scottish, and Cockney) were intertwined with the story of the water carrier, and in Alf Goulding's 1931 dramatic composition four rough-hewn soldiers (á la D'Artagnan and the three musketeers) find Gunga Din and he shares in their escapades. But all of these mergers of elements from *Soldiers Three* and "Gunga Din" were dissimilar to the Hecht and MacArthur story line, for the most part.

The underlying basis for the new script was a plot device from the highly successful Hecht and MacArthur play, *The Front Page* (1928). In that

---

* Not *two* comrades, as producer-director George Stevens recalled in references to the Hecht and MacArthur script years later.

comedy-melodrama about the newspaper business, a star Chicago reporter announces to his editor that he is going to quit his job and go to New York to get married. His editor spends a good deal of the play trying one way or another to prevent this. After listening to a touching farewell speech by the editor and accepting the latter's gift of his watch, the newspaperman at last leaves for New York with his bride. The editor picks up the phone and asks the New York police to arrest the reporter and send him back as soon as he arrives. Why? "The son of a bitch stole my watch."

The basic parallel in Hecht and MacArthur's *Gunga Din* script is in Ballantine's announcement to his comrades Cutter and MacChesney that he is resigning from the service to marry Emmy and go into the tea business. His friends try to thwart this plan in various ways throughout the narrative. At one point, Cutter is captured by the religious fanatic and his followers. MacChesney decides to go alone to rescue his friend. Ballantine wants to accompany him, but MacChesney will not allow it. He has been released from the army and cannot go as a civilian. In despair, Ballantine offers to reenlist, provided that MacChesney tears up the papers after Cutter is saved. So the two, with Gunga Din, set off.

Up to this juncture the original screenplay by Hecht and MacArthur follows the finished film in general outline. But the final third of the narrative differs considerably. In the original script, Ballantine disguises himself as a native and he and Din pretend that they have captured MacChesney. The three are thus allowed to enter Sufi Khan's (the original name of the religious fanatic) temple. MacChesney is placed in a cell with Cutter. Ballantine, with Din's aid, captures the Khan and places him in the same cell. They hold him as hostage, knowing that he is sacred and that while he lives they too are safe. However, the Khan kills himself to deliver the English into the hands of his followers. The only way out is for Din to masquerade as the Khan until they can get safely out of the grounds. Din, however, is very ill, and during their escape he collapses. In the free-for-all that follows the three comrades and Din manage to get away. Most of the above has structural parallels with *The Front Page*.

In the original Hecht and MacArthur script, Ballantine and Emmy at last are married. They bid a fond farewell to Cutter and MacChesney and depart for their honeymoon and a life of leisure. But no sooner are they out of sight than MacChesney takes Ballantine's reenlistment form, reads it carefully, and wires ahead to arrange his arrest—for desertion (*The Front Page* again). In the final version, this ending was not used. Instead, Ballantine gladly renounces domestic life and voluntarily stays in the service.

After two revisions of their own script, Hecht and MacArthur were off the project by February 1937. In April, slight incidental changes were made by

RKO staff writer Dudley Nichols and by Howard Hawks, but the narrative remained the same. During this period there was some discussion about using British actor Roger Livesey (*Drums*) for one of the leading roles, and Hawks suggested to Sam Briskin that the studio try to borrow Robert Montgomery from MGM for the role of Ballantine and Spencer Tracy for MacChesney. Briskin had tried to convince Louis B. Mayer to lend RKO Clark Gable, Spencer Tracy, and Franchot Tone in exchange for the rights to *Rio Rita*, an old RKO property that MGM wanted to make with Nelson Eddy and Jeanette MacDonald. Mayer was adamant about not releasing Gable, but left the door open for discussions regarding the other players.

By mid-1937, producer Edward Small, being somewhat disenchanted with his set-up at RKO, went back to being an independent producer for United Artists, and Howard Hawks had departed RKO under less than agreeable circumstances—mostly concerning the high cost, long schedule, and only fair box-office results of his *Bringing Up Baby* (1938). The *Gunga Din* project sat on the shelf. Then after studio head Sam Briskin left in November 1937, Pandro S. Berman, RKO's new vice-president in charge of production, took it over.

Berman assigned staff writer Anthony Veiller to cut the previous script, but nothing was changed—merely pruned somewhat. RKO was going through difficult times. In late 1937, the studio even considered selling the *Gunga Din* property. Earlier, in June, MGM claimed that the Hecht and MacArthur script infringed on their rights to Kipling's *Soldiers Three*, recently acquired from Gaumont-British, which had planned to make it with Victor McLaglen and Maureen O'Sullivan. Second-unit material, which was never used, had already been photographed in India. The infringement claim was discarded along the way, but then MGM thought that by buying the rights and scripts of *Gunga Din* from RKO, they would be able to meld it with *Soldiers Three*, eliminate similar competitive material from another studio, and get a wanted property—*Rio Rita*—in the bargain. MGM made an offer to RKO, but after careful consideration, it was rejected. For various reasons *Soldiers Three* was dropped from MGM's schedule until many years later.

Pandro Berman recalls that "the [*Gunga Din*] script needed a lot of work, and before we got around to actual production on the picture I began to get awfully worried about cost." According to Berman, Hawks was still being considered to direct the film. "But Howard was rather slow and difficult, and I was afraid. We were quite limited in our own money situation at RKO in those days, and I was afraid he would go over budget so much that I would be in trouble. So I didn't go with Howard. I went with George Stevens who, up to that time, had made pictures quite reasonably for us."

Stevens, since making *Alice Adams* with Katharine Hepburn in 1935, had become RKO's most valued director. Having just completed *Vivacious Lady* with Ginger Rogers and James Stewart, which was a success commercially and critically, he was scheduled to do, of all things, *Room Service* with the Marx Brothers, who were on loan from MGM. In April 1938 he was given *Gunga Din* instead, and the project was reactivated. Joel Sayre and Fred Guiol were assigned to rework the script with Stevens,* and Cary Grant (as Ballantine) and Jack Oakie (as Cutter) were discussed as possible leading players. Oakie was under contract to RKO and Grant had a nonexclusive agreement with the studio. Berman recalls Grant originally being offered the role of Ballantine, but the actor really wanted the role of the Cockney, Cutter (the Oakie part), who was considered at that time to be secondary. With his customary shrewdness Grant was right. His comic, offbeat portrayal of Cutter opened up new dimensions for him, and he wound up stealing the show. Grant had previously portrayed a Cockney in *Sylvia Scarlett* (1936).

Meanwhile, Victor McLaglen was borrowed from Twentieth Century-Fox to portray MacChesney. McLaglen was hardly a stranger to this kind of material; most of his professional screen career had been spent playing tough, earthy officers or enlisted men with a heart of gold—the prototype being Captain Flagg in *What Price Glory?* (1926). As far as the British in India were concerned, McLaglen first saw duty in *The Black Watch* (1929), an adaptation of Talbot Mundy's *King of the Khyber Rifles*, and he later did the 1937 version of Kipling's *Wee Willie Winkie*.

Director George Stevens wanted to make *Gunga Din* primarily on location. "I knew where that location should be," Stevens said. "In California around Lone Pine . . . . We designed the set before the script was [re]written. I flew up there with a fellow named Perry Ferguson [art director] and laid out the three sets; the temple, the town, and the parade ground . . . . It is a rather remarkable area because there are the Sierras at their best; Whitney and the other two peaks flank left and right. There are these Alabama hills, this strange rugged rock formation that relates to various other localities, certainly locations in Persia, Afghanistan, the Khyber Pass in India. They really are eroded mountains." The area around Lone Pine had been used previously as a substitute for India's northwest frontier, most notably in *The Lives of a Bengal Lancer* (1935) and *The Charge of the Light Brigade* (1936).

Stevens and writers Joel Sayre and Fred Guiol then went to Arrowhead

* There have been some references in recent years regarding William Faulkner being engaged to "doctor" the script, but there is nothing that substantiates this in the very extensive RKO files. In any case, it would have been highly unlikely, given his previous association with the project.

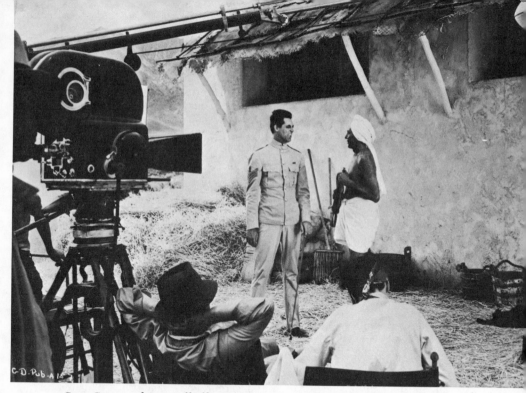

Cary Grant and Sam Jaffe filming a scene for Gunga Din *on location near Lone Pine, California. Director George Stevens (with hat) seated next to camera.*

Springs to work on the script. Time was a factor. Because of actors' commitments and other considerations, the start of shooting was set for late June 1938—only a few weeks away. Sayre concentrated on research, having brought a miniature library on India with him, while Guiol and Stevens talked over ideas. Guiol was an ex-comedy director and an old associate of Stevens, going back to their days at Hal Roach in the 1920s (at the time Stevens was a cameraman). Sayre, like Hecht and MacArthur, had been a newspaperman. His first novel, *Rackety Rax*, was made into a Fox picture with Victor McLaglen in 1932. He had worked on RKO's *Annie Oakley* (1935), directed by Stevens, among many other films.

"We had an essential thing necessary to glue this whole thing together and Joel came upon it," Stevens has said. "That was the cult of the Thugee that existed in India . . . . a cult of assassins . . . . Getting hold of that, we worked it into the theme." Sworn by the most binding oaths to commit murder as an honor to Kali, a Hindu goddess associated with death and destruction, the organization whose members were known as "Thugs" brought terror to people in India between the thirteenth and the nineteenth centuries. They disguised themselves as ordinary travelers and carried small pickaxes with which they dug graves for those whom they planned to kill, and light cloths with which they strangled their victims. These details were all planted in the modified script.

The Thugs' leader, played by Eduardo Ciannelli, compares himself to Caesar, Hannibal, and Napoleon and predicts that his cult will sweep from village to town and from town to city, eventually engulfing all of India. As in so many pictures of the time, a parallel was being drawn with fascism in general and Hitler in particular.

Sabu, the young Indian who had played in *Elephant Boy* (1937) and *Drums* (1938), seemed the logical choice for the role of Gunga Din, but producer Alexander Korda did not want to lend him as at that time he was preparing *The Thief of Bagdad* (1940) for Sabu. Then there was an attempt to find an unknown Indian player for the role, and tests were made of various actors. Garson Kanin suggested that character actor Sam Jaffe test. Jaffe told me that he had thought about his approach to the character and decided to pattern his performance after Sabu; he won the role. Douglas Fairbanks, Jr., who had a nonexclusive agreement with RKO, was signed for Ballantine only a week before shooting began.

For the thankless part of "the girl," Berman and Stevens decided on Joan Fontaine, who had been under contract to RKO for almost two years, but who after a promising start had proved a disappointment in the films in which the studio had cast her as part of its grooming for stardom program (*A Damsel in Distress* [1937] with Fred Astaire being the most notable failure). Jules Levy, RKO's general sales manager, strongly protested Berman and Stevens's decision to cast Fontaine in *Gunga Din*, and stated that the studio's field men felt that the actress showed "little promise," was "a very colorless personality," and that she should be released from her contract. She was, shortly after *Gunga Din*. Two years later she starred in *Rebecca* for David O. Selznick, and the course of her career changed.

In July 1938, an exceptionally large company headed for the location, 220 miles northeast of Los Angeles. The village of Tantrapur had been built by the studio in the Sierras. Six miles out on the California desert a cantonment and parade ground for British troops had been laid out, and a few miles away, in the higher ground of the Sierras, the Thug temple was erected.

Eduardo Ciannelli as the fanatical Guru in Gunga Din *having body makeup applied.*

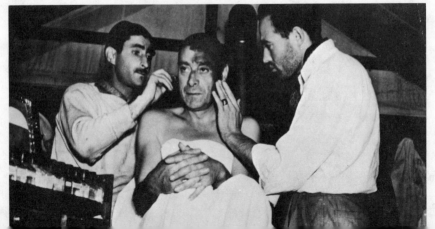

In March 1938, just prior to Stevens's being assigned to the picture, $1,493,000 was estimated for the cost of production—an enormous budget for a picture in those days, and for the relatively modest RKO, an unprecedented fortune. Most of the studio's pictures during that period had cost well under a million—even the Astaire-Rogers musicals.

Six weeks had been scheduled for location work. Stevens, Sayre, and Guiol were still working on the script day and night while they were shooting, and the last third of the picture had yet to be finalized. According to Pandro Berman, prior to *Gunga Din* Stevens had always brought pictures in on budget, but "lo and behold, when Stevens got on *Din* he changed, and he became as slow as Hawks ever was and perhaps a little slower—in fact, quite a bit slower."

The location junket lasted approximately two weeks longer than originally scheduled. Director of photography Joseph August—*The Informer* (1935), *The Hunchback of Notre Dame* (1939)—said at the time:

> The wild assortment of weather during our . . . weeks on location in the Sierras gave the camera crews the most trouble. Because of the heavy expense of maintaining a large company so far from Hollywood it wasn't feasible to shoot the story in sequence. And it was our problem to reconcile the photography to keep the weather cinematically consistent. Here are a few weather notes . . . .

George Stevens (left) directing a scene for Gunga Din *with Joan Fontaine and Douglas Fairbanks, Jr.*

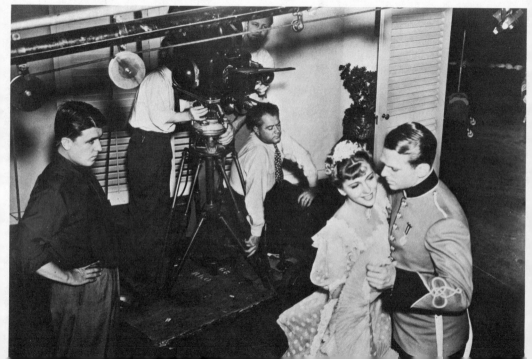

Temperatures which for weeks ranged from 105 to 115 degrees, beneath cloudless, empty skies. A pre-season snowstorm that swooped down from nearby Mt. Whitney skirted our sets, changed our majestic background of rugged peaks to solid white. (While subsequent warm weather brought the background back to normal we confined ourselves to closeups.) A freak windstorm which damaged some of the sets, and actually took the roof off a nearby mountain cabin. Dust storms which lasted three days, obscuring all but the closest objects. (Again we stuck to closeups till the weather cleared.) Several rain storms, preceded by some of the most beautiful cloud formations I've ever seen.

Because the script was still being revised, Stevens improvised and embellished material just before and during the shooting of a scene. Not only Stevens and his writers but also principal members of the cast contributed ideas, bits of business, and changes in dialogue. Each evening on location was spent working out what in general was going to happen the next day. This was essentially the procedure of many silent-picture makers, and Stevens reverted to those days when he had photographed two-reel Laurel and Hardy comedies and Hal Roach features.

Berman and the New York office were worried and apprehensive over the escalating costs. Finally, Stevens and the entire company were ordered to return, even though all of the required scenes were not finished. Some exteriors were shot at nearby Chatsworth and Lake Sherwood. Interiors and scenes on top of the temple were then photographed on the main RKO lot in Hollywood. The last part of the picture was still a dilemma. Then it was

Producer-director George Stevens (left) and visiting executive producer Pandro S. Berman on location in the Sierras during the filming of Gunga Din.

decided, based on the quality of the material shot thus far, and the need to make this a truly spectacular production, to go all-out and stage a magnificent battle finale. This was photographed after all the other material had been completed and required another two-week trip to the Sierras. By now it was October, and the company encountered a preseason snowstorm and some rainstorms.

Shortly after the film's completion Stevens said:

> The [final] battle scenes constituted our biggest problem. The job was to use 1,500 men, several hundred horses and mules— to say nothing of four elephants—most effectively for scenes of utmost confusion, and still plan the action to obviate accidents and possible injuries.
>
> To do this we first fought on paper the entire battle, the charge, and the headlong retreat of the Thugs. Then we transferred our activities to Mt. Whitney's rugged slopes, and rehearsed the cast in small detachments and in slow motion until the mechanics of the action were established. As the scene took shape the number of people and animals was gradually increased, the action speeded up until we had the scene going at top speed. Then we shot it.
>
> Just beyond the range of the cameras were posted first-aid facilities as well as wranglers to re-capture frightened riderless animals. Behind various rocks assistant directors kept in touch with me by field telephone, and relayed my "commands" to the groups nearest them.

Stevens also used a public-address system while setting up the battle details. These mass scenes were photographed from various vantage points concurrently with a number of cameras.

For dramatic purposes it was decided to give Gunga Din a hero's death, following the self-sacrifice tradition of *The Lives of a Bengal Lancer*, in which one of the leading players (Gary Cooper) dies nobly to save his regiment, *The Charge of the Light Brigade*, in which the character portrayed by Errol Flynn is killed while avenging the massacre of a British garrison in India, *Beau Geste* (1939), in which Beau dies a valiant death at a Foreign Legion desert outpost, and so on. The final shot is a closeup of Gunga Din in corporal's regalia—his fondest wish was to be a soldier—superimposed over a dawn background of the regiment's camp. Shades of the ending of *Trader Horn* (1931): The faithful native gunbearer in that film (Mutia Omoolu) has died gallantly, and just before the final fade out he is superimposed over a jungle landscape as Horn brushes back his tears.

At last *Gunga Din* was completed. Instead of the originally planned 64 days of shooting, there were 104. While the final editing was taking place, Pandro Berman approached Erich Wolfgang Korngold about scoring the film. In a wire to George Schaefer in New York on November 2, Berman said:

> WITH REGARD TO MUSICAL SCORE "GUNGA DIN,"
> DESIRE MAKE IT EXTRAORDINARILY FINE AND
> HAVE MANAGED TO OBTAIN KORNGOLD, GREAT
> MUSICIAN WHO DID "ANTHONY ADVERSE" AND
> "ROBIN HOOD," BUT UNABLE TO USE HIM IF
> PICTURE IS TO BE RELEASED CHRISTMAS . . . .
> WILL ASSIGN KORNGOLD TO PICTURE IF YOU ARE
> GOING TO HOLD UP CAMPAIGN UNTIL YOU HAVE
> SEEN NEARLY COMPLETED PICTURE, WHICH
> WILL BE THREE WEEKS OFF WITHOUT MUSICAL
> SCORE, AND REQUIRE APPROXIMATELY FIVE OR
> SIX WEEKS FOR MUSIC THEREAFTER.

In a November 10 letter to Ned Depinet at RKO in New York, J. R. McDonough said:

> We are concluding a deal with Korngold . . . and he is insisting
> that he have at least six weeks time for his work after the final
> cut of the picture is delivered to him. The final cut of the
> picture has not been made yet . . . .
> We have been unwilling to talk of any deferred release date
> for fear that such news might tend to slow down the cutting
> and editing of the picture.

When Korngold finally saw the film later in November he turned it down because, we can presume, there was not enough time. However, according to his son George, he did compose a theme for the water carrier before seeing the film. Also, according to George Korngold, Korngold did not want to compose for yet another picture with a superabundance of battle scenes (such films drown out the music and are time-consuming to write for because of the fast tempi), and he never had done a film away from Warner Bros., where he felt comfortable. On November 25 Alfred Newman was signed to compose the score, which he did in a more than competent manner in a little over three weeks in order to meet the release date of January 12.

Although there had been earlier thoughts about utilizing the music Gerard Francis Cobb had written in 1897 to the poem of "Gunga Din," Newman composed an original theme for the regimental water carrier, as well as new thematic material for the majority of the picture. He did, however, employ "Will Ye No Come Back Again," by Finlay Dunn, for considerable dramatic effect, when the entire regiment, with Scottish pipe band, was proceeding to rescue the comrades at the temple. Other traditional or patriotic material incorporated into the original score by Newman included "God Save the King," "Her Majesty's Colors," "Lochiel's Welcome," "Bonnie Dundee," "Auld Lang Syne," "The Barren Rocks of Eden," "Roast Beef of Old England," "Lord Lovat's Lament," "Last Post," "Pibroch of Donald Dhu," and a paraphrase of "The British Grenadiers." Newman's "The Three Comrades" motif, as he called it, was used in a variety of colorful interpretations and variations throughout the film.

There were no drastic changes made to the film following three successful previews (in Whittier, Huntington Park, and Inglewood), only the usual tightening here and there. Pandro Berman told me that both Din's climb to the top of the temple to warn the approaching regiment and the subsequent final battle scene ran much longer at this point. Stevens finally agreed to cut the material down after the previews.

The final negative cost of *Gunga Din* listed in the RKO books was $1,909,669.28. Very few pictures produced in the 1930s at any studio cost that much. The film did not make back its negative cost (plus advertising and release prints) on its initial release, but went on to ensure an excellent profit with each reissue beginning in 1941.* It did exceptionally well abroad, but was banned in India for its obvious imperialistic, white supremacy overtones.

In February 1939, the film critic for *The Bombay Chronicle*, Khwaja Ahmad Abbas—later a director, producer, and screenwriter of films made in India—wrote for the magazine *Filmindia* a special article that carried the headline: "*Gunga Din* Another Scandalously Anti-Indian Picture!" It went on to say:

> *Gunga Din* is imperialist propaganda of the crudest, the most vulgar sort and depicts Indians as nothing better than sadistic barbarians . . . .
>
> All the British characters are honest, jolly souls while all the "natives" are scheming, treacherous, unscrupulous devils. All but one!! The solitary exception is Gunga Din, the faithful water carrier—loyal unto death, despite the insults and curses that are invariably showered on him by his White Masters. He is always cringing before them . . . . That is how all loyal "natives" must behave in the presence of their rulers! . . .

* The film has been in almost continuous distribution since 1939.

> The scenarists who wrote *Gunga Din* seem to have heard of Pathans [Afghans], of Kali, of idols and priests and temples, of elephants, of loin-cloth, and of upright British soldiers. And in *Gunga Din* they have put them all together in a most amazing jumble . . . . It is all like producing a film of Hollywood life and showing glamour girls riding on the back of Alaskan bears and cigar-chewing producers going about with feathers stuck in their hair like the Red Indians!

In addition, the whole idea of British soldiers looting a temple was considered repugnant by the Bengal Board. And, it was pointed out in a letter from N. M. Durant, the manager of RKO's office in Calcutta, to RKO executives in December, 1939, Thuggery was *not* a religion. The great majority of Thugs were Hindus by religion, but Thuggery was not confined to Hindus only.

> Kali is not and never has been a Goddess exclusive to Thuggery. Kali is a Hindu goddess and is commonly known as "the Destroyer" . . . . Thus on the eve of a marauding expedition we might expect Thugs to worship Kali to gain strength for their enterprise, but to depict the Goddess as being the peculiar deity of Thuggery is not only misleading but likely to give offense to all orthodox Hindus.
>
> Kali is the Mother Goddess and as such is as real and is reverenced by all good Hindus as much as the Virgin Mary is revered by Catholic Christians.

When the film opened in England in March 1939, shortly after its American release, Mrs. Caroline Kipling, the author's widow, demanded that RKO eliminate for the British market any shots showing the actor Reginald Sheffield impersonating Kipling. He appeared as the journalist accompanying the regiment on its way to rescue the prisoners at the temple. Later, after the battle, he was seen composing his poem, "Gunga Din," which is then read by the colonel (Montagu Love) while Din is being buried with full military honors and Kipling is standing by. Mrs. Kipling claimed that Kipling looked incongruous in the midst of such proceedings, that people were inclined to laugh when he appeared on the screen, and that all of this held him up to ridicule. Kipling was not witness to any battles during the years he served as a young journalist in India. Indeed, the frontier was unusually quiet at that time. Without losing critical scenes, RKO quickly modified the negative (for the American version as well) to eliminate the actor playing Kipling and any reference to Kipling other than his name in the credits. The Colonel still reads the poem, but Mr. Kipling was matted out via the optical printer. Fortunately, the American Film Institute has uncovered the deleted footage, thus making available once again the version originally released.

The initial running time of the film was one hour and fifty-seven minutes, but for the large-scale 1954 reissue *Gunga Din* was cut to ninety-four minutes. Nothing of great consequence was eliminated. Before the opening titles, there was originally a prologue showing a monument of Victoria. An off-camera voice intoned the first six lines from Kipling's poem:

> Now in Injia's sunny clime,
> Where I used to spend my time
> A-servin' of 'Er Majesty the Queen,
> Of all them black-faced crew
> The finest man I knew
> Was our regimental bhisti, Gunga Din.

Immediately following the credit titles a sequence was deleted that depicted a group of Thugs disguised as pilgrims asking the leader of a British patrol if they could follow it for safety. That night at camp the Thugs strangle members of the detachment. Also cut was a scene at the regimental dance having to do with MacChesney trying to prevent the colonel and major from drinking out of the punch bowl that had been diluted by Cutter and MacChesney with a powerful elephant medicine specifically intended for Ballantine's replacement, Higginbotham (Robert Coote); and a sequence showing MacChesney and Ballantine going off to bring back Annie the

This sequence depicting Rudyard Kipling (Reginald Sheffield) composing his poem "Gunga Din" was deleted shortly after the film went into release.

This sequence with Douglas Fairbanks, Jr. and Joan Fontaine was cut from Gunga Din.

elephant. Emmy (Joan Fontaine) and Sergeant Higginbotham meet them
en route. She surprises Ballantine by bringing his discharge papers, and
Higginbotham is there ready to replace Ballantine. Other small cuts were
made throughout the film.

There has been no official remake of *Gunga Din*, although *Sergeants
Three* (1962) with Frank Sinatra, Dean Martin, Sammy Davis, Jr., and Peter
Lawford, transplanted the basic plot, more or less, to the West. MGM's
Soldiers Three, finally made in 1951, was an extremely free adaptation of
Kipling's stories that has been erroneously described at various times as a
remake of *Gunga Din*. Actually, it has little or nothing to do with that film
(or Kipling, for that matter) in story line, style, or quality.

George Stevens referred to *Gunga Din* as "The Rover Boys in India."
Certainly the film was not based on reality. Although it reflects distorted
and—for many—repugnant attitudes and ideas of a different time, such as
jingoism, British imperialism and colonialism, "the white man's burden,"
and so on, *Gunga Din* was not conceived or designed as anything more
weighty than a vigorous and rowdy romp done in the grand manner. It is
still—in its sometimes naive and corny way—just that.

6

BRET HARTE IN MONUMENT VALLEY: STAGECOACH
(1939)

In the spring of 1937, director John Ford happened to read a short story by Ernest Haycox called "Stage to Lordsburg" in the April issue of *Collier's* magazine. He liked it and purchased the film rights for less than $7,500.

Ford had made scores of westerns, beginning in 1917, but it had been eleven years since he had made his last, the silent *Three Bad Men* in (1926). "Stage to Lordsburg," although brief and sketchy, provided a cross-section of characters brought together while traveling in a stagecoach during perilous times in the late nineteenth century when the Apache Indians fiercely opposed the white intrusion into the Southwest. Ernest Haycox was a prolific writer of short stories and novels about the West, some of which were transferred to the screen: *Union Pacific* (1939), *Canyon Passage* (1946), and *Bugles in the Afternoon* (1952). John Ford thought that Haycox's "Stage to Lordsburg" had been inspired by Guy de Maupassant's classic short story, "Boule de Suif," which dealt with a prostitute and various bourgeois passengers traveling across occupied France in a coach during the Franco-Prussian War of 1870.

Ford worked with his old collaborator Dudley Nichols (*The Lost Patrol*,

104

The Informer) on the adaptation. When Nichols first read the story he said
he "thought it was a mixture of *Grand Hotel*, *The Covered Wagon*, and *The
Iron Horse*, so I called it 'The Grand Covered Iron Stagecoach' . . . . Our
first problem was to get a group of characters. The characters in the story
weren't well drawn, they were just outlines."

Although the basic Haycox plot was retained, some of the characters were
changed, and considerable elaboration of the narrative took place. The
passengers on Haycox's stage to Lordsburg were a cowboy, a prostitute, a
whiskey salesman, a gambler, an Englishman, a cattleman, and a woman
traveling to her fiancé, who was an Army officer. Atop the coach were John
Strang, riding shotgun, and Happy Stuart, the driver. Nichols and Ford
dropped the cattleman and Englishman, replacing them with a banker and
doctor. In their adaptation, the woman was already married to the officer
and carrying his child.

Writer Dudley Nichols and director John Ford preparing Stagecoach.

Malpais Bill, the cowboy on his way to Lordsburg to "wipe out a grudge" in the original short story, was transformed into the fictitious Ringo Kid, whose manners and morals seem to suggest Owen Wister's Virginian, while his name is similar to the real Johnny Ringo, a notorious gunfighter who had many confrontations with Wyatt Earp—detailed in Stuart N. Lake's book, *Wyatt Earp, Frontier Marshal* (1931). Ford had known Wyatt Earp, and he liked Lake's anecdotal biography based on the aging lawman's own reminiscences, which later became the basis for Ford's *My Darling Clementine*. Lake's book seems to have influenced certain names in Nichols's adaptation of "Stage to Lordsburg": Wes Wilcox became Curly Wilcox (George Bancroft), who rode shotgun; the name Lou Rickabaugh from the book suggested Buck Rickabaugh, the driver (Andy Devine); and Jim Peacock became Samuel Peacock, the whiskey salesman (Donald Meek).

Both Doc Boone (Thomas Mitchell) and Hatfield (John Carradine) owe a lot to the town drunk, Uncle Billy, and the gentleman gambler, John Oakhurst, in Bret Harte's short story "The Outcasts of Poker Flat." And in that same story there is also the prostitute with heart of gold called the Duchess. Ford and Nichols were admirers of the stories and characters of Bret Harte, whose work is marked by sentimentality, humor, and a penchant for showing thieves and vagabonds as more admirable than conventional, law-abiding people. In 1919 Ford had directed a film version of *The Outcasts of Poker Flat*.

Ford, who was then free-lancing, found it difficult to interest any studio or independent producer in the story. But Merian C. Cooper (producer-director of *Chang* and *King Kong* and producer of *The Last Days of Pompeii*), at the time vice-president of Selznick International, signed Ford with the company and became enthusiastic when Ford told him about "Stage to Lordsburg." Cooper chose this property as his first personally produced film for Selznick International, and it was to be made in the then relatively new three-color Technicolor process with Ford directing.

In late 1937, John Ford asked his old friend John Wayne to spend a weekend aboard his yacht. Ten years earlier, while working as a prop boy, Wayne had met Ford at Fox. Ford liked the USC football player and had him play bit parts in a few of his films, in addition to using him as a prop man on others. Director Raoul Walsh took a chance on Wayne for the lead in a Fox special called *The Big Trail* (1930), which proved to be less than successful. Wayne was then relegated to acting in quickie westerns at various studios throughout the thirties.

During the 1937 weekend on Ford's yacht, the director handed Wayne the "Stage to Lordsburg" short story and an early version of the script to read. Afterward Ford asked him who, in his opinion, would be right for the Ringo Kid. According to Wayne: " 'Well, there's only one actor I can think of who could play it,' I said, 'and that's Lloyd Nolan.' 'Why, you stupid son of a bitch,' he [Ford] said, 'I want *you* to play it.' And I was hoping like hell that *he* wouldn't say Lloyd Nolan.

"Pappy wanted me, but nobody else did. There was a lot of resistance to my playing the part—and with good reason. After all, a theater could get me in a Republic Western for five dollars. So why should they pay two hundred dollars for me in *Stagecoach*?"

Then Ford approached Claire Trevor, who had just finished a five-year contract at Fox. "For some reason, Ford was interested in me as an actress," she said in 1971. "I couldn't understand why, because I had [done] nothing at Fox that would have shown any promise."

Merian C. Cooper agreed with Ford on the casting. In Cooper's correspondence he tells about going with Ford to David Selznick's house for dinner to talk about the picture. Cooper's deal with Selznick International allowed him to choose his own projects and have full authority for producing them, with Selznick to have veto power of any project if he thought it would not be profitable.

Selznick listened, but was not impressed. According to Cooper, he thought "Stage to Lordsburg" was "just another Western," and that they would do a lot better if they made "a classic." In a memo dated June 29, 1937, Selznick stated that "we must select the story and sell it to John Ford, instead of having Ford select some uncommercial pet of his that we would be making only because of Ford's enthusiasm."

Both Ford and Cooper argued that the very reason they liked the story so much was that it was a perfect vehicle in which to use some of Bret Harte's and other classic characters. Finally, Selznick agreed and gave them the go-ahead. But, according to Cooper, Selznick changed his mind the next morning, telling Cooper he felt it was necessary to put stars in the leading roles in order to make the picture commercially viable. He indicated that he could sign Gary Cooper and Marlene Dietrich. Merian Cooper said that both he and Ford had made verbal commitments with Wayne and Trevor, and that, in their opinion, this was as binding as a written contract.

In a memo dated July 16, 1937 Selznick commented: "Ford apparently has no desire to go through with his commitment with us, evidently being annoyed because he could not do *The Stage To Lordsburg* . . . . He is an excellent man, but there is no point in treating him as a god, and if he doesn't want to be here I'd just as soon have some other good director." According to Cooper, because of this impasse, both he and Ford left Selznick International, Cooper to go to MGM as a producer and Ford to sign nonexclusively with Fox and Goldwyn. Though Cooper remained active behind the scenes until the film eventually was completed, he did not take or claim any credit for it. Ford and Cooper were partners for many years afterward.

No studio seemed interested in taking on the project. Finally, Walter Wanger, who was making independent films for release through United Artists, decided to take a chance after Ford and Cooper convinced him that the picture could be brought in for the relatively low figure of $546,000, according to Wanger's negative-cost report. This could be accomplished by eliminating Technicolor, by using no stars, and by carefully working out the logistics of the location and studio shooting. The distributors, United Artists, had invested $2,000,000 in Wanger's company from July 1936 to the end of the 1938 season. Seven pictures had been released, but none had returned a profit. After that debacle, financing was to come primarily from the Bank of America, and Wanger had to budget very economically and carefully. Therefore, the timing was right. The plan for *Stagecoach* (the new title for *Stage to Lordsburg*) seemed a good gamble under the circumstances.

Revisions continued to be made on the screenplay. John Wayne considered Ford a fine script editor. Regarding this particular script, Wayne recalled that Ford would "make Nichols write a scene five or six times till Nichols was just about drenched. And then he'd find three lines out of three scenes that Dudley had written and use them for that particular speech. He knew how to draw lines out that give character and progress your story at the same time."

Ford began assembling his cast. With the exception of Louise Platt, who played the pregnant wife of the officer and who was under contract to Walter Wanger, all of the major supporting players had been hired previously by Ford, in some cases repeatedly. Andy Devine, cast as the driver of the coach, recalled that "the first time I worked for John Ford was in 1919, when he came to Arizona to make *Ace of the Saddle* with Harry Carey. I was working on a ranch then, wrangling cattle and horses, and he gave me a job in the picture." Berton Churchill, who played the embezzling banker, was doing a virtual repeat of his role in the first film version of *Frontier Marshal* (based in part on Stuart Lake's book) in 1934 with George O'Brien.

Prior to filming, some tests were made. Clarie Trevor recalled that when Wayne was being tested, "at one point, Ford took Duke by the chin and shook him. 'What are you doing with your mouth?' Ford demanded. 'Why are you moving your mouth so much? Don't you know that you don't act with your mouth in pictures. You act with your eyes!' It was tough for Duke to take, but he took it. And he learned eight volumes about acting in that picture."

It was that way throughout the entire shooting schedule. "Sure he got me angry," Wayne said, "but he knew what he was doing. First of all—he was makin' me feel emotions. He knew he couldn't get a good job of work out of me unless he shook me up so damn hard I'd forget to worry about whether I was fit to be in the same picture with Thomas Mitchell . . . . By deliberately

On location for Stagecoach: *Andy Devine and John Wayne in the foreground, John Ford (with glasses) in the background.*

Monument Valley as seen in Stagecoach.

kickin' me around, he got the other actors on my side and hatin' him
. . . . Mr. Ford only wanted to do one thing and that was to make good
pictures, and to do this he would do anything, anything."

Walter Reynolds, who was the sound man on *Stagecoach*, recalled that
"John Wayne was having a lot of trouble with a scene he was doing with
Claire Trevor. He just couldn't get it. So Ford told him: 'Just raise your
eyebrows and wrinkle your forehead.' Wayne's been doing that ever since."

Ford wanted to use varied locations for the picture, but in those days,
because of the costs, it was not standard procedure to take all of the cast and
crew on extended junkets. Therefore the passengers inside the coach (other
than Wayne) did not make the trips to the various sites, with the exception
of those nearby in the San Fernando Valley.

The most spectacular and memorable location was Monument Valley, a
Navaho Indian tribal park astride the Utah–Arizona border. A desert land
of approximately two thousand square miles, set off by towering sandstone
buttes, Monument Valley was for all practical purposes first introduced to
filmgoers in *Stagecoach*, although it is possible that it was used briefly on
a rare occasion earlier. Awesome landscape such as this tends to elevate
even the relatively routine into epic status.

There are at least three versions of how Monument Valley came to be
used in *Stagecoach*: John Ford, in the most succinct account said years
later, "I had driven through Monument Valley, and I thought it would be
a good place to shoot a Western." John Wayne's version is considerably

different. As recounted in Maurice Zolotow's biography of Wayne, *Shooting Star* (1974), Wayne said:

> It was back in '29, and I was proppin' and stuntin' on a George O'Brien location, out in Arizona.* One Sunday, I wanted to get away by myself. I took a car and went drivin'. I went out on this Navaho reservation . . . .
>
> I never forgot about it, and when Mr. Ford was talkin' about locations on *Stagecoach* I told him about Monument Valley and he looked at me as if I was stupid because he thought he knew the Arizona and Utah country and he never heard of the Valley. [Later] I was with him on a party when he was scoutin' locations in Arizona . . . . Well, we were drivin' along and finally came to the reservation . . . . Mr. Ford pretended to see the buttes and said, 'I have just found the location we are going to use.'
>
> It was Monument Valley.

The third version is that of Harry Goulding, who ran the Indian Trading Post at Monument Valley after 1924. As Goulding tells it, "The Navahos were desperate by 1938. They were starving and had to get money in." Having heard about *Stagecoach* and armed with still photographs, Goulding went to Hollywood to see if he could interest the studio location manager in Monument Valley. After Goulding refused to budge from the reception area of the Goldwyn Studio, Ford's location manager finally came down, saw the photographs, and introduced Goulding to John Ford. Ford was immediately intrigued.

Ford chartered a plane and flew to the valley the next day. Goulding told me that Ford had positively never been to or heard of Monument Valley previously. He also stated that to the best of his knowledge no earlier motion picture company had ever shot there. The director decided immediately after seeing the spectacular site to film some of *Stagecoach* there.

Some time later, in November 1938, by plane, train, and automobile, eightly members of the crew began arriving in Kayenta, Arizona, headquarters for the troupe while shooting in and around Monument Valley. Harry Goulding met Ford, John Wayne, and Ward Bond (who was along just for the trip) at the Flagstaff train station and drove them 175 miles on the rough, unpaved road to the remote valley (no other place in the

* *The Lone Star Ranger* may have used Monument Valley—at least fleetingly—in the background, judging from stills from the picture. Negatives or prints of the film itself are missing.

continental United States is farther from a railway line). Goulding's Trading Post was and is the only place one can stay in the valley, aside from camp sites. Most of the crew stayed in tents or in Depression-style prefabricated housing.

In the early days, Monument Valley was one of the most picturesque and hazardous spots in the long trek from the Mississippi Valley to the California gold mines. And it was here that some of the last Indian uprisings took place. For *Stagecoach*, thousands of dollars were paid in salaries to the Indians who worked as laborers and movie extras. Although some Apaches were recruited from elsewhere for the close-ups, for the most part Navahos (and stuntmen) were outfitted to appear as Apaches.

Many people assume that most of the location work in *Stagecoach* was done in Monument Valley, but actually only a few scenes in the finished picture utilized the unique high-desert tableland, with its natural obelisks and many miles of uncultivated alkali-whitened sand and clay. Monument Valley became Ford's favorite location; he featured it in six additional Western pictures—*My Darling Clementine* (1946), *Fort Apache* (1948), *She Wore a Yellow Ribbon* (1949), *The Searchers* (1956), *Sergeant Rutledge* (1960), and *Cheyenne Autumn* (1964).* Producer Edward Small sent a unit to Monument Valley for *Kit Carson* in 1940, and MGM was the first to photograph the location in Technicolor for *Billy the Kid* (1941).

It had been decided to film the crossing of the river sequence for *Stagecoach* at the Kern River near Kernville, California; and the old wagon cut at Newhall, California (also called Fremont Pass)—which Ford had used as far back as *Straight Shooting* in 1917 and again in *The Iron Horse* in 1924—provided the entrance to the dry lake. Other filming areas in California were Chatsworth and Calabasas.

One of the original sturdy Concord stagecoaches that traveled the route over mountains and deserts when the coach was the Southwest's only means of transportation was transported to each location. During the years 1876 to 1889 the stagecoach carried hundreds of pioneers to new and often dangerous frontiers.

The big Indian attack was filmed at Muroc Dry Lake near Victorville, California. Wayne had recommended that Ford hire Yakima Canutt, his cohort from the cheap Westerns, to function as stuntman, double, and hirer-ramrod of the other stuntmen for this sequence. During the Indian attack, Ford asked Canutt to do a trick of his that he had performed in B Westerns and serials. According to Canutt, the plan was to have him jump from his pony onto the lead horse of the stagecoach and try to take the reins. The

* A few shots in Ford's *Rio Grande* (1950) were photographed in the valley, but most of the film was made elsewhere.

driver shoots him, and he drops to the tongue between the lead horses, drags awhile, then lets go, the horses and coach passing over him:

It was kind of a tricky thing to do, because you only had two and a half to three feet between horses and you had to be flat to get clearance under the stagecoach.

First I did the transfer, and it wasn't easy. The pinto I was riding shied away from the team, and I had a long jump to make . . . .

Next we shot the drop. Wayne shot me from the coach, and I dropped to the lead tongue. I swung under it and got hold of a long, slender bar I had fastened to the bottom of it. As I dragged along the ground I let my legs go limp from the waist down. Then he [Wayne] was to shoot me again, and I was to drop off. It was kind of spooky, dragging along and looking back at the horses' hooves. But they were running straight, so I let go.

I kept my legs together and my arms flat against my body [on my chest and stomach], and nothing hit. As soon as the coach passed over me, I did a little roll and got up, then fell back again and laid still . . . .

I never used any pads for that gag. To see how fast I could be dragged along the ground and then turn loose without rolling, I tied a support on the back of an automobile and practiced at different speeds. I could do it up to 45 miles an hour and slide to a stop. But you had to kill your legs. If you stiffened them you'd go into a roll.

Stagecoach: *The Indian attack, filmed at Muroc Dry Lake.*

But that wasn't all. Next Canutt assumed the role of the Ringo Kid (Wayne), who had climbed to the top of the stagecoach. The driver was wounded. The reins had dropped and the horses were runaways. Ringo (Canutt) leaped to the wheel team, then to the swing team, and finally to the lead horses, which he brought under control not too long before the bugle of the rescuing cavalry was heard. Canutt performed an amalgamation of these stunts for Warner Bros.' *Virginia City* about a year later. Other variations were used in *Young Bill Hickok* (1940) and *Sunset in Eldorado* (1945). Canutt says that the first time he did part of his stagecoach stunt was in *Lightning Warrior*, a 1931 Mascot serial. Other serials that featured the entire routine of Canutt dropping between the horses and the coach passing over him were Republic's *The Vigilantes Are Coming* (1936) and *Zorro's Fighting Legion* (1939).

The splendidly realized attack sequence in *Stagecoach*, punctuated with spectacular running falls, undoubtedly owes a great deal to Canutt's particular talent for setting up and arranging this kind of material. With the camera covering the action from cars, ground level, coach, and just below the surface looking up at thundering hooves, it is a marvelous synthesis of time-honored elements (reused as stock footage in various other films). The big but rather dull production of *Wells Fargo* just a year or so before *Stagecoach* had been one of the more recent epics to include an Indian attack on a coach, but the attack was relatively brief and unexciting. At the other end of the budgetary spectrum was Monogram's modest *Riders of the Dawn* (1938), with a climactic and well-done race across the salt flats, including Canutt's stunts.

After the company returned from the various locations, the Republic Studio Western Street (rented for a few days) doubled for the town of Tonto by day, as shown at the beginning of the film. The fragmentary exterior of Lordsburg, shown at night for the conclusion, was shot on a stage at Goldwyn, with lighting units used from behind doors, windows, and in an occasional street lamp.

Ford has said that the final shoot-out in Lordsburg between the Ringo Kid and the Plummer brothers was based on a similar sequence he had done once before in a silent Harry Carey film. Ford was to do yet another variation in *My Darling Clementine*. The shoot-out was, of course, a Western staple that was popularized early in fiction in dime novels and in 1902 with Owen Wister's novel *The Virginian*. In the shoot-out, the hero classically avenges the killing of a friend or a relative.

The interiors for *Stagecoach* were filmed on the Goldwyn lot. Cameraman Bert Glennon photographed in a dramatically effective manner some low-ceilinged sets designed by Alexander Toluboff. Ceilings on sets were not common at the time. They were regarded as an unnecessary expense, and they also precluded the positioning of lighting units from above. Two years later Orson Welles's *Citizen Kane* (1941) was praised for its innovative use of ceilings, among many other things, in the photographic compositions. Welles was a great admirer of Ford's style. When he first came to Hollywood in 1939, he screened Ford's films to learn about movies in general. According to Welles and several of his associates at the time, he ran *Stagecoach* every night for a month, each time with a different member of his staff present. Cameraman Bert Glennon, interviewed during the filming of *Stagecoach*, stated that the photographic idea behind the film was to "reproduce the method of lighting as used in the Sargent paintings of the early West."

There were also a good number of rear projection shots in *Stagecoach*, as was common at the time. The many dialogue scenes in the coach were done on a sound stage with a coach mock-up on rockers placed in front of a process screen showing background footage shot for the picture by a second unit under the direction of the film's editorial supervisor, Otho Lovering.

Ford always had live music played on the set while lighting and rehearsing. This was a throwback to the silent era, when music was provided off-camera to get the players into the proper mood for the upcoming scene. Over the years Danny Borzage (brother of director Frank Borzage) regularly played Ford's favorite nostalgic and sentimental tunes on his accordian for the entire company, whether on location or in the studio. His playing was

The Stagecoach *cast rehearses the song "Ten Thousand Cattle" at the studio. The filmed sequence, which took place in the stagecoach, was cut. Left to right: John Carradine (cropped), Andy Devine, Berton Churchill, Donald Meek, George Bancroft, John Wayne, Claire Trevor, and unidentified pianist.*

sometimes augmented by that of other musicians, to make up a trio or quartet. Often some of the tunes played formed the basis of the score for a Ford film, such as "Red River Valley" in *The Grapes of Wrath* (1940), "Harbor Lights" in *The Long Voyage Home* (1940), and "Bury Me Not on the Lone Prairie" in *Stagecoach*.

Although Ford could be autocratic, militaristic, and sarcastic while filming, there was another side: John Wayne recalled that "there has never been enough credit given to Mr. Ford as to how far he'd go to make an actor feel comfortable. Like havin' Danny play accordian music, so we wouldn't get bored." On another occasion Wayne told interviewer Scott Eyman:

> It's easy to talk an actor into a scene that way. Ford, while they're lighting a set, talks to the actors very quietly, puts them through a scene. Now he calls the cameraman over. He watches them go through the scene. He talks to them. "Do you think you can go down over there instead of here?" "Yeah, sure." Now, when you start to do the scene you're at complete ease. You've walked through it, and as you're setting your lines you're in the right position. Some directors line the whole scene up the night before and say, "You stand here and you stand there and when you say that line come over here." Well, when you say "Come over here on that line," instinctively it affects your performance. The other way, you're eased into it so beautifully you're where he wants you for composition but you're also where you want to be for the lines. Ford wants the action to come out of the actor in a manner that is comfortable to him. After that's done, then he gives you the little touches that he wants. But he gets you at ease first.

Cameraman Bert Glennon said while making *Stagecoach*: "Ford knows what he wants and when he has it, so I had better be right the first time because he will not take a scene more than once if he gets it the first time."

Stagecoach finished shooting after forty-seven production days on December 23, 1938—four days over schedule, according to Wanger's cost-report sheet of the time. Film editor Dorothy Spencer confirmed that Ford "cut in the camera," meaning that he did not cover each scene all the way through from a variety of angles, a technique that gives considerable choice and flexibility in the editorial process. Rather, Ford shot and printed only what he knew in advance he wanted to use, allowing the cutter (or himself) little or no opportunity for second thoughts.

Editor Spencer also stated in 1971 that "unlike most other directors, he never even went to the rushes [the screening of the material shot the preceding day]."

The score was originally to have been done by Louis Gruenberg, a composer of concert works, but either after his writing was completed, or at some point along the way, it was decided that things were not working out. Because of the early release date, several film composers were brought in to rewrite the score, a great deal of which was based on American folk songs of the period.

According to the music cue sheets in the files at Paramount (where the score had been farmed out), John Leipold, Leo Shuken, Gerard Carbonara, W. Franke Harling, and Richard Hageman all contributed, but for some reason, the official credits eliminated Carbonara's name and included Gruenberg's, whose music was not in the final score. However, the Academy Awards for best score went to all but Gruenberg and Carbonara. It was obviously correct to eliminate Gruenberg, but Carbonara contributed as much and more, in some cases, as some of the credited and awarded composers—according to the cue sheets, at any rate.

Although such nineteenth-century favorites as "My Lulu," "Shall We Gather at the River," "Gentle Annie," "The Trail to Mexico," "The Union Forever," Owen (*The Virginian*) Wister's "Ten Thousand Cattle," and others are quoted at varying lengths throughout the score, it is the somewhat altered "Bury Me Not on the Lone Prairie," the rolling and sweeping theme of the stagecoach itself, that is so enormously effective in all its variations, juxtaposed with the beautifully framed shots of the coach going through nostalgic and varied landscapes. The song literally came out West with the pioneers. The original title when it first appeared in 1850 was "The Ocean Burial" ("Bury me not in the deep, deep sea"); the words were then revised to suit the waterless terrain.

Lucy Mallory's (Louise Platt) theme is Stephen Foster's "Jeanie with the Light Brown Hair." When all appears lost near the conclusion of the Indian attack, Lucy cries and prays, while the gallant gambler (John Carradine) aims his last bullet at her head to spare the lady from what would inevitably follow. The "Jeanie" theme takes over in a moving manner from the Indian attack music. The gambler drops his gun before he is able to use it, having been shot by the Indians seconds before the bugle of the rescuing cavalry is heard. (This visual idea was no doubt inspired by a similar situation in D.W. Griffith's 1914 Western, *The Battle at Elderbush Gulch.*)

Stagecoach was previewed at the Fox Westwood theater on February 2, 1939, following which there were some cuts made here and there. One scene that was deleted took place shortly after Ringo joins the coach. There is unpleasantness between Hatfield (Carradine) and Doc Boone (Mitchell). To break the tension, the whiskey salesman suggests singing a hymn. But Boone launches into "Ten Thousand Cattle" instead. For a moment the others listen. Then one after another they join the song, humming when they do not know the words, until finally even the aloof Lucy Mallory adds her soprano. The singing grows louder from within the coach, and at last Buck, the driver, and Curly, riding shotgun, join the vocalizing. The scene then dissolves to a distant shot of the coach and the escorting cavalrymen as they go along the trail in Monument Valley (still in the film).

The surprising success of the unheralded *Stagecoach* ushered in a new cycle of large-scale Westerns, some shot in part on distant locations. In 1939 alone *Dodge City, Union Pacific, Jesse James, Destry Rides Again, The Oklahoma Kid, Man of Conquest*, and *Geronimo* were released, in addition to *Stagecoach*.

In 1966, Martin Rackin bought the rights to Dudley Nichols's script and induced Twentieth Century-Fox to back a remake in color, with most of the exteriors to be photographed in the Colorado Rockies instead of Monument Valley. The cast included Ann-Margret in the Claire Trevor role, Alex Cord in John Wayne's part, Bing Crosby substituting for Thomas Mitchell, Mike Connors for John Carradine, Red Buttons for Donald Meek, Bob Cummings for Berton Churchill, Stephanie Powers for Louise Platt, Van Heflin for George Bancroft, and Slim Pickens for Andy Devine.

There were some modifications to the characters and situations (for example, Crazy Horse was substituted for Geronimo), but the basic story line was unaltered. Although handsomely produced, the picture did not capture the imagination of the public and was not particularly successful.

Dudley Nichols stated in 1939 that he and John Ford wanted to make the original *Stagecoach* a picture "that recovers all of the old feeling that they had for films before sound came in. We tried to make a picture that would be practically a textbook on the old ways of making pictures."

The original *Stagecoach* was also a textbook of themes and ideas that Ford loved and adapted from Bret Harte and other writers and interpreters of a mythological West—or mythological anyplace. Laced with sentimentality, humor, and local color, there are, as Andrew Sarris says, "the redemption of the harlot (Claire Trevor), the regeneration of the drunkard (Thomas Mitchell), the revenge of the bereaved brother [and son] (John Wayne), the self-sacrifice of a self-condemned aristocrat (John Carradine), and the submergence of the group in the symbolic conveyance of a cause (the stagecoach itself). Above all, there is the sense of an assemblage of mythical archetypes outlined against the horizon of history." And if that isn't enough, there is the ever popular idea of the love between a good-bad man and a good-bad girl.

"WE'RE THE PEOPLE":
THE GRAPES OF
WRATH
(1940)

"It's a story of the survival of the fittest," said Nunnally Johnson, the eminent screenwriter who did the adaptation of John Steinbeck's major novel *The Grapes of Wrath*. That was the way Steinbeck explained it to Johnson, and that was how Johnson saw it. "The fit survive, the weak fall by the wayside, the incompetent wander off."

Johnson's approach to the art of adaptation was summed up when he said: "I have learned to look for the backbone, the skeleton, what this fellow was setting out to tell, so that actually he could have told it in a night letter, almost. The story line [of *The Grapes of Wrath*] was clear—the migration of a people forced from their homes. It is old as the Bible."

Published in March 1939, *The Grapes of Wrath* moved to the top of the best-seller list in early May, stayed there for the rest of the year, and remained on the list another year. Shortly after publication, screen rights were purchased by Twentieth Century-Fox for $70,000. One clause in the contract that had been a subject of considerable discussion stated:

> The producer agrees that any motion picture based on the
> said literary property shall fairly and reasonably retain the
> main action and social intent of said literary property.

ARRYL F. ZANUCK'S PRODUCTION OF

THE GRAPES OF WRATH

BY *John Steinbeck*

ASSOCIATE PRODUCER, AND SCREEN PLAY BY NUNNALLY JOHNSON

WITH

HENRY FONDA AND JANE **DARWELL** JOHN **CARRADINE** CHARLEY **GRAPEWIN**

DORRIS **BOWDON** RUSSELL **SIMPSON** O. Z. **WHITEHEAD** JOHN **QUALEN** EDDIE **QUILLAN** ZEFFIE **TILBURY**

DIRECTED BY **JOHN FORD**

A 20ᵀᴴ CENTURY-FOX PICTURE

This was important to Steinbeck. A native Californian, he had been working toward *The Grapes of Wrath* since the beginning of the Depression, when his second published novel, *The Pastures of Heaven* (1932), established his primary subject—farm life in the central valleys of California. Specific preparations for *Grapes* began with a trip by Steinbeck in September 1936 to observe the migrant farmworkers' camps near Salinas and Bakersfield, California. The following year he went to Detroit, bought a car, and drove to Oklahoma. There he joined a group of migrant workers heading west, lived with them in their collection of huts and shacks (called Hoovervilles after Herbert Hoover), and worked with them when they got to California. In March 1938, Steinbeck and photographer Horace Bristol toured the migrant camps, gathering material for a *Life* magazine picture story that appeared in the June 5, 1939, issue, and for a picturebook project that was dropped. Then Steinbeck wrote his novel.

Steinbeck threw away his first version of what was to become *The Grapes of Wrath* because he thought it dishonest. Starting over, he created an exceptionally moving proletarian novel that told of the hardships of the Joad family. These Okie* farmers were forced out of their homes in the Oklahoma

* "Okie" was a derogatory term for any poor white migrant who came west. It referred not only to the 100,000 that traveled to California from Oklahoma but also to the 250,000 other rural migrants from Texas, Arkansas, the Dakotas, eastern New Mexico, and Missouri.

dust bowl region by economic desperation brought on by drought, dust storms, machine farming, and land banks. They drove to California in search of work as migrant fruit pickers. After deaths, harassments, and disillusionment, the Joad family was defeated but still resolute.

The book, with its left-wing implications, ranging ideologically from New Deal liberalism to revolutionary socialism, was extremely controversial and one of the most talked about in this country's history. No American novel since *Uncle Tom's Cabin* had created such an immediate reaction on so many levels. Denounced as obscene and subversive, it was banned in several places, actually ordered burned in East St. Louis, Illinois, attacked by an Oklahoma congressman, and condemned by the California Chamber of Commerce. The Agricultural Council of California and the Associated Farmers of California conducted in rural newspapers a campaign against the filming of the novel, calling for a boycott of all Twentieth Century-Fox releases. It was even rumored that "powerful interests" had ordered Darryl F. Zanuck, in charge of production at Fox, to buy the rights in order to shelve the work.

Determined to check on the validity of Steinbeck's presentation of the deplorable conditions he described in the migrant camps, Zanuck hired a private investigating firm; it reported that the book's facts were understated. Zanuck admitted that many people advised against producing the film, arguing that it would be inflammatory and widely censored. Undaunted, he assigned staff writer and associate producer Nunnally Johnson to work on the script. Johnson, a former newspaper reporter and short-story writer for *The Saturday Evening Post*, had worked for Zanuck since 1934. Some of his previous credits include *The House of Rothschild* (1934), *The Prisoner of Shark Island* (1936), *Slave Ship* (1937), and *Jesse James* (1939). By 1939 he was one of the highest paid screenwriters in Hollywood.

Johnson simplified the narrative of *The Grapes of Wrath*, eliminating most of the material that did not concentrate specifically on the Joad family and their trek. The religious satire inherent in the book was eliminated and the politics muted. Dropped entirely were the author's sometimes angry interludes and explicit indictments. The profanity was deleted and the dialogue heavily pruned.

Johnson was quoted by Hollywood correspondent Philip K. Scheuer on July 30, 1939: "The picture will not editorialize. If you rationalize the novel, there are two viewpoints. The 'other side' (forces opposing the migrants) has one too. You can't blame the bankers for trying to get back their investment in the dust bowl. You can't blame Willy, the Okie, who backslides onto a tractor, for taking two dollars a day to keep his family from starving . . . . The only people whose 'side' is indefensible are the labor recruits who passed out handbills among the Okies, urging them to come to the Promised Land—California."

The most significant change had to do with the transposition of two major episodes and the addition of an upbeat epilogue. George Bluestone in his incisive book, *Novels into Film* (1957), points out: "Instead of ending with the strike-breaking episodes in which Tom [Henry Fonda] is clubbed, Casy [John Carradine] killed, and the strikers routed, the film ends with the Government Camp interlude. This reversal, effected with almost surgical simplicity, accomplishes, in its metamorphic power, an entirely new structure which has far-reaching consequences . . . . In place of the original ending, we find a line that appears at the end of chapter twenty, exactly two-thirds of the way through the book. It is Ma's [Jane Darwell] strong

Generic handbill made up for The Grapes of Wrath *film is suggestive of the many different kinds of handbills that lured migrants to California.* (COPYRIGHT © 1940 TWENTIETH CENTURY-FOX FILM CORP. ALL RIGHTS RESERVED.)

800 PICKERS
WANTED

Work in California.

GOOD WAGES.   TENTS AND CABINS FURNISHED FREE. STORE ON CAMP GROUND

Busy From October to February.
COME AT ONCE!

BILL MACEY, LABOR CONTRACTOR.

assurance, 'We'll go on forever, Pa. We're the people.' . . . The affirmative ending implies that action is not required since the victims of the situation will automatically emerge triumphant." (The line from the book actually reads: "Why, we're the people. We go on.")

One could interpret the novel as a call to action, a support for revolutionary tactics as perhaps the only realistic way to deal with the situation. It has been related in some previous books and articles that the epilogue delivered by Ma Joad was not in the original script and was added by Zanuck and photographed after the picture was finished. But, included in the earliest draft of the screenplay (July 13, 1939) and all subsequent versions on file at Fox are the scene and speech as they appeared in the final film.

Nunnally Johnson said at the time that "the only real change I made—and I had to make it—was in the ending. There had to be some ray of hope— something that would keep the people who saw it [the film] from going out and getting so drunk in utter despondency that they couldn't tell other people that it was a good picture to see. Steinbeck agreed on the necessity for a more hopeful ending."*

Johnson in his University of California-Los Angeles/American Film Institute Oral History (1969) stated that Steinbeck understood that an adaptation for the screen was intended for a different medium than the novel. He did not interfere and was pleased when he read the script. Evidently this is true, as Steinbeck defended his position on the grounds that a novelist's final statement is in his book.

At the time Johnson was completing the first draft of the screenplay in July, Zanuck sent a memo to him in which he said:

> I want complete secrecy in reference to *The Grapes of Wrath* script. Instead of having the first script mimeographed, as in our usual custom, I want you to make only three copies—one for yourself and two for me. A number of more or less unfriendly newspapermen are waiting to grab our first script to actually find out what we have done with this great book.

The screenplay was finished on July 13. Julian Johnson, the head of Fox's story department, sent a memo to Zanuck the next day:

> I have read this script twice.
> It is a sincere and impressive transcription of Steinbeck's book . . . . If there is any Hays Office poppycock about having

---

* The ending of the novel, which for obvious reasons was eliminated in the script, is as follows: Under impossible conditions, Rose of Sharon gives birth to a dead baby. Rains had made the family's old car useless. They come to a barn, which they share with a boy and his starving father. Rose of Sharon, bereft of her baby, nourishes the famished old man with the milk from her breasts.

> justice overtake Tom (for killing two men) I think it is superbly
> answered in that great scene of farewell between Tom and his
> mother . . . . He isn't getting away. He can't get away. He
> knows it. He is merely moving on, to do what he can, before
> his certain fate overtakes him elsewhere.

Johnson went on to point out that the picture had to "set up *its own* standard of censorship, different from anything that has ever been done before," and to note that the book's general social significance would provide the politically minded with fuel for their arguments: "The Fascists will say it is purely Communistic because it shows nothing but greed, villainy and cruelty in the minds of all who are not paupers. The Communists will say it tends to Fascism, because it subtly shows that the country ought to be regimented, regulated and controlled from the top, so that such utter and crushing poverty in the midst of surplus and plenty could not take place." But this struck him as being of no importance. The story created a profound sensation "by a presentation of dreadful, inescapable facts and does not suggest any infallible answer."

Also in the files at Fox is Zanuck's initialed and marked copy of the July 13 screenplay. Zanuck's procedure was to go through a script and make his notations with strong pencil markings. Here and there would be material crossed out with the word "dull" in the margin. On July 19, all the notes made on Zanuck's script were discussed at a story conference, the distillation of which was typed and distributed. The conference notes started by saying, "Mr. Zanuck is very enthusiastic about the script. The changes to be made are few. There are several places where we can heighten the drama and suspense." There followed twelve pages of comments, most of which were reflected in Johnson's revised screenplay of a few weeks later. One instance of Zanuck's creative contribution had to do with a section after the family had entered California and Grandma had died. Zanuck said:

> Before we come to Hooverville, we need a scene in a town.
> Their money practically gone—gas low—and the terrible
> realization that what they were told is true. The fellow was
> right.
>   We come in on them driving into town and asking somebody
> where they should go about finding work—maybe showing
> the fellow the handbill. The man just looks at them and laughs.
> Someone else comes along and they ask him. We see the
> fellow look at the car and down at the license plate. "Oh—
> Oklahoma. There's a camp on the edge of town—maybe
> somebody there will tell you . . . ."

Their hopelessness and terrible disillusionment, they drive into the Hooverville camp and their hearts drop at the terrible sights. The futility of what has occurred. They just look at each other as the stark truth dawns on them. "Don't seem very encouragin', does it?" "All this and for what?" etc. Ma snaps them out of it—they'd better pitch the tent, etc. And as they start working we *FADE OUT* and *FADE INTO* Scene 142.

In the original script, there is no scene in the town, and the Hooverville episode begins with an establishing shot followed by the scene showing Ma Joad fixing breakfast and the hungry camp children watching. Johnson has said that Zanuck generally did not expect his story conference ideas, improvised dialogue, and descriptions to be used just as he spoke them, but rather they were to be regarded as suggestions and guidelines. The scene in the town, as written by Johnson, evolved somewhat differently, but according to Johnson, "When I came back in with the revised version . . . it didn't matter to him [Zanuck] whether I'd followed anything he suggested or not. Not as long as it made dramatic sense." The Hooverville introduction, as directed by John Ford and photographed by Gregg Toland, became one of the most powerful scenes in the film, with the camera being the eyes of the Joads as the truck entered and moved through the camp.

Many of Zanuck's notes had to do with clarification, proper motivation, or dialogue that was not convincing. Also, he wanted to drop some peripheral material, such as Uncle John's getting drunk and the reason for it. Jason S. Joy, Fox's director of public relations, suggested through Zanuck that "we incorporate a line to show that not all of the migrant workers were sharecroppers originally." Zanuck said that "Colonel Joy feels we must express the doubt where the handbills came from—so we don't give [the] definite impression that the big growers did it. Get in the idea that they might have come from the fly-by-night labor contractors." And under general notes: "Be sure to characterize caretaker of Government Camp [Grant Mitchell] as being a particularly fine, good man." And lastly, "Make more of an issue of Al [Tom's younger brother] trying to go out and get girls." The latter request was made, presumably, to fulfill the need for some comic relief.

Back in April, when the motion picture rights were being finalized with Fox, John Steinbeck met with Joseph Moskowitz, the studio's New York representative. Julian Johnson reported to Zanuck in a memo that Steinbeck had "mentioned Jack Ford as his ideal director for such a subject." Moskowitz told him, however, "that it was too early to predict any production set-up of any kind."

John Ford, under nonexclusive contract to Fox, had just directed two very well received pictures in a row: *Stagecoach* (1939) and *Young Mr. Lincoln* (1939) and was shooting *Drums along the Mohawk* for Fox. Zanuck assigned him in late June to *The Grapes of Wrath* while Johnson was completing the first draft of the script.

Then casting began in earnest. Handwritten by Zanuck on the inside back cover of his personal copy of the July 13 screenplay were some preliminary casting notes: opposite "Tom" was scrawled Henry Fonda, "Pa"—Walter Brennan, "Ma"—Beulah Bondi, "Al"—James Stewart, "Grandpa"—Frank Craven. At the top of these notes is the name of an MGM contract director, Clarence Brown, with a question mark after it. He recently had finished *The Rains Came* for Fox on loan. Although Ford had been announced as director of *The Grapes of Wrath* a few weeks before, it is possible that there was still some uncertainty.

A few days later, attached to the July 19 story conference notes, was a tentative cast sheet:

Tom	Henry Fonda
Ma	Beulah Bondi
Pa	⎰ Walter Brennan ⎱ Warren Hull* ⎰ James Barton ⎱ Charles Grapewin
Grandpa	(Probably one of the suggestions for Pa will be used for Grandpa)
Grandma	Zeffie Tilbury
Al	Jimmy Stewart
Connie	Eddie Quillan
Rose of Sharon	Dorris Bowdon
Muley	John Qualen
Uncle John	Victor Killian
Casy	John Carradine
Government Caretaker	Grant Mitchell

The final casting differed in some instances: Jane Darwell played Ma, Russell Simpson played Pa, Charles Grapewin, Grandpa, O. Z. Whitehead, Al, and Frank Darien, Uncle John.

Although Henry Fonda was wanted from the beginning—contrary to some reports, there is no indication in the Fox files that contract players Tyrone

---

* This presumably should have read Henry Hull. Warren Hull was a relatively young radio announcer and film actor.

Power or Don Ameche were considered—he was not set until two weeks before filming began on or about September 28, 1939. At the time, Fonda was not interested in signing a seven-year contract with a studio, preferring to free-lance. Fonda told Mike Steen that *The Grapes of Wrath* had been offered to him as bait in exchange for signing a long-term contract:

> Zanuck had tried to get me under contract even before *Jesse James* [1939], and I had resisted it. I was very happy doing free-lance. I was working a lot at Twentieth Century, but it was my choice of pictures . . . . I did want the part. It was a choice part! It was another picture with Ford, and Ford wanted me. I had a long meeting with Zanuck. Obviously I fell for what he said because I signed his contract. He had a lot of reasons. You know: This was the plum part, and it was going to be the big feature of the year for Fox, and if he put me in that, he didn't want to jeopardize the product by having me go to MGM to do a film with Joan Crawford. I remember he used that . . . . I did sign the contract, and I regretted it from the day we finished *Grapes of Wrath*. Oh, I did some good films during my contract period at Fox, but they were almost all on loan-out.

Beulah Bondi tested for the role of Ma Joad, and according to her, both Ford and Zanuck were lavish with praise and she was led to believe that part was hers. The actress then acquired an old jalopy, dressed appropriately, and left Hollywood: "I had gone up to Bakersfield and I lived with the Okies incognito . . . . I visited five different camps as an unknown. I was an Okie. I lived with them . . . to get the feeling of the role." Then she learned that Jane Darwell, a Fox contract player, had been given the role on September 10. According to Miss Darwell, she asked to test for the role and did.

Before Ford started shooting in California, staff director Otto Brower headed a second unit to shoot background material. With a well-running jalopy, later used by the first unit at the studio, they were to travel along the route through Oklahoma, Texas, New Mexico, and Arizona that 350,000 Okies had taken over several years. Charles G. Clarke, the cameraman on the unit, later recalled gathering at McAlester, Oklahoma, where the shots of the family (doubled) leaving the farm were filmed. Then the scenes of the jalopy chugging along Route 66 were photographed. Backgrounds had been selected that were typical of the country, in order to establish identity and change of locale. As there was considerable controversy regarding the story, Oklahoma did not particularly like the idea of its country being depicted as a run-down state from which its people had to migrate. So on the scripts for

Beulah Bondi almost played Ma
Joad in The Grapes of Wrath.

Jane Darwell was cast as Ma Joad in
The Grapes of Wrath. (COPYRIGHT ©
1940 TWENTIETH CENTURY-FOX FILM
CORP. ALL RIGHTS RESERVED.)

the second unit the cover page was entitled *Route 66*. As it was necessary to get local permission to film on the streets and highways, that name was given for the work that was being done. "One interesting sidelight," recalls Clarke, "was the use of other cars in the caravan besides our own jalopy. We did not want to show just one car making this migration, so our business manager would stop other migrants and offer them $5.00 to drive along with our car for a short distance—then they could go on their way. This meant holding them, say, for possibly ten minutes." Frequently the migrants wanted no part of this, suspecting, Clarke thought, that there was "some hoax about making this money so easily. Most of them wouldn't do it, though they surely needed the money. A few others seized on this as a blessing." Very little of the second-unit footage remains in the final version, but enough is there to give the necessary ambience and a sense of authenticity.

Ford started shooting in early October on the Fox Pico Boulevard lot. Although there was some filming at various California locations by the Ford unit, most of the picture was shot in the studio or on the backlot, where the Hooverville settlement of shacks and the model government camp (which was copied from an actual one) were built.

In a letter to his literary agent, Elizabeth Otis, on June 22, 1939, Steinbeck said: "I saw [Nunnally] Johnson in Hollywood . . . and apparently they intend to make the picture straight, at least so far, and they sent a producer into the field with Tom Collins and he got sick at what he saw and they offered Tom a job as technical assistant which is swell because he'll howl his head off if they get out of hand."

Tom Collins for seven years headed the U.S. camps for the migratory workers. The government agreed to loan him for the duration of the filming. Collins had done some of Steinbeck's research, and he was the "Tom" to whom the author dedicated his book. Collins had encouraged Steinbeck to write the novel, and he took him into the migrant camps, where Steinbeck lived for some time. Collins coached the cast in the proper idiom, checked on the sets and wardrobe, and generally served as consultant.

According to Dorris Bowdon (Mrs. Nunnally Johnson), who played Rose of Sharon, the cast never received complete scripts, but worked from mimeographed sides of dialogue only as part of the overall security program. She also recalls John Ford trying to convince Zanuck to use a different ending (she doesn't remember what, exactly) from the one in Johnson's script (Ma Joad's "We'll go on forever, Pa. We're the people.").

Between scenes of The Grapes of Wrath *on the back lot at Twentieth Century-Fox. Henry Fonda, director John Ford, and visiting Alice Faye, who was working on* Little Old New York *(1940).* (COPYRIGHT © 1940 TWENTIETH CENTURY-FOX FILM CORP. ALL RIGHTS RESERVED.)

Filming The Grapes of Wrath *at Fox: John Ford in director's chair; Joe Sawyer and Henry Fonda playing scene.* (COPYRIGHT © 1940 TWENTIETH CENTURY-FOX FILM CORP. ALL RIGHTS RESERVED.)

Zanuck borrowed cinematographer Gregg Toland from Samuel Goldwyn for this important assignment. His low-key work on Zanuck's *Les Miserables* (1935) had impressed the studio head, and he later borrowed him on two other occasions. In almost every picture Toland photographed, his treatment differed. For Goldwyn's *Wuthering Heights* (1939), he decided on a romantic pictorial style, with heavy diffusion and a soft candlelight effect. For *The Grapes of Wrath,* a stark, naturalistic approach was necessary. Toland's picture quality for *Grapes* was sharp and hard; the skies were unfiltered, and faces were lit in a harsh manner that matched the bleak background. A year later Toland photographed *Citizen Kane* in yet another strong style.

The Saturday-night dance sequence at the government camp was considerably elaborated on by Ford with improvisational material not contained in the screenplay. Tom Joad sings "Red River Valley" while dancing with his mother, and there are other incidents during this sequence, such as Al's attempts "to look for girls" (per Zanuck), that provide a light interlude before a return to the generally somber tone. Ford staged a somewhat similar dance sequence in his earlier *Drums along the Mohawk* (1939) and later in *My Darling Clementine* (1946). All three scenes in a way suggest a country dance in D. W. Griffith's *Way Down East* (1921) and served the same "audience breather" purpose. Ford, years later, said, "I like folk dances; they're very amusing."

In late November, after approximately seven weeks, the shooting was completed. Ford immediately took off on vacation, and Zanuck, as was his custom, supervised the editing. The first cut ran long, and some scenes were omitted and others were tightened. One of the deletions left the audience with the unexplained disappearance of Tom's brother Noah (Frank Sully) from the film after he had been established in the early scenes as part of the migrating family. There had been material photographed that explained Noah's taking off, and there had been a scene of him swimming in the Colorado River at the California-Arizona border after leaving the family. Also dropped was a speech of Ma's near the end suggesting that Rose of Sharon's baby had been miscarried or stillborn, which left the audience without any explanation about what became of the baby. Other than these deletions, as author Warren French states, "the total effect of the changes from the screenplay to the film . . . is to soften things up a bit for the audience—to give it less to think about, a little more to cry over, a little more action to enjoy."

The decision was made to be sparing with the background music. With the exception of the opening and closing titles and the scene depicting the family starting on its trek, all of which was scored for a relatively small contingent of the Fox orchestra, the music—mostly "Red River Valley"—

was played by solo accordian or banjo and guitar. The folk tune "Red River Valley" was originally written about the Mohawk Valley in New York state ("Bright Mohawk Valley"), but with the westward migration it underwent countless changes. As played on accordian, the plaintive melody offers a cushion of sentimentality that aids in softening the social protest element.

In early December 1939, about seven weeks before it premiered in New York City, the completed *Grapes of Wrath* was shown to Steinbeck at the Fox studios. In a letter to his literary agent, Elizabeth Otis, shortly afterward he said:

> Zanuck has more than kept his word. He has a hard, straight picture in which the actors are submerged so completely that it looks and feels like a documentary film and certainly it has a hard, truthful ring. No punches were pulled—in fact, with descriptive matter removed, it is a harsher thing than the book, by far. It seems unbelievable but it is true . . . . It opens sometime in January. There is so much hell being raised in this state that Zanuck will . . . . open in N.Y. and move gradually west, letting the publicity precede it. He even, to find out, issued a statement that it would never be shown in California and got a ton of mail, literally, in protest the next day. He has hired attorneys to fight any local censorship.

Without a single preview, *The Grapes of Wrath*, made at an approximate cost of $850,000, opened to generally outstanding reviews and business. But in the January 27 issue of the trade paper *Motion Picture Herald*, publisher Martin Quigley, coauthor of the Hays Office Motion Picture Production Code and supporter of a major censorship body, the Catholic Legion of Decency, took a hard line:

> The motion picture version of *Grapes of Wrath* . . . is a new and emphatic item of evidence in support of the frequently repeated assertion in these columns that the entertainment motion picture is no place for social, political and economic argument. It is a stark and drab depiction of a group of incidents in human misery, told against a chaotic jumble of philosophic and sociological suggestion and argument . . . .
> It may be wondered why . . . such an unpromising field of material was prospected. The answer perhaps is a situation of reaction rather than initiative. Pressure has been heavy and unrelenting. Mr. Zanuck, while issuing a series of fine popular

entertainments, probably had the term "escapist" hissed so often in his ear that he finally—and we hope reluctantly—decided to give them that which they like loosely to label as "significant." This he has done and well done.

There remain, however, to be measured the consequences to the screen and the consequences to reasoned judgment on those problems—political, social, economic and religious—which the screenplay, guided by the heavy and designing hand of John Steinbeck, treats with.

Back in May, Zanuck had been quoted as saying, "If they [the Hays Office] interfere with this picture I'm going to take full-page ads in the papers and print our correspondence."

It is interesting to note that Steinbeck had what was referred to as his radical, left-wing work adapted for the screen by the conservative and apolitical Johnson; produced by Zanuck, a man who generally voted Republican, although he seems to have been rather eclectic politically, and had at least on occasion evidenced liberal instincts, and lastly, directed by Ford, who at the time called himself "a definite social Democrat—always left," but who also moved more and more into the area of conservative

Filming a sequence for The Grapes of Wrath *in the Colorado River at the California-Arizona border. A large percentage of this material was dropped in the editing room. Henry Fonda in bathrobe on shore.* (COPYRIGHT © 1940 TWENTIETH CENTURY-FOX FILM CORP. ALL RIGHTS RESERVED.)

traditionalist. Ford, when asked in the mid 1960s by Peter Bogdanovich what attracted him to *The Grapes of Wrath*, replied in part:

> The whole thing appealed to me—being about simple people— and the story was similar to the famine in Ireland, when they threw the people off the land and left them wandering on the roads to starve. That may have had something to do with it— part of my Irish tradition—but I liked the idea of this family going out and trying to find their way in the world.

In 1964 Ford said that he was concerned with the Joad family only as characters. "I was not interested in *Grapes* as a social study . . . . I am apolitical."

Apparently the ending of the film was suppressed in the European versions, and the picture concluded with the departure of Tom from the government camp, thereby eliminating the family setting out for Fresno and Ma meditating on what has happened ("We're the people"). This deletion gave the impression that the family was safe at last in the good government camp.

The Grapes of Wrath was that rarity—a social protest drama with a message (albeit a watered-down social protest and message) that the public in large quantities wanted to see. And, what may seem remarkable on the surface, the film and the novel have had continued interest and popularity to the present day, although the specific problems relating to migratory farm workers from the dust bowl were no longer an issue not long after the film was released.

But what is important and enduring is that the theme, the structure, the ideas, the emotions, and specifically the sentiments, are not merely indicative of the last phase of the Depression but are timeless and relate to no particular geography. The family sticking together despite overwhelming problems, the migration to the Promised Land, obstacles along the way, gradual disenchantment, the exploitation of simple and good people, the tenacity— the "We're the people" philosophy, and above all, the love of land and family—these elements all endure. They are perpetuated in Bible stories, myths, history, and sagas. And there is an underlying sense of nostalgia in both the immediate and the larger view of *The Grapes of Wrath*.

"THE STUFF THAT DREAMS ARE MADE OF": THE MALTESE FALCON

(1941)

In an apartment on Nob Hill, a few blocks west of the Mark Hopkins Hotel in San Francisco, Dashiell Hammett wrote perhaps the best of all private-eye novels. *The Maltese Falcon* originally appeared as a five-part serial in the pulp detective magazine *Black Mask* beginning in September 1929. In 1930 the book was published and became a best seller. It has remained so over the years.

Warner Bros. bought the rights to *The Maltese Falcon* the year it was published in book form for $8,500 and produced two film versions within the next six years. By 1941, John Huston, the son of actor Walter Huston, was doing particularly well at Warners collaborating on the scripts for such films as *Jezebel, The Amazing Dr. Clitterhouse, Juarez, Dr. Ehrlich's Magic Bullet, High Sierra,* and *Sergeant York.* But he wanted to direct. When he occasionally visited sets and watched directors working with his material, he realized he would never be happy unless he could interpret the ideas himself.

135

"They indulged me rather," Huston told author Gerald Pratley. "They liked my work as a writer and they wanted to keep me on. If I wanted to direct, why they'd give me a shot at it, and if it didn't come off all that well, they wouldn't be too disappointed as it was to be a very small picture. They acted out of friendship for me, out of good will. This was Jack Warner, but largely [executive producer] Hal Wallis and [producer] Henry Blanke." When Huston was asked what subject he would like to do he told them *The Maltese Falcon*, which the studio still owned and which could be done in a relatively inexpensive manner. "There was something in the *Falcon* that attracted me," Huston has said, "that hadn't been done in the other versions."

Henry Blanke by his own account was at first apprehensive about a third time around with the material, having produced the less-than-successful 1936 version. But Huston wanted to stick closely to the novel. "We took two copies of the book, tore each page and just pasted it together on script pages, and edited it a little," Blanke has said. The producer understood what Huston wanted to do with the material and became a strong supporter. Huston had worked with Blanke on *Jezebel* (1938) and *Juarez* (1939), and they had become good friends.

An account given by Huston and verified by writer Allen Rivkin, who at the time shared a secretary with Huston, goes as follows: Huston gave the novel to the secretary and told her to recopy the text, but to break it down routinely into script format with the usual scene numbers and shot descriptions. According to this version, a copy somehow appeared on Jack Warner's desk. Warner looked over the "adaptation," was pleased, and gave Huston a go-ahead.

Eventually Huston tightened the narrative and eliminated a few scenes, a rather lengthy parable, and two minor characters—the daughter of the Fat Man, Casper Gutman (one scene), and Sam Spade's attorney (two scenes)—but he retained an unusually large amount of the dialogue, style, and ambience used by Hammett, the founder of the hard-boiled school of detective fiction. Fortunately, the novel lends itself to dramatization, being primarily a series of brilliant dialogues.

As was the custom, the temporary script was sent automatically for approval to the Production Code Administration, the film industry's self-regulatory body. Joseph I. Breen wrote back to Jack L. Warner that while the basic story was acceptable under the code, there were certain objectionable details. Too much drinking, a few damns and hells, and instances of "gruesomeness"—meaning brutality. The point was made that "it is essential that Spade should not be characterized as having had a sex affair with Iva [his partner's widow]. Accordingly, we request that you cut down

Executive producer Hal B. Wallis and associate producer Henry Blanke in the projection room at Warner Bros. at the time of The Maltese Falcon *(1941).*

the physical contact indicated . . . and that the following lines must be deleted or changed to get away from such inference: 'You shouldn't have come here today, darling. It wasn't wise,' and Iva's line, 'You'll come tonight?' with Spade's reply, 'Not tonight.' "

Regarding the character subsequently played by Peter Lorre, the letter stated that "we cannot approve the characterization of Cairo as a pansy as indicated by the lavender perfume, high pitched voice, and other accoutrements. In line with this, we refer you to page 148, where Cairo tries to put his arm around the boy's [Wilmer] shoulder and is struck by the boy for so doing. This action, in the light of Cairo's characterization, is definitely unacceptable . . . .

"There must be no indication that Brigid [Mary Astor] and Spade are spending the night together in Spade's apartment," and, referring to a later scene in the script, "Brigid's line, 'Not after what we've been to each other . . . ' should be changed to get away from the reference to an illicit sex affair."

The final script and film reflected these requests for changes. One scene from the novel that was used in the 1931 film version, when the old production code was quite loosely enforced, had been dropped early in the 1941 adaptation due to the strong censorship situation at that time: In Spade's apartment, the detective forces Brigid (or "Miss Wonderly")* to remove her clothes in front of him (off camera) in order to find out if she stole a thousand-dollar bill from an envelope containing several thousand dollars brought by Gutman.

Huston has said that Warner, Wallis, and Blanke "helped me marvelously with the casting." As was the custom, the casting department drew up a list of possibilities for each of the roles and circulated the sheet to Huston and the key executives. The list is an interesting one for various reasons, not the least of which is speculation on how certain roles would have been played by other performers. At the top of the roster of possible actors to play Sam Spade was George Raft, then under contract to Warners; in second position was Bogart, followed by Edward G. Robinson, Richard Whorf, Franchot Tone, Fred MacMurray, Fredric March, Henry Fonda, Brian Donlevy, Warner Baxter, Paul Muni, and some others.

On May 19, 1941, Hal Wallis sent a memo to Henry Blanke instructing him to send George Raft his two weeks' notice to report for work. "It will not be necessary for you to tell Raft at this time what his picture is to be, but for your own information, he will do *The Maltese Falcon*." Raft turned down the role on the advice of his agent. Also, Raft was uneasy about working with an inexperienced director, and his contract called for no remakes.

So, once again Bogart was second choice after a Raft refusal. The interesting and convoluted sequence of events leading up to Bogart being cast in *The Maltese Falcon* is worth noting in some detail: A few years earlier, producer Samuel Goldwyn and director William Wyler had wanted Raft for the role of the gangster in *Dead End* (1937), but Raft turned it down because he thought the character unsympathetic, and he had an aversion to being killed at the picture's conclusion. Arrangements were made to borrow Bogart from Warners. Then Raft was wanted for *It All Came True* (1940) at Warners. On October 17, 1939, Raft wrote to Jack L. Warner:

> When I saw you at your house you told me . . . that I would not have to play any dirty heavies and if anyone at your studio ever submitted a script to me in which I was to play a dirty heavy I was to bring the script to you and you would take me out of it. I remarked at the time to you that I was afraid the

* In the novel and in the Huston version, "Miss Wonderly's" real name is revealed to be Brigid O'Shaughnessy. In the 1931 version she was referred to only as "Miss Wonderly" or "Ruth Wonderly."

studio would put me into parts that Humphrey Bogart should play and you told me that I would never have to play a Humphrey Bogart part.

Bogart did *It All Came True* and then *High Sierra* (1941), which Paul Muni and other Warners players had refused, followed by the lead in *The Wagons Roll at Night* (1941). Raft had turned down that one also. On January 16, 1941 Bogart wired Jack Warner:

DEAR JACK: IT SEEMS TO ME I AM THE LOGICAL PERSON ON THE LOT TO PLAY "GENTLE PEOPLE." I WOULD BE VERY DISAPPOINTED IF I DIDN'T GET IT.

Bogart was referring to the important role of the gangster in the studio's upcoming adaptation of Irwin Shaw's 1939 play, which later was retitled *Out of the Fog* (1941). However, there was some disagreement at the studio regarding the casting. Ida Lupino was slated to play the leading woman's role, and she did not want to work with Bogart again (they recently had made *High Sierra* together). Hal Wallis, Henry Blanke, and Lupino favored John Garfield for the part. Jack Warner wanted Bogart to do it, and Bogart agreed. Blanke said in an interoffice memo to Jack Warner on January 31, 1941 that "casting Garfield for the part of Goff would, as you know, relieve us of the problem of convincing Lupino to play with Bogart." And on February 3, Blanke wrote to casting director Steve Trilling that "you witnessed my last conversation with Mr. Warner in which he insisted it was Bogart, and you had better straighten out the Lupino–Bogart situation."

Ida Lupino was in a strong position at the time, having just completed outstanding performances in three particularly good Warner films in a row: *They Drive by Night* (1940), *High Sierra* (1941), and *The Sea Wolf* (1941). (George Raft turned down the part eventually played by John Garfield in *The Sea Wolf*.) She won her point regarding Bogart, and Garfield was cast opposite her in *Out of the Fog*. Then Bogart was assigned to *Manpower* (1941) with George Raft and Marlene Dietrich. Bogart sent a telegram to Hal Wallis on March 6, 1941:

DEAR HAL: . . . I HAVE NEVER HAD ANYTHING BUT THE VERY FINEST FEELINGS OF FRIENDSHIP FOR GEORGE. I UNDERSTAND HE HAS REFUSED TO MAKE THE PICTURE IF I AM IN IT . . . . GEORGE HAS ALSO TOLD MY AGENT SEVERAL

WEEKS AGO THAT HE DIDN'T THINK I SHOULD DO
THIS PART AS IT WAS COMPLETELY WRONG FOR
ME . . . . I FEEL VERY MUCH HURT BY THIS
BECAUSE IT'S THE SECOND TIME I HAVE BEEN
KEPT OUT OF A GOOD PICTURE AND A GOOD PART
BY AN ACTOR'S REFUSING TO WORK WITH ME.

Bogart was replaced in *Manpower* by Edward G. Robinson. On March
13, a script of *Bad Men of Missouri* (1941) was delivered to Bogart and he
was notified that he had been given the role of Cole Younger in that
production. On March 17, a messenger returned the script with a memo
attached to Steve Trilling: "Are you kidding? This is certainly rubbing it in.
Since Lupino and Raft are casting pictures maybe I can."

For refusing *Bad Men of Missouri*, which was given to Dennis Morgan,
Bogart was placed on suspension. Meanwhile, after finishing *Manpower*,
George Raft was assigned to *The Maltese Falcon*. He wrote Jack Warner on
June 6: "As you know, I strongly feel that *The Maltese Falcon*, which you
want me to do, is not an important picture and, in this connection, I must
remind you again, before I signed the new contract with you, you promised
me that you would not require me to perform in anything but important
pictures." Bogart was put in *The Maltese Falcon* shortly before filming was
to begin on June 9th. He had been on suspension for two months.*

Possibilities for the role of Brigid were Olivia de Havilland, Loretta
Young, Rita Hayworth, Geraldine Fitzgerald, Mary Astor, Paulette Goddard,
Brenda Marshall, Janet Gaynor, Joan Bennett, Betty Field, Ingrid Bergman,
and a few others. Geraldine Fitzgerald (*Dark Victory*, *Wuthering Heights*)
seemed to be favored for a time. But on May 19, Blanke sent a memo to
Wallis saying:

> I had Mary Astor in on Friday and gave her the script on
> *Maltese Falcon* . . . . She called me this morning saying that
> she thinks *Maltese Falcon* is a "humdinger" and would love
> to do it . . . . We are waiting to hear from [Geraldine]
> Fitzgerald today . . . so that we can then make up our minds.

Later that day, in a memo to Blanke, Wallis said, "If we do not get an
okay from Geraldine Fitzgerald on *The Maltese Falcon*, we will use Mary

* Later, in July, Raft was assigned to *All through the Night* (1942), which he refused. Bogart's
agent, Sam Jaffe (not the actor), wrote Steve Trilling: "I had a long discussion about *All Through
the Night* with him [Bogart], and I felt this would make a pretty fair picture though he didn't
exactly think so . . . . A story should be prepared for which they have Bogart in mind and no
other actor because it seems that for the past year he's practically pinch-hitted for Raft and
been kicked around from pillar to post." Bogart did *All Through the Night*, but soon afterward
when it came time for *Casablanca*, the tables were turned (see chapter 9).

The 1941 Maltese Falcon: *Humphrey Bogart (Sam Spade), Peter Lorre (Joel Cairo), Mary Astor (Brigid or "Miss Wonderly"), and Sydney Greenstreet (Gutman).*

Astor." The inference is that Fitzgerald had certain contractual approvals, since almost immediately thereafter the decision was made to go with Mary Astor. She had recently signed a two-picture contract with Warners. Mary Astor had been in films since 1921. While still a teenager, she had played opposite John Barrymore in *Beau Brummel* (1924) and *Don Juan* (1926) and Douglas Fairbanks in *Don Q Son of Zorro* (1925). Other memorable films include *Red Dust* (1932), with Gable; *Dodsworth* (1936), with Walter Huston; *The Prisoner of Zenda* (1937); and *Midnight* (1939). At the time Mary Astor was set for *The Maltese Falcon,* she had just scored a considerable success with a major role in a Bette Davis vehicle, *The Great Lie* (1941).

Peter Lorre was first choice for Joel Cairo in *The Maltese Falcon,* with Martin Kosleck, Sam Jaffe, Curt Bois, and Elia Kazan as follow-ups. (Kazan was also considered for Wilmer.)

Sydney Greenstreet, who at the age of sixty-one had never made a film, was the prime choice for the Fat Man, Casper Gutman. Other possibilities included Laird Cregar, Edward Arnold, George Barbier, Lee J. Cobb, Gene Lockhart, Eugene Pallette, Akim Tamiroff, S. Z. Sakall, Guy Kibbee, Alan Hale, Broderick Crawford, and Billy Gilbert, the character comedian whose trademark was his crescendo sneeze. Greenstreet had been acting on the stage, both in his native England and in America, since 1902. He had spent over six years with Alfred Lunt and Lynn Fontanne and was touring with them in *There Shall Be No Night* when John Huston saw him at the Biltmore Theater in Los Angeles and persuaded him to break his rule about doing films. He was primarily a character comedian on the stage, but his

The 1931 Maltese Falcon: *Bebe Daniels (Miss Wonderly), Dudley Digges
(Gutman), Otto Matiesen (Joel Cairo).*

screen career was to consist mainly of villains. Warners signed Greenstreet
for $1000 a week with a four-week guarantee. The principal players were
now set for *The Maltese Falcon.*

In the first film version of the novel, *Dangerous Female**, made in early
1931, Ricardo Cortez played a tough but rather suave and elegant Sam
Spade, given to wearing a silk lounging robe in his apartment. Bebe Daniels
was a more vulnerable Ruth Wonderly, Dudley Digges a less ominous
Gutman, Otto Matiesen a relatively colorless Joel Cairo, and Dwight Frye
a rather perfunctory Wilmer (Elisha Cook, Jr., in 1941), compared with the
portrayals in the Huston version.

Although it was reasonably faithful to Hammett's novel in plot, the first
film did not have the advantage of the style, marvelous casting, and beautiful
mesh of elements that prevail in the classic 1941 version. A 1936 Warners
variation on the theme, called *Satan Met a Lady*, took considerable liberties

* Retitled for TV to avoid confusion with the 1941 version.

The 1936 version of The Maltese Falcon *called* Satan Met A Lady. *Left to right:*
Alison Skipworth (the Gutman role), Arthur Treacher (Joel Cairo's equivalent),
Warren William (Sam Spade's counterpart), Bette Davis (Brigid or Miss
Wonderly's counterpart), and Maynard Holmes (Wilmer's equivalent). The falcon
was changed to an ancient ivory horn crammed with jewels.

and transposed an item or character here and there. Warren William was
a slick, flamboyant Spade (changed to Ted Shane), Bette Davis a revamped
Miss Wonderly, or Brigid, called Valerie Purvis, and the Fat Man had the
most dramatic metamorphosis—he became a woman, Madame Barabbas, in
the person of Alison Skipworth. The Falcon was now an ancient hunting
horn crammed with jewels, and the whole enterprise emerged as a misguided
attempt at comedy-melodrama.

Dashiell Hammett had based some facets of his *Maltese Falcon* characters
on real people he had encountered while working as a Pinkerton detective
for several years: "I followed Gutman's original in Washington," Hammett
said, "and I never remember shadowing a man who bored me so much. He
was not after a jeweled falcon, of course; but he *was* suspected of being a
German spy. Brigid was based, in part, on a woman who came in to
Pinkerton's to hire an operative to discharge her housekeeper." And she
was also patterned on Peggy O'Toole, Hammett's assistant in the advertising
department of Albert Samuels's jewelry company in San Francisco, where
Hammett worked after leaving Pinkerton's. "The Cairo character I picked
up on a forgery charge in 1920. Effie, the good girl [Spade's secretary,
played by Lee Patrick], once asked me to go into the narcotic smuggling
business with her in San Diego. Wilmer, the gunman, was picked up in
Stockton, California; a neat small smooth-faced quiet boy of perhaps twenty-

one. He was serenely proud of the name the papers gave him—'The Midget Bandit.' " Hammett stated that Sam Spade had no original. He was "idealized . . . in the sense that he is what most of the private detectives I've worked with would *like* to have been."

Hammett told author James Thurber that he was influenced by Henry James's 1902 novel *The Wings of the Dove* when writing *The Maltese Falcon*. James, with his polished prose styling, influenced the history of the novel by emphasizing psychological character analysis. "In both novels," related Thurber, "a fabulous fortune—jewels in *Falcon*, inherited millions in *Dove*—shapes the destinies of the disenchanted central characters, and James's designing woman, Kate Croy, like Hammett's pistol-packing Brigid O'Shaughnessy, loses her lover in a Renunciation Scene."

Concentrating on abiding moral themes, James admitted into his stories and novels only what could be represented as the perception or experience of his characters. Huston followed this technique. He said that "the book was told entirely from the standpoint of Sam Spade, and so too is the picture, with Spade in every scene except the murder of his partner. The audience knows no more and no less than he does. All the other characters are introduced only as they meet Spade, and upon their appearance I attempted to photograph them through his eyes."

Recalling his initial opportunity to direct a film, John Huston told Gerald Pratley: "I still remember going on the floor for the first day . . . . As I hadn't been on the set very often when I was a writer, directing was something that came instinctively. I knew almost exactly what I was going to do. I made drawings of every set-up, through the whole picture from beginning to end. I made the drawings myself. I showed the pictures and the drawings to [director] Willy Wyler and he criticized them, and whatever ideas he had I incorporated them if they seemed to be good." Wyler was an old friend and professional associate. He had directed the first film Huston worked on as a writer, *A House Divided* (1931), and was directly responsible for bringing Huston to Warners to work as a writer on *Jezebel* (1938).

"Before going on the set," said Huston, "Henry Blanke gave me the best advice I ever had, that any young director could have, in my opinion. That was: each scene, as you go to make it, is the best scene in the picture . . . the most important." Blanke worked closely with Huston and helped him with the fundamental techniques of film making before he stepped on the stage.

But, as shooting began, there was some concern on the part of the executives. Hal Wallis, in a memo sent to Blanke on June 12, 1941 (with a copy to Huston), said, in part, that:

Huston's second day's dailies* are better than the first, but I still feel that they are too leisurely in tempo. I think my criticism is principally with Bogart, who has adopted a leisurely, suave form of delivery . . . . Bogart must have his usual brisk, staccato manner . . . . All of the action seems a little too slow and deliberate . . . . The actual scene, the set-ups, etc. are fine. It is primarily a matter of tempo and delivery.

Huston replied to Wallis in a memo:

I am shrinking all the pauses and speeding up all the action. You understand, of course, that so far I have done only the slow scenes of the picture . . . . After the sequence I am doing at present—Brigid's apartment—the story really begins to move. By the time we reach the Cairo-Brigid-copper sequence in Spade's apartment, it will be turning like a pinwheel . . . . As I am making each scene, I am keeping the whole picture in mind. This picture should gain in velocity as it goes along . . . . Nevertheless, I am . . . making Bogart quick and staccato and taking the deliberateness out of his action.

Blanke recalls screening for Huston the daily scenes of a picture director Anatole Litvak was shooting on the lot at the same time, *Blues in the Night*, and pointing out the difference in pacing, with Litvak's fast tempo being presented as an example.

Of course, the dominant aspect of the Warners style during the 1930s and 1940s was the furious pacing. The credo was to move everything as fast as possible without anything remaining on screen a fraction of a second longer than necessary. Scripts were usually pared down to the minimum prior to shooting, performers talked rapidly and picked up their cues, and editors ruthlessly cut frames; next Hal Wallis (and, before he left Warners in 1933, Darryl Zanuck) trimmed even more footage. Then Jack L. Warner had his crack at it. There were exceptions to this, particularly after the initial release of *Gone with the Wind* (1939) and during the World War II years, when long-drawn-out features were in vogue.

Mary Astor thought that "it helped a great deal that we shot the picture [to a large extent] in sequence . . . . Because John's script was well prepared, and because he took time in rehearsal, the shooting went very quickly. Often there is much time lost in lack of preparation. There was and is too

* The material shot the previous day that had been developed and printed.

much of 'Let's rehearse with film,' in the hopes that something might happen that would be spontaneous and fresh, and wouldn't happen again."

One of Mary Astor's approaches to the role of Brigid, the slightly psychopathic, congenital liar, was to breathe rather rapidly to emphasize the unstable quality. "So, I hyperventilated before going into most of the scenes. It gave me a heady feeling, of thinking at cross purposes."

In a memo to Henry Blanke on June 24, Wallis said:

> The scene in the apartment with Bogart, Astor and Peter Lorre is very good. I don't think it is too slow . . . . One thing that bothers me, however, is the way in which Mary Astor is speaking her lines. She seems to be playing it just a little too coy and ladylike. I think she is going overboard a little on this, in the soft quality of her voice, and obviously playing a part for all the characters with whom she comes in contact in the picture, and I think she overdoes it to the point of where the people she is playing with would know that she was putting on an act.

On June 30, Wallis said in another memo to Blanke that "Sydney Greenstreet is wonderful in the part, but just a little difficult to understand. Will

Actor William Powell, author Dashiell Hammett, and director W. S. Van Dyke II at the time of MGM's The Thin Man *(1934). Hammett wrote* The Thin Man *novel four years after his* The Maltese Falcon.

you ask Huston to watch him a little on this, and have just a little clearer enunciation."

As a good-luck gesture, Walter Huston worked one day in the unbilled bit role of Captain Jacobi, who staggers into Spade's office and hands the Falcon over before dying. Most people in the audience did not recognize him.

After thirty-four days of filming, on July 18, 1941, *The Maltese Falcon* completed shooting—two days ahead of schedule. Jack Warner requested a few changes after the film was edited. First, there was a very brief additional scene—not in the book, script, or any previous movie version— showing Spade's partner, Archer (Jerome Cowan), being murdered. This was to be photographed using the subjective camera technique, with the camera being the killer. Second, there was a new ending. The ending originally planned was the same as that of the book: After Brigid is turned over to the police in Spade's apartment, the scene shifts to the next morning in Spade's office. There is a short dialogue between Sam and his secretary, Effie. She says to him, "Iva is here" (Gladys George). Spade, looking at nothing, nods almost imperceptibly and says, "Yes . . . . " He shivers, and then says, "Well . . . send her in." Fade out.

In the revised ending, the latter part of the scene in Spade's apartment was reshot in early August, including a new non-Hammett line in reference to the Falcon—"the stuff that dreams are made of." Lieutenant Dundy (Barton MacLane) and Brigid exit the room first, but this time they continue in the corridor to the elevator. Spade follows. As Brigid descends in the open elevator, Spade takes one last look at her from the corridor and starts down the stairway. The end.*

This revision contributes to the general softening of Sam Spade's character, some of which was already accomplished by the necessary editing of the overall text, some of which was implicit in Bogart's somewhat vulnerable manner. The new ending allows the audience to believe that, although he may have seemed as corrupt as Gutman, Spade was always playing a role in order to solve the crime.

James Naremore in his 1973 essay, "John Huston and 'The Maltese Falcon,'" points out that "Bogart is the visual opposite of Hammett's Sam Spade. Spade, Hammett tells us, is a tall man with an 'almost conical' body. When he takes off his shirt, 'the sag of his big rounded shoulders' makes him resemble 'a bear' . . . .

---

* In the 1931 version, the audience learns by means of a newspaper insert shot that at the trial Spade produced a Chinese merchant, the only eyewitness to Archer's murder, who positively identified Ruth Wonderly as the murderess. Then Spade visits her in jail, announcing that he has been made a special investigator for the district attorney's office. "You helped me get it," he says. "If they don't hang you, I'll be waiting for you." The picture ends with Spade leaving the jail.

"Sydney Greenstreet . . . is not so flabby or bombastic as the Gutman of the novel, and he lacks 'dark ringlets' of hair. Peter Lorre is properly Levantine, but less effeminate and less bejeweled than Hammett's Joel Cairo . . . . Hammett's Brigid O'Shaughnessy is little more than a sexy dame . . . . Mary Astor, on the other hand, has a lovely but almost matronly face and build, and she brings a sophistication to the role that is entirely lacking in the novel."

Jack Warner also requested a short written prologue giving the background and history of the Falcon on a title following the opening credits. The background was partially based on fact. Hammett stated that "somewhere I had read of the peculiar rental agreement between Charles V [of Spain] and the Order of the Hospital of St. John of Jerusalem [the Knights of Malta]." This agreement of 1530 specified that rent for the island of Malta would be an annual tribute on All Saint's Day of a single falcon. The rest of the history seems to be Hammett's romantic embellishment.

Warners staff composer Adolph Deutsch was assigned the film and created a subtle and properly mysterious score that was devoid of bombast. The Warners music style of that time usually was thick textured, with heavy

Left to right: Walter Huston (father of John) playing Captain Jacobi, an unbilled bit role; Humphrey Bogart (back to camera), Lee Patrick (Effie), and director John Huston on the set of the 1941 Maltese Falcon.

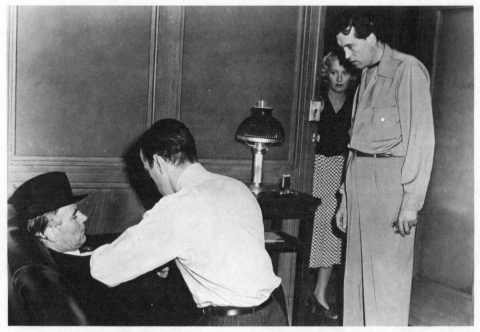

The Maltese Falcon: *A deleted scene in an elevator on the way to Sam's (Bogart) apartment to see Joel Cairo (Peter Lorre). Mary Astor is Brigid.*

brass and strings surging to the foreground. Deutsch was relatively unobtrusive in his approach and gave the edge more to the mood and colorings his use of woodwinds evoked. He told me recently that he consciously avoided "the Wagnerian approach" and that he did not want obvious leitmotifs overpowering the picture. He said that he did not screen the film with Huston, Blanke, or Wallis and Warner, but discussed the music and where it would be used in the film only with Leo F. Forbstein, the head of the studio's music department.

The Maltese Falcon was previewed on September 5, 1941, and the next morning Jack Warner sent a memo to Hal Wallis in which he said:

> Last night after the preview, I thought for about an hour, and believe we should positively make over the opening closeups of Mary Astor [in Spade's office] and tell the audience what the hell it is all about instead of picking up with a lot of broken sentences with confusing words. . . .
>
> Many of the [preview] cards stated they were very confused in the beginning, and I am sure we throw them off. Therefore,

why be so clever, as we have a hell of a good picture under the name *The Maltese Falcon*, which I have already wired New York we are going to use.* We should do these retakes the first thing Monday.

On September 10, Bogart was excused from the shooting of his next picture, *All through the Night,* and along with Mary Astor and Jerome Cowan, reported to Stage 6 to retake the opening scene in the office of Spade and Archer. Brigid's speech regarding her sister and Floyd Thursby was rewritten and simplified by Huston. For example, in the original shooting the dialogue began:

SPADE

Now what can I do for you, Miss Wonderly?

MISS WONDERLY
(*hurriedly*)

Could you—? I thought—I—that is—

SPADE

Suppose you tell me about it from the very beginning.

MISS WONDERLY

That was in New York.

SPADE

Yes?

MISS WONDERLY

I don't know where she met him in New York. She's five years younger than I—only seventeen—we didn't have the same friends. I don't suppose we've ever been as close as sisters should be. Mama and Papa are in Europe. It would kill them. I've *got* to get her back before they come home.

In the revised scene, the exposition was much clearer:

SPADE

Won't you sit down, Miss Wonderly?

MISS WONDERLY

Thank you. I inquired at the hotel for the name of a reliable, private detective. They mentioned yours.

---

* There had been some thought given to calling the film "The Gent from Frisco."

SPADE

Suppose you tell me about it from the very beginning.

MISS WONDERLY

I'm from New York.

SPADE

Uh-huh.

MISS WONDERLY

I'm trying to find my sister. I have reason to believe that she's here in San Francisco with a man by the name of Thursby, Floyd Thursby. I don't know where she met him. We've never been as close as sisters ought to be. If we had, perhaps Corinne would have told me that she was planning on running away with him. Mother and Father are in Honolulu. It will kill them. I've got to find her before they get back home. They're coming home the first of the month.

The entire scene up to Archer's entrance was modified in this way. Seven camera set-ups—photographed by Ernest Haller, substituting for the original cameraman, Arthur Edeson, who was on another assignment—were completed by 4:00 P.M.

Less than a month later, this modest little film, which cost $381,000, according to the studio records, opened in New York. Within two days Wallis wrote Jack Warner, who was on vacation in Hot Springs, Arkansas:

> According to some of the reviews and other press notices from New York on *The Maltese Falcon*, the picture came in "under wraps," "on rubber heels," "was a delightful surprise because it came in unheralded," etc., etc.
>
> You probably have seen the reviews, which are wonderful, and have seen the figures, which are also wonderful, and it is too bad that they [Warners' New York headquarters] were apparently not sufficiently sold on the picture in New York to get behind it importantly.
>
> Now that it has opened and has proven to be a hit, I thought perhaps you might want to give them a slight goose and let them get behind this picture in other situations and give it the importance which it deserves.

The Maltese Falcon was the forerunner of a number of films over the next several years that were a direct, if somewhat belated, result of its influence.

Hammett, Raymond Chandler, James M. Cain, and similar authors of the hard-boiled school became fashionable in Hollywood. *The Glass Key* (1942), *Murder My Sweet* (1944), *Double Indemnity* (1944) and others were big box office. Bogart even returned to the private detective genre a few years later as Philip Marlowe in Chandler's *The Big Sleep* (1946).

In early 1943, Henry Blanke wrote Roy Obringer, head of the studio's legal department that

> several years ago we purchased an original, called *Three Strangers*, from John Huston . . . .
>
> To the characters John Huston had, we have added a private detective on the order of the one played by Humphrey Bogart in *The Maltese Falcon*. It would enrich my story manifold if we could make him identically the same character as in *The Maltese Falcon* and even give him the same name . . . .
>
> The question . . . is whether or not I have the legal right to use this character's name.

Obringer replied (in part):

> I find that "Detective Spade" is a character which has been used on more than one occasion by Dashiell Hammett . . . .
> In other words, the author did not divest himself of the privilege of using the character "Spade" when he sold us *The Maltese Falcon*, as this character is one which appears to have established a secondary meaning in the public mind, and which character cannot be used by the buyer of a book containing such character for the purpose of sequels. We have no sequel rights on *The Maltese Falcon*.

When Warner Bros. first announced their intention of filming *Three Strangers* in October 1942, the plan was to reunite Bogart with Sydney Greenstreet and possibly Mary Astor, if she could be borrowed from MGM by the time filming was to begin. John Collier had been signed to write the screenplay and Blanke was to produce. By the time the picture was released in early 1946, it had a new producer and writer, there was no character named Sam Spade, and Mary Astor and Bogart were not in the cast.

Before becoming a star of the first magnitude, Humphrey Bogart spent several years under contract to Warner Bros. playing mostly tough, ruthless gangsters. He supported Warners' main gangster fixtures—James Cagney, Edward G. Robinson, George Raft—in addition to carrying the load by himself in a few minor films. These were all stock roles with little opportunity for dimension and shading, but Bogart played them better than anyone else and built a reputation as a reliable actor with a distinctive style. *The Maltese Falcon* solidified further aspects of the emerging Bogey character that had been tentatively projected in *Dead End* (1937) and *High Sierra* (1941). In *The Maltese Falcon* Bogart presented the classic loner: weathered, tough, disillusioned (or perhaps nonillusioned), somewhat sadistic, cutting right through to the bare bones of his women, and yet true to his own sense of ethics and professional integrity.

According to Mary Astor, Bogart "was a hard working guy, a good craftsman . . . . His technical skill was quite brilliant. His precision timing was no accident. He kept other actors on their toes because he *listened* to them, he watched, he *looked* at them. He never had that vague stare of a person who waits for you to finish talking, who hasn't heard a word you have said."

Following *The Maltese Falcon*, all that was now needed to complete the Bogart mystique was a strong romantic element. Bogart's love interest in the *Falcon*, brilliantly played by Mary Astor, was a tough and striking figure of feminine deceit and betrayal, but the relationship, while intriguing and offbeat, did not project the necessary romantic aura to capture the public's imagination. Then came *Casablanca*.

GEORGE RAFT IN
CASABLANCA?
(1943)

The enduring appeal of *Casablanca* probably results from the perfect melding of various elements one associates with the better films of Hollywood's golden age: colorful characters involved in what is essentially a love story, an exotic locale, first-rate supporting players, melodramatic incidents, tough, humorous, cynical repartee, sentimental interludes, and idealism and heroic commitment to a cause. But *Casablanca* had a rather inauspicious beginning as an unproduced play called *Everybody Comes to Rick's*.

Playwright and New York City high school teacher Murray Burnett and his wife went to Europe in the summer of 1938, stopping first in Brussels to visit her relatives. Then, in order to check on some other relatives, they traveled to Vienna. In March Hitler's forces had entered the city. Burnett was able to observe closely the grim realities of the "New Order" and the plight of refugees. Later, the Burnetts visited a small town in the south of France where they went to a nightclub that overlooked the Mediterranean. A black pianist played jazz for a mixed crowd of French, Nazis, and refugees. Burnett remarked to his wife that the nightclub would be a marvelous setting for a play.

Back in New York, Burnett and Joan Alison, his collaborator, wrote a melodrama during the summer of 1940 that dealt directly with the problem

154

of the refugees and took place in a fictitious nightclub called Rick's Café Américain, in Casablanca, French Morocco. Casablanca was one of the key stops on the refugee trail Burnett had learned about in Vienna.

The play was optioned for production by Martin Gabel and Carly Wharton, who felt that rewriting was required. Specifically, Wharton objected to the fact that Lois, later renamed Ilsa (the role eventually played by Ingrid Bergman), sleeps with Rick (the Bogart part) in order, as interpreted by Wharton, to obtain exit visas. Burnett and Alison, unhappy at the prospect of making changes, took back the play and gave it to their agent, who then submitted it to various Hollywood studios.

On December 8, 1941, the day after the Japanese attack on Pearl Harbor, a story analyst for Warner Bros., Stephen Karnot, read his assignment, *Everybody Comes to Rick's*. Later he sent off his synopsis to Hal B. Wallis, who for many years had been in charge of the making of most of Warners' major films (under Jack L. Warner), but who now was beginning to produce personally a few films a year for Warners. In his comments attached to the synopsis, Karnot said:

> Excellent melodrama. Colorful, timely background, tense mood, suspense, psychological and physical conflict, tight plotting, sophisticated hokum. A box-office natural—for Bogart, or Cagney, or Raft in out-of-the-usual roles and perhaps Mary Astor.

Wallis read the short synopsis and a twenty-two page synopsis. On December 22, Wallis asked for reactions from some of his associates on the lot. Writer Jerry Wald said that "it can be easily tailored into a piece along

Playwrights Joan Alison and Murray Burnett celebrating the sale of their play Everybody Comes To Rick's *to Warners. The title was changed to* Casablanca *for the film.*

STAGE PLAY
Rec'd Ms from NY
12/8/41

EVERYBODY COMES TO RICK'S
Reader: Karnot
12/11/41

IMPORTANT!
RETURN STORY DEPT.

EVERYBODY COMES TO RICK'S
by
Murray Burnett & Joan Alison

Rick Blaine, American owner of de luxe Rick's Cafe in Casablanca, French Morocco, is a taciturn man of mystery to his patrons -- wealthy French expatriates; refugees; French, German and Italian officers. Cynically indifferent, Rick enforces an atmosphere of strict neutrality in his powderkeg of political tension. Only Rinaldo, French Prefect of Police, Rick's professed friend, knows of his background as a famous criminal lawyer in Paris, his affair with a woman, his divorce from his wife and children in '39, his abandonment of career and flight into oblivion. But only Sam, Rick's devoted Negro entertainer, knows what's in Rick's embittered heart. Ugarte, peddler of stolen exit visas, asks Rick to hold a pair of priceless letters-of-transit signed by Weygand. He plans to sell them for a fabulous sum this evening, and quit Casablanca and the racket. Rinaldo enters with Strasser, Gestapo agent, seeking to prevent recently arrived Victor Laszlo -- wealthy Czech patriot hunted by the Nazis for his fearless underground activity -- from buying the letters from Ugarte. Rick plays dumb, but Ugarte is arrested. On their exit enters Laszlo, accompanied by beautiful Lois Meredith. Rick is almost visibly shaken by her presense -- their casual greeting betrays their past connection. Strasser privately gives Laszlo an ultimatum. Unless he signs over his foreign-banked millions to Germany, he will never leave Casablanca. Laszlo calmly defies him. Later, after all have left, Sam begs Rick to avoid re-entanglement with Lois. But Rick cannot. She soon returns alone, and spends the night with him. In the morning, torn between unquenchable love and deep distrust, Rick challenges her motives. Frankly admitting admiration for valiant Laszlo, she insists she loves Rick, wants to stay with him. But she owes Laszlo a debt. Rick promises to help Laszlo. Rinaldo enters, and with one remark makes it clear to Rick that Lois is playing him for a sucker. Rick tersely, viciously, rejects her reassertion of love. That evening, when Laszlo, followed by Lois, comes seeking Ugarte, Rick, now drinking heavily, insults them both. Rinaldo brings news of Ugarte's suicide -- bluntly charges Rick with possession of the letters, but Rick outbluffs him. Rinaldo introduces Jan and Annina Viereck, young, bewildered, newly-wed Bulgarian refugees. When Annina confides to Rick she has agreed to yield to Rinaldo for the sake of an exit visa for Jan, Rick's cynicism is pierced; he begins to understand Lois. Rinaldo makes passes at Annina, Jan knocks him down. As he screams for his gendarmes, the lights go out. When they come on, the Vierecks have disappeared. After a vain search, Rinaldo summarily closes the cafe, promising Rick trouble. Later Rick brings the Vierecks from hiding, refuses to let them leave. In the morning, as Sam brings plane tickets for Lisbon, Rinaldo appears, warning Rick he is closed and will not leave town until the Vierecks are found. On his exit Lois appears; she is leaving Laszlo for Rick. Without explanation he demands her aid in helping the Vierecks. She agrees. He calls Rinaldo, offers to surrender the Vierecks. Rinaldo arrives to find Rick and Lois in rapturous embrace. Rick makes another offer; he will trap Laszlo for him, with one of the letters, if the Vierecks are allowed to leave with the other. Convinced by the lovemaking, Rinaldo agrees, calls off his police, and the Vierecks leave with the letter and plane tickets. Rick then calls Laszlo, who comes immediately for the letter. Rinaldo emerges to arrest him as he takes the letter, but Rick covers Rinaldo with a gun. Just realizing that Rick is practically committing suicide, Lois frantically tries to prevent him, but Rick insists that she accompany Laszlo. Despairing, she does. Rick, his self-respect redeemed, surrenders to Rinaldo and furious Strasser.

Warner Bros. story analyst Stephen Karnot's synopsis of the play, Everybody Comes To Rick's (Casablanca).

the lines of *Algiers* [made in 1938 with Charles Boyer and Hedy Lamarr]."
Robert Buckner, another writer under contract, answered a few days later
that he didn't like the play at all and thought that the main situations and
the basic relations of the leading characters were highly censorable and that
"its big moment is sheer hokum melodrama of the E. Phillips Oppenheim*
variety; and this guy Rick is two parts Hemingway, one part Scott Fitzgerald,
and a dash of cafe Christ."

One of Wallis's associate producers, Robert Lord, replied that the material
was a very obvious imitation of *Grand Hotel*, but suggested that since it was
written as a play some money could be contributed to its theatrical production
in exchange for priority on the motion picture rights. If it turned out to be
successful, the property would then be worth doing as a picture. "Somehow
most of these characters and situations seem very conventional and ster-
eotyped. If we buy this thing, I would not pay much money for it."

Screenwriter Aeneas MacKenzie in his answer of January 3 was more
enthusiastic:

> I think we can get a good picture out of the play. But it isn't
> a pushover; because certain characterizations—such as Rinaldo
> [the character eventually played by Claude Rains] need very
> definite strengthening, and certain basic situations present
> problems from the censorship angle. . . . These, however,
> can be overcome, I believe, because behind the action and its
> background is the possibility of an excellent theme—the idea
> that when people lose faith in their ideals they are beaten
> before they begin to fight. That was what happened to France
> and to Rick Blaine.

Two days later MacKenzie and Wally Kline, his collaborator on the recent
Errol Flynn—Olivia de Havilland vehicle *They Died with Their Boots On*
(1942), were assigned to work on the screenplay of *Casablanca*, the project's
new title since December 31. Warner Bros. had purchased the property for
$20,000. MacKenzie wrote a follow-up memo on January 6 in which he said
that he had taken *Casablanca* to pieces and analyzed its structure and
movements. The results caused him to revise the favorable impression he
had felt after his first reading of the play. "It presents some very serious
problems indeed, and has certain defects which are slurred over in its
present form but which will become very apparent in a picture. In my
opinion this material will require some drastic revision."

* A prolific British writer of early-twentieth-century mystery novels about secret international
documents, shifty diplomats, and seductive adventuresses.

Producer Hal B. Wallis (left) and production chief Jack L. Warner.

Aeneas MacKenzie and Wally Kline spent approximately six weeks on their adaptation of the play. For the most part, the plot of their screen treatment of *Casablanca* was based on the play, but they modified some of the characters and added a number of scenes and minor roles. The characters in the play were drawn mainly from composites of people the playwrights had known, according to Murray Burnett.

The Epstein twins, Julius and Philip, were assigned to work on the adaptation. They had recently finished scripting a good deal of *Yankee Doodle Dandy* (uncredited), and before that such popular films as *Four Daughters* (1938), *No Time for Comedy* (1940) and *The Man Who Came to Dinner* (1941). Their forte was bright dialogue.

Following MacKenzie and Kline's lead, the Epsteins developed still further the character of the corrupt Vichy official, Luis Rinaldo—changed to Louis Renault (Rains)—giving him some marvelously witty lines and building up his offbeat relationship with Rick. The Epsteins also addressed themselves to the problems inherent in the love scenes, which everyone regarded as unsatisfactory.

Meanwhile, Hal Wallis was thinking about a director. He was interested in borrowing William Wyler, who had directed *Jezebel* (1938) and *The Letter* (1940) for Warners on loan from Samuel Goldwyn. Wallis sent an early draft of the script to Sun Valley, where Wyler was vacationing. Writer-producer

Norman Krasna, also at Sun Valley Lodge working on *Princess O'Rourke* (1943) for Warners, wrote Wallis:

> [Darryl F.] Zanuck leaves here tonight and Wyler probably will be forced to read *Casablanca*. They both play gin rummy until 2:30 AM, which, you can see, leaves little time for anything else. He hasn't read Goldwyn's story either, so you can't feel slighted.

Shortly afterward, Wallis decided to go with Warners' top director, Michael Curtiz (*Yankee Doodle Dandy*, *The Adventures of Robin Hood*, *Angels with Dirty Faces*).

On February 14, about the time the Epsteins started work on the script, Wallis sent a memo to Steve Trilling, head of casting at Warners, asking him to "please figure on Humphrey Bogart and Ann Sheridan for *Casablanca*, which is scheduled to start the latter part of April." (On January 5, 1942, Warners announced in the trade paper *The Hollywood Reporter* that Ann Sheridan, Ronald Reagan, and Dennis Morgan—all under contract to the studio—were to be in *Casablanca*.)

Anyone recalling Ingrid Bergman's portrayal of Ilsa Lund in the final version of *Casablanca* would be hard-pressed to conceive of Ann Sheridan in the role. But in the play and in the early drafts of the scripts (including an April 2 Epstein version), the girl was called Lois Meredith and presumably was American. Her background is sketchy in the play, but while she was having a romance in Paris with Rick, a prominent American criminal lawyer residing there with a wife and children, she was living with another man—not Victor Laszlo, the Czech patriot. Rick did not know this until they all accidentally met one evening in a cafe called La Belle Aurore. Shaken by his discovery, he departed without leaving a forwarding address.

Four years later, when Lois and Victor Laszlo enter Rick's place in Casablanca, Rick slips Lois the key to his room, and later she returns alone to spend the night with him. In the play, as distinguished from the final screen version, Lois does not meet Victor Laszlo until after the affair in Paris with Rick, and Lois and Laszlo are not married.

Just a few days after Wallis contacted Trilling regarding the casting of Bogart and Sheridan, a new approach developed. It was decided that the leading lady should be a lovely European. Wallis thought of Ingrid Bergman, under contract to David O. Selznick. Discussions commenced but were not productive. He then considered Hedy Lamarr, who had made such a success with a somewhat similar role in *Algiers*. But she was under contract to

MGM, and Trilling reported that "L.B. Mayer is opposed to loaning her out to anybody" (February 23, 1942). Other names were discussed: Edwige Feuillere, the distinguished French actress, who had impressed Wallis in a fairly recent Max Ophuls film; and Michele Morgan, another French actress, who had done only one film since arriving in America—RKO's *Joan of Paris* (1942). Then Tamara Toumanova tested in April. Warners screenwriter Casey Robinson has said in his American Film Institute Oral History (conducted by Joel Greenberg) that it was his idea to change the American Lois Meredith to a European. "Something very specific gave me this idea," he said. "I was falling in love with a Russian ballerina named Tamara Toumanova; writers sometimes have such personal reasons. She had movie ambitions."

Meanwhile, Selznick had been stalling regarding the loan of Bergman because he was hoping that she would be cast as Maria in Paramount's major enterprise, *For Whom the Bell Tolls*. But then that part temporarily went to Vera Zorina. Wallis recalls in his memoirs (1980) that "knowing I wanted and needed Bergman, Selznick avoided me. He failed to return my phone calls. When I learned he was in New York at the Hotel Carlyle, I flew back, checked in there and called him on the house telephone. It paid off. He agreed to see me."

Wallis persuaded Selznick to listen to the Epsteins tell him the story of *Casablanca* in early April. Many of the script problems had not been solved, so it was thought that the Epsteins, whom Selznick admired, would do the best job selling the story verbally. After Selznick listened, he brought in Ingrid Bergman to discuss the project with himself, the Epsteins, and director Michael Curtiz, for whom Selznick also had great respect. Some modifications were recommended.

On April 14, Steve Trilling advised Hal Wallis in a memo that the only deal Selznick would consider for loaning Ingrid Bergman "is an even swap for Olivia de Havilland . . . . They will give us eight weeks time on Bergman and we in turn are to give them eight weeks on de Havilland." This was later agreed to, and Bergman was set for the role of Ilsa Lund.

Ingrid Bergman had come to Hollywood from Sweden to replay for David O. Selznick's 1939 version of *Intermezzo* the role she had originated in the 1936 Swedish production. Although she was well received in her first film in this country, her next three pictures (*Adam Had Four Sons*, *Rage in Heaven*, and *Dr. Jekyll and Mr. Hyde*—the Spencer Tracy version) did not appreciably advance her career. She did have a unique freshness and projected a natural beauty. She was a healthy, intelligent, and charming continental heroine—a welcome contrast to the usual glamour and exotica.

On April 2 Jack L. Warner sent a note to Wallis: "What do you think of using Raft in *Casablanca?* He knows we are going to make this and is starting a campaign for it." George Raft had been under contract with Warners since 1940, but he had turned down more pictures than he had made. The next day Wallis replied:

> I have thought over very carefully the matter of George Raft in *Casablanca,* and I have discussed this with Mike [Curtiz], and we both feel that he should not be in this picture. Bogart is ideal for it, and it is being written for him, and I think we should forget Raft for this property.

And that, apparently, was that, refuting the legend that Raft was offered *Casablanca* first and turned it down.

Philip Dorn was wanted for the role of Victor Laszlo, the Czech underground leader. However, MGM advised that Dorn was going into *Random Harvest* and would not be available. Carl Esmond was tested. On April 22, Wallis sent a note to Curtiz saying that he had gone over with Trilling the possibilities for the part of Laszlo. Aside from Philip Dorn, "whom we cannot get, and Paul Henreid, who I am sure will not play the part when he reads it, there is no one else that I can think of." Wallis then mentioned that Curtiz should begin to adjust himself to the possibility that they might have to use Dean Jagger, Ian Hunter, Herbert Marshall, or someone of a similar type without an accent.

Thoughts then turned to Joseph Cotten, and a test was made of Jean-Pierre Aumont. But Henreid was the man they wanted. He was currently filming *Now, Voyager* on the Warner lot for Wallis, and everyone was impressed with the footage. A Viennese actor who had been discovered by Max Reinhardt, Henreid had appeared on the London stage (*Victoria Regina*) and screen (*Goodbye, Mr. Chips, Night Train*) before coming to America in 1940. Henreid was persuaded to accept the role when Warners took over part of his RKO contract and he was promised costar billing along with Bogart and Bergman.

Wallis had considered changing the important role of Sam, the black singer–piano player and Rick's confidante from the play, to a black woman. In a February interoffice communication to Steve Trilling, Wallis said, "When I was in New York I saw Hazel Scott at the Uptown Cafe Society. She would be marvelous for the part." Shortly afterward it was decided to go back to the original concept of the character. Dooley Wilson, who had created the role of Little Joe opposite Ethel Waters in the Broadway

To **MR. HAL WALLIS**   April 2, 1942
    Confidential Correspondence

What do you think of using

Raft in "CASABLANCA"?

He knows we are going to

make this and is starting a campaign

for it.

                                                              JACK

Inter-office note from Jack Warner to Hal Wallis.

Wallis's reply.

FORM 10

WARNER BROS. PICTURES, INC.
BURBANK, CALIFORNIA

INTER-OFFICE COMMUNICATION

To MR._____ **WARNER** _____   DATE _____ **April 3, 1942** _____

FROM MR._____ **WALLIS** _____   SUBJECT _____ **"CASABLANCA"** _____

Dear Jack:

   I have thought over very carefully the matter
of George Raft in "CASABLANCA", and I have
discussed this with Mike, and we both feel
that he should not be in this picture. Bogart
is ideal for it, and it is being written for
him, and I think we should forget Raft for
this property.

   Incidentally, he hasn't done a picture here
since I was a little boy, and I don't think
he should be able to put his fingers on just
what he wants to do when he wants to do it.

HW:og   HAL WALLIS

VERBAL MESSAGES CAUSE MISUNDERSTANDING AND DELAYS
(PLEASE PUT THEM IN WRITING)

George Raft in Casablanca?

production of *Cabin in the Sky* (1940), was tested. Wallis thought the test "pretty good. He isn't ideal for the part but if we get stuck and can't do any better I suppose he could play it." Then he asked what happened to the test that was to be made of Clarence Muse for the same role (Muse had played in films since 1928). Eight days later, on May 1, Wallis wrote to Trilling that "Clarence Muse is okay with me, and in view of the interest elsewhere, I think we should sign him." But by June 3 the situation changed, and Dooley Wilson was borrowed from Paramount at $500 per week.

Wilson could not play the piano, so a staff musician, Elliot Carpenter, dubbed all the piano playing by working on the sidelines during shooting. Several weeks after filming began, Wallis had second thoughts about Wilson's particular style of singing. He requested Leo Forbstein, the head of the music department, to "begin looking immediately for a Negro with a good crooning voice to double all of Dooley Wilson's songs." Fortunately, Wallis changed his mind after listening to several candidates, and Wilson's voice was retained.

The cast was set. Claude Rains, an ex–Warner Bros. contract player, now free-lance, was firm from the outset for Renault. British-born Rains had been an outstanding film actor—and earlier a stage actor—since his debut as *The Invisible Man* (1933). Although he did some leads, his wide-ranging and colorful assortment of supporting roles brought him the most recognition.

Peter Lorre and Sydney Greenstreet, lately of *The Maltese Falcon*, were ideal for Ugarte and Ferrari, two characters left more or less intact from the play. Although Otto Preminger tested, Conrad Veidt eventually was borrowed from MGM for the key role of Major Heinrich Strasser. In the play and in the early drafts of the film script, Strasser is young, fresh-faced, a captain, and the new attaché to the German consulate. After director Michael Curtiz read a preliminary draft, according to Julius Epstein, he felt that the role should be built up considerably and Strasser represented as an older, sophisticated, and autocratic high Nazi official, in order to provide the film with a potent villain. The director also suggested the insertion of some additional vignettes depicting the anxieties and frustrations of refugees—Curtiz could relate to this, having gone through the rigors of trying to get some of his family out of Hungary.

The picture was due to start on May 25, but there were still script problems. Another contract writer, Howard Koch, had been assigned on April 6. Koch had previously worked on the screenplays for two Warner films, both of which were well received: *The Sea Hawk* (1940) and *The Letter* (1940). Earlier he had been associated with Orson Welles's Mercury Theater productions for radio, and he had written the adaptation for the sensational *War of the Worlds* radio dramatization in 1938. Koch was instructed to start all over again on *Casablanca*, paying particular attention to the trouble spots: the ending, certain aspects of Rick's character, the flashback to Paris, and other romantic scenes.

Bogart, according to Julius Epstein, had felt that in the early drafts Rick's character was heavy with self-pity and that he was too cold, too suspicious, and too hostile. Also, his background needed filling in. The Epsteins and MacKenzie and Kline had dropped all references to Rick's past, the wife and children, his former career as a lawyer (inherent in the play). His life

Veteran character actor Clarence Muse, who almost was chosen to play "Sam" in Casablanca.

was left purposely vague. After listening to Bogart's objections, the Epsteins went back over the script and softened Rick's character somewhat, substituting a controlled manner and a philosophy of independence and neutrality for many of the former negative characteristics. And Koch worked on evidences of his humanity and sentimental nature. He inserted a reference to Rick's having "fought on the side of the Loyalists in Spain" and the fact that he "ran guns to Ethiopia."

On May 11, Wallis wrote Koch that he would "appreciate anything you can do to speed up the balance of the script. We are starting production next Monday . . . . I think this next batch of the Epsteins' stuff is for the most part good . . . and . . . almost everything is usable." Koch answered that same day:

> Although the Epstein script follows in a general way the new story line, I feel it is written in a radically different vein from the work I've just finished on the first half of the picture. They apparently see the situations more in terms of their comic possibilities, while my effort has been to legitimize the characters and develop a serious melodrama of present day significance, using humor merely as a relief from dramatic tension.

Koch went on to say that, to a large extent, he had been writing and would go on writing a new screenplay, gladly availing himself of whatever material he felt he could use from the Epsteins' script and from the original play. In conclusion, he said that he "would continue to work hard, but I can't turn out a third of the screenplay in three days—not the kind of screenplay I thought you and Mike wanted."

Koch and the Epsteins kept on developing their versions independently. In mid-May, just before shooting was to commence, Casey Robinson and Lenore Coffee, Warners contract writers, were asked individually to read over the Epstein and Koch versions and offer a critique. Wallis and Curtiz were still trying to strengthen the "love interest." Both writers came up with suggestions, and Robinson included a good many ideas to improve the construction and development of the Rick–Ilsa relationship. Robinson was a favorite of Wallis's. His first script for Warners had been *Captain Blood* (1935), followed by such impressive credits as *Dark Victory* (1939), *Kings Row* (1941), and *Now, Voyager* (1942). On each of these he received solo screenplay credit. In his May 20 notes to Wallis, he began by saying that he felt the melodrama and humor in the script were well done but that the love story was deficient. He suggested that the first meeting between Rick and Ilsa alone occur late at night in the cafe when she comes back to talk to him. It is Rick's bitterness and his brutality, springing from his wounded pride, that stops Ilsa from telling him about Laszlo. Her disillusionment in Rick and what he has become is for the moment enough to turn her away from him. In the play she spends the night with Rick.

Robinson recommended another scene between them in Rick's apartment above the cafe that afternoon. Ilsa returns because she wants to clarify their relationship. She loves Rick; the days they had together in Paris were the most beautiful in her life. She tells him that Laszlo is her husband and discloses all the background of their marriage and the real reason she didn't come to the train in Paris. Ilsa explains the quality of her love for Laszlo— her admiration, respect, and veneration for him. To her Laszlo is the personification of the best ideals of her nature, of honor, of sacrifice for a great cause. Rick understands, softens, and is ashamed of himself.

Next Robinson outlined the scene between Laszlo and Rick. Rick now feels that Ilsa had been softening him up for a touch. He suspects he has been played for a sucker, so Rick turns down Laszlo's request for help, and when Laszlo wants to know why, he says, "Ask your wife."

Then Robinson moved to the end of the next scene between Rick and Ilsa:

> Ilsa comes for the visas. She tries to be hard boiled. She can't be. She breaks down completely. But completely. She tells Rick that she loves him and will do anything he wants. She will go anywhere, stay here, anything. She is absolutely helpless in the great passionate love she has for him. She will leave Victor. Rick can get him out of Casablanca. She knows that she's doing wrong, she even says so. She knows that in a way it is a violation of all the high idealism and honor of her nature. She knows she is being wicked but she can't help herself. This is a great scene for a woman to play.

At the end of the scene, Ilsa says that she will go home to her husband and tell him. With an enigmatic look on his face, Rick tells her not to do it. Better that she come with Laszlo to his place for the letters without telling her husband first, for otherwise he might not come. Better, anyway, that they tell him together. Robinson concluded:

> Now you're really set up for a swell twist when Rick sends her away on the plane with Victor. For now, in doing so, he is not just solving a love triangle. He is forcing the girl to live up to

the idealism of her nature, forcing her to carry on with the work that in these days is far more important than the love of two little people. It is something they will both be glad for when the pain is over.

Casablanca began shooting on May 25 without a completed script. According to the studio files, Howard Koch continued writing for another two weeks, after which he was taken off the project when his work presumably was finished. The Epsteins officially finished their work three weeks after the start of shooting. But of course they were all under contract to Warners, and consequently on call.

Wallis asked for Casey Robinson to be put on the picture for two weeks' work (which stretched into three and a half) starting the day filming began. Robinson did not receive credit on the finished film. Many years later he said:

> I wouldn't put my name on the screen with another writer. I was very proud of the fact of my solo screenplays. Except in the case of where somebody came on after me, as in *This Is the Army* [1943], or *The Corn Is Green* [1945], where Jack Warner ordered it rewritten, or where I rewrote somebody else—that's fine.
>
> But to go on the screen with three other writers with my piece—because I regarded it as *my piece!** And I wouldn't put my name on the screen. It was a very bad mistake, because the boys proceeded to earn an Academy Award.

Neither Aeneas MacKenzie nor Wally Kline received screen credit. The Screen Writers Guild ruling specified that a maximum of two writers or writing teams could be allowed credit on a screenplay. If necessary this would be arbitrated and measured by the writers' contributions. But often a writer would merely decide for whatever reason not to take credit.

Jack L. Warner sent Michael Curtiz a letter just prior to the picture's start, saying, "These are turbulent days and I know you will finish *Casablanca* in top seven weeks. I am depending on you to be the old Curtiz I know you to be, and I am positive you are going to make one great picture."

The primary setting of *Casablanca* was the interior of Rick's cafe, but whereas the entire action of the play took place in the main room, the film moved from there to the gambling room in back, to the exterior of the entrance, upstairs to Rick's quarters, out into the streets of Casablanca, and

* Robinson claimed that he had read the play while traveling east with Wallis, urged him to buy it, and was disappointed when he was not assigned the screenplay at first.

to Rick's competition, The Blue Parrot. The backlot street and fragments of other sets were appropriated from Warners' 1943 version of *The Desert Song*. There was a scene in Victor and Ilsa's hotel room, another in Captain Renault's office, the climactic airport sequence, and the Parisian episode. The important railway station scene in Paris was shot on a set that was designed and used for *Now, Voyager* and then revamped for *Casablanca*. All of this was what was and still is referred to as "opening up the play" from the confines of a theatrical presentation.

Everything in the film was photographed at Warners' Burbank studios, except one brief sequence depicting the arrival of Major Strasser at Casablanca's airport. This was shot at the old Metropolitan Airport in Van Nuys. The concluding airport sequence was photographed on Stage One at the studio.

Wallis continued to work on improvements as the picture was being shot—even wardrobe details. After several days of shooting, he sent a memo to Curtiz regarding the scene in which Victor Laszlo and Ilsa make their entrance at Rick's. Wallis was concerned about whether Ilsa should appear in an evening outfit: "After all, these two people are trying to escape from the country. The Gestapo is after them; they are refugees, making their way from country to country, and they are not going to Rick's Cafe for social purposes." He thought it incongruous for Ilsa to dress up in evening clothes as though she had carried a wardrobe with her. It would be better for

The script for the love scenes in Casablanca *presented some major problems.*

Henreid to wear a plain sports outfit, or a Palm Beach suit, and for Bergman to wear a simple street suit. Both recommendations were followed.

On Sundays, Wallis and Koch would meet with Curtiz at the latter's ranch to go over the script and try to improve some of the troublesome aspects. Julius Epstein recalls that Michael Curtiz, with whom he and his brother did six pictures, was a very fine director, "although he never learned the English language. Curtiz was marvelous on the visual side of directing. He knew just when the cigarette smoke should curl backwards; when to move; when not to move . . . . We all knew, of course, that the night before the story conferences Mike would get his directions [regarding the script development] from his wife, Bess Meredyth, who was one of the great silent screenwriters, and then come in and tell us what Bess had said. But sometimes Mike would forget what to say! I wish I had a tape recording of those story conferences!"

Casey Robinson had similar recollections: "I think Mike was one of the great directors of scenes. He was one of the great directors with people, especially young people. He knew nothing whatever about story. To talk story with Mike was hopeless . . . . He didn't get along with writers, because you couldn't talk to him, you know? He didn't know what the hell you were talking about. He saw it in pictures, and you supplied the stories."

Under the studio system, it was highly unusual for a writer to be on the stage or location during filming. Howard Koch says that "at the time . . . writers were supposed, when they finished a script, to disappear and get on another assignment and not bother their producer and director and actors." Casey Robinson notes: "I was practically never present on the stage during the shooting of a picture." And Julius Epstein: "In the old days writers weren't allowed on the set."

Koch recalled in 1973 that approximately two-thirds of the way through production he was getting the scenes down to the *Casablanca* set on the morning they were to be shot. As the distance between script and shooting narrowed and the pressures increased, disagreements between Curtiz and Koch erupted into quarrels. In 1973 Koch recalled:

> I realize the difference between us was mostly a matter of emphasis. Mike leaned strongly on the romantic elements of the story, while I was more interested in the characterizations and the political intrigues with their relevance to the world struggle against fascism. Surprisingly, these disparate approaches somehow meshed, and perhaps it was partly this tug-of-war between Curtiz and me that gave the film a certain balance.

A specific area of disagreement between Koch and Curtiz was the Paris flashback. According to Koch, he felt that those scenes were superfluous and that they would dissipate the tension in the primary narrative. Curtiz insisted on using them, and they were written and shot in accordance with his and Wallis's ideas. There are no Paris scenes in the play (and no recurring line, "Here's looking at *you*, kid"—probably written by the Epsteins).

Finally, Curtiz was running out of things to film. The picture was due to finish, but its ending still had not been resolved. In the play, Rick sends Laszlo and Ilsa off to the airport with the exit visas and then, his self-respect redeemed, he surrenders to Renault, the prefect of police, and Strasser. Other possibilities were discussed: Rick leaves Casablanca with Ilsa, Ilsa stays with Rick, Rick is killed while helping Laszlo and Ilsa escape. None seemed right. In one of Howard Koch's early treatments, after Rick sends Lois (Ilsa) off to the airport with Laszlo, he continues to cover Renault with his gun. Rick suggests they finish their chess game until the plane leaves:

RENAULT

It was my move, I believe.
(*He studies the board*)
Mmm—a very difficult position.

He moves a piece, then backs away as Rick advances to the board, still covering his friend with the gun.

RICK

That doesn't leave me but one move.
(*He makes it*)
Again the Prefect advances to the board, studies it.

RENAULT

There is no move. The Kings can't get out. We're checkmated.

RICK
(*grimly*)

I guess the game's finished.

At this moment the plane carrying Lois and Laszlo roars over the roof of the cafe. The gaze of Rick and Renault sweeps the ceiling. The SOUND of the plane diminishes.

RENAULT

Ricky, I was right. You *are* a sentimentalist.

FADE OUT.

With only a week to go in the filming schedule, the Epsteins came up with the solution to the ending (according to Julius Epstein). Ron Haver has described in his article on *Casablanca* in the June 1976 issue of *American Film* magazine what Julius Epstein told him: Late one night as they were driving down Sunset Boulevard toward Beverly Glen, he and his brother turned to each other at exactly the same time and shouted, "Round up the usual suspects." (This phrase, which is not in the play had been used by Renault throughout the film to show his disdain for the functions of his job.) The Epsteins immediately called Wallis and told him of their idea: Rick was to shoot Major Strasser at the airport, while Renault looks on. When the police arrive, the prefect announces "Major Strasser's been shot." A pause, Renault looks at Rick, and then says, "Round up the usual suspects." Renault and Rick go off together with the exit line, "[Louis], I think this is the beginning of a beautiful friendship."

This was actually an alternate line to the first choice: "Louis, I might have known you'd mix your patriotism with a little larceny." Obviously, the alternate line played better. Casey Robinson said in his Oral History that "the last line in the picture—'Louis, I think this is the beginning of a beautiful friendship'—that's Hal Wallis. He wrote that line, and it was marvelous!"

Everyone was delighted with the ending. It was upbeat, inspirational, and provided an ironic twist. Koch—not the Epsteins (or Casey Robinson) for some reason—was put back on the picture to rewrite the last two scenes in order to incorporate the new approach. Then another problem was eliminated. Wallis wrote to Curtiz on July 6 that "I think we have successfully

Bogart, Bergman, and director Michael Curtiz on the set of Casablanca.

licked the big scene between Ilsa and Rick at the airport by bringing Laszlo in at the finish of it." Wallis went on to say that it was difficult to write a convincing scene between the two in which Rick could persuade Ilsa to leave without him. However, bringing Laszlo in for an additional few lines made it impossible for Ilsa to protest further.

On July 17, when the company was shooting the climactic airport sequence involving Bogart, Bergman, Henreid, and Rains, Al Alleborn, the unit manager, in his report said in part:

> Report for Friday, 7-17-42. 45th shooting day.
>
> Company had a 9:00 o'clock call on Stage 1 to shoot the EXT[ERIOR] AIRPORT. First shot at 9:50 a.m. and the last one at 6:14 p.m. . . .
>
> During the day the company had several delays caused by arguments with Curtiz the director, and Bogart the actor. I had to go and get Wallis and bring him over to the set to straighten out the situation. At one time they sat around for a long time and argued, finally deciding on how to do the scene.
>
> There were also numerous delays due to the cast not knowing the dialogue, which was a rewritten scene that came out the night before.

After fifty-nine days of filming (eleven days over schedule), *Casablanca* finished on August 3, and Owen Marks completed editing the film a short while afterward. Max Steiner, Warners' prodigious and prolific composer since 1936, had been assigned to do the music on July 11, per Wallis's request. Steiner's custom was not to pay heed to a script or a film until it was shot, edited, and ready to be scored. Then he would sit in a projection room and watch—absorbing the material from a fresh, open vantage point with few or no preconceived ideas.

The song "As Time Goes By," written by Herman Hupfeld and originally sung by Frances Williams in a Broadway revue of 1931 called *Everybody's Welcome*, had been an integral part of *Everybody Comes to Rick's* and the photographed script. It stemmed from playwright Murray Burnett's visit to the nightclub in France where a black piano player was featured. According to Burnett, the music played there evoked his college days. At that time he was particularly fond of "As Time Goes By" (then current and popular), and he played it constantly on his record player in the fraternity house at Cornell.

Posed publicity photograph: Paul Henreid, Bergman, and Bogart.

Steiner, after viewing the film, did not like the idea of using "As Time Goes By." According to an interview with Steiner by Mark Schubart in either the August 2 or August 21, 1943 (the exact date is not clear on the clipping) edition of the New York newspaper, *PM*, he didn't care for the tune, didn't think it would make a good theme for Rick and Ilsa, and, most importantly and more to the point, would rather have composed an original melody to suit the occasion.

Naturally, film composers prefer to write their own songs in addition to the background score, because songs are published, played, and earn royalties for the composers, whereas in those days background scores were relegated to oblivion after the film had been shown for a few months.

Supposedly, Wallis went along with Steiner. With a new song, portions of a few scenes referring specifically to "As Times Goes By" would have to have been reshot, but it was confirmed that Ingrid Bergman had already had her hair cut very short for the role of Maria and was filming *For Whom the Bell Tolls* (she replaced Vera Zorina after a considerable number of scenes had been photographed). So reshooting was out of the question, and Steiner had to use "As Time Goes By." In the 1943 *PM* interview he was quoted as saying that he still didn't think much of the tune but admitted that it must have something to attract so much attention.

Steiner's use of the song in his background scoring is a classic example of how to dramatize and develop a piece of material to serve the needs of the picture. Also sprinkled throughout the evocative score are appropriate quotations from "Deutschland über Alles," Germany's national anthem, "Die Wacht am Rhein," a patriotic German song, and "La Marseillaise," the French national anthem. The Morocco milieu set forth in the main title music was a reorchestration of Steiner's North Africa desert music composed for *The Lost Patrol* (1934), which in turn is suggestive of Ippolitov-Ivanov's use of a folk tune in his *Caucasian Sketches*.

Wallis sent some music notes to Leo Forbstein, head of the music department, on September 2. Two excerpts from a much longer memo give an insight into his thinking about the scoring details:

> Start the piano as Ilsa and Laszlo come in the door . . . . [Later,] when Rick and Ilsa exchange glances, on the first of their closeups, start an orchestration using "As Time Goes By." And *score* the scene. Let Steiner do this. And carry this until right through the Exterior until the lights go out . . . .
>
> On the *Marseillaise*, when it is played in the Cafe, don't do it as though it was played by this small orchestra. Do it with a full scoring orchestra and get some body to it . . . . In the last reel, the last time that Bogart looks off and we cut to the

plane, I would like to see a dramatic pause in the music, just before the cut to the plane. Then as we cut to the plane, emphasize the motor noises and then, when you cut back to the scene, resume the music.

Casablanca cost approximately $950,000 (it was budgeted at $878,000)—not a cheap picture, but by no means an extremely expensive one for that time. There were two previews, one in Pasadena and the other in Huntington Park. Hal Wallis says in his memoirs that the audience seemed to like it but didn't rave. "And indeed several cards suggested we should show Rick and Louis escaping Casablanca as it looked as if they would be arrested when they got back to town."

On November 11, Wallis sent a memo to production manager Tenny Wright regarding a proposed epilogue scene:

There will be a retake on *Casablanca* involving Claude Rains and Humphrey Bogart, and about 50 or 60 extras. Free French uniforms will be required for all of these.

We will need the deck of the freighter on Stage 7. The scene is to be a night sequence with fog.

We will also require the interior of the Radio Room of this same ship.

Rains is in Pennsylvania, and I am asking Levee [his manager] to get him out here as quickly as possible as I want to make these scenes this week if possible.

Curtiz will shoot and . . . . I think it will probably take two nights to complete—shooting from 7:00 until 12:00 or 1:00.

Then the next day David O. Selznick wired Wallis:

DEAR HAL: SAW "CASABLANCA" LAST NIGHT. THINK IT IS A SWELL MOVIE AND AN ALL-AROUND FINE JOB OF PICTURE MAKING. TOLD JACK [L. WARNER] AS FORCIBLY AS I COULD THAT I THOUGHT IT WOULD BE A TERRIBLE MISTAKE TO CHANGE THE ENDING, AND ALSO THAT I THOUGHT THE PICTURE OUGHT TO BE RUSHED OUT . . . . I HAVE A FEW MINOR SUGGESTIONS TO MAKE, AND IF BY ANY CHANCE YOU WOULD CARE TO HAVE THEM I WILL BE GLAD TO PASS THEM ALONG, ALTHOUGH I AM SURE THAT YOU WILL FIND OUT THESE THINGS FOR YOURSELF AT PREVIEW.

The release date had been announced for June 1943, but in early November 1942 the Allies landed in North Africa—at Casablanca. After deciding not to film the new ending, Warners immediately planned to open the film in New York on Thanksgiving Day, only eighteen days after the landings. The general release date, January 23, 1943, came during the Roosevelt-Churchill-Stalin conferences at Casablanca.

The superb entertainment, the capturing and distillation of various moods then current, and the unplanned timing made the picture an outstanding success. It won the Academy Awards for best picture, direction, and screenplay. For the second time, Hal Wallis was presented the Irving Thalberg Award "for the most consistent high quality of production."

Ingrid Bergman was now, thanks to *Casablanca*, an extraordinarily popular star. Soon afterward she made her biggest hits: *For Whom the Bell Tolls*, *Gaslight*, *Spellbound*, *Saratoga Trunk*, *Notorious*.

As for Bogart, *Casablanca* established him as a romantic star and brought him to a high level of popularity that he maintained for seven years. And not too long after *Casablanca*, his new Warners contract made him the highest-paid actor in the world.

10

THE FACE IN THE MISTY LIGHT:
LAURA
(1944)

Through most of his life, Petrarch, the fourteenth-century Italian poet and scholar, kept writing and rearranging his poems about his beloved Laura. The dominant theme of his collection of lyrics is hopeless love, a spiritualized passion for the unattainable. Upon Laura's death, as described in the lyrics, the poet finds that his grief is as difficult to live with as was his former despair.

These poems of Petrarch dominated lyric poetry for centuries after, and the name Laura has been used by poets ever since in love poems addressed to similar idealized ladies. Robert Tofte entitled his 1597 collection of love lyrics *Laura;* Lord Byron used the name in his poem "Laura," and Schiller wrote a series of poems to Laura in the eighteenth century.

However, novelist, playwright, and screenwriter Vera Caspary, the author of the book *Laura,* answered when I asked if she had been influenced by this heritage, "There is no significance to my choice of the name 'Laura.' I've always liked the name. There's no more than that to it."

Sometime around 1940, Caspary had been struggling with an idea for a story about a detective who falls in love with a presumably dead idealized

woman whose life he investigates. But she didn't know how to solve the problem until she read an item in the newspaper about a young woman whose face was destroyed in an explosion. Now it was solved; Vera Caspary's heroine wasn't killed at all. Another person, whom everyone presumed to be Laura, was to have her face blown away by gunfire. And later Laura would come back to confront the lovelorn detective.

With these elements in mind Caspary wrote a play, but she was dissatisfied with it. The basic situation was worked out—acts one and two—but the solution and act three were not right. And she had not found the cynical columnist Waldo Lydecker. Putting the manuscript in a suitcase, she went to Hollywood: "I don't know when or how I discovered Waldo, but I thought of the character during some ordeals in the studios. And there came to mind the real killer; the man who does away with what he can't possess." The author didn't know anyone who would shoot a woman whom he couldn't own, so for a while the character eluded her.

Caspary denies that Waldo was based on Alexander Woollcott.* She told

* Woollcott was a well-known critic, commentator, and occasional actor who achieved strong influence on literary tastes beginning in the 1920s thanks to his strong-willed, iconoclastic, witty observations.

me that she had been reading several of Woollcott's books while living in a house, in Studio City, near Hollywood, whose owners had a Woollcott collection, so that she let herself be influenced by Woollcott's style. "Then I discussed the character with my friend [writer] Ellis St. Joseph, and he was so fascinated that he sat up with me night after night discussing the life and habits of the man. He *was* Waldo. Of course, he would never murder anyone, but my understanding of the character was deepened by Ellis's conversations."

When I spoke to Ellis St. Joseph about *Laura*, he told that his good friend Vera Caspary did have Alexander Woollcott in mind when they first began to talk about the book. "But the world of Waldo was not Vera's world, and I was able to discuss and describe aspects of that kind of person to her in considerable detail." As time went on, he noted, Waldo became increasingly villainous in Vera's eyes. "She was not sure how to present the story in narrative form, and I suggested that she read Wilkie Collins's novel, *The Moonstone*, and use that technique." Vera Caspary confirmed this to me.

The Moonstone (1868) is often called the first detective novel. This recounting of the theft of the fictitious Moonstone diamond is told by several different people who are judged best able to describe the various phases of the solution of the novel's plot.

In the novel *Laura*, the events came to be described in the first person

Vera Caspary, author of Laura.

by Waldo, then by Mark McPherson—the detective—and finally, in the last third of the book, by Laura. The book was published in early 1943 to great success, having been previously serialized in *Collier's* magazine in October and November of 1942 under the title *Ring Twice for Laura*. A synopsis of the serial appeared in the mimeographed story bulletins of all the major studios prior to the book's publication. Although it was recommended by some of the analysts in the story departments, apparently no producer or executive was interested.

Vera Caspary recalls that Hollywood's indifference did not break her heart, as she was working on the second version of the play at the time. Meanwhile, her agent, Monica McCall, who was handling the dramatic rights, had given a typescript of the book to a Broadway producer and director who liked the story and wanted not only to produce it but to collaborate with Caspary on the revised play. "I was flattered because he had a Broadway reputation, because he offered all of his Middle European charm along with an elegant lunch of blinis and caviar. His name was Otto Preminger."

> Mr. Preminger did not agree with me about one element
> in the dramatization. He wanted to make it a conventional
> detective story. I saw it as a psychological drama about people
> involved in a murder. We fell out over this, and I asked my
> old friend and collaborator George Sklar [the playwright and
> novelist] to work with me.

Years later, when asked what particularly interested him about *Laura*, Preminger responded: "The gimmick . . . . A girl you thought was dead automatically becomes a murder suspect by walking into her own apartment."

Despite the success of the novel, backers stayed away from the play project. Marlene Dietrich, who had read the book, expressed interest in playing the role in a film. "It seemed odd casting," said Vera Caspary, "but George [Sklar] and I, dazzled by Marlene in blue jeans and quantities of perfume, decided that, with certain adjustments, the idea was not impossible. In character this beautiful woman came closer to the independent girl who earned her living and pampered her lovers than anyone who has yet played the part."

Since the writers still wanted a theatrical production before movie rights were sold, they discussed a pre-Broadway tour with Miss Dietrich, who agreed to consider the idea. That night, after their meeting, Vera Caspary "remembered too vividly the time I had been incurably maimed by a [pre-Broadway] tryout," and with dire thoughts of all the potential disagreements with producer, director, and star, she decided—against the wishes of George Sklar—"to offer *Laura* as a movie and be done with the bitch." According to Caspary, only two studios showed even faint interest: MGM, with plans for a B mystery, and Twentieth Century-Fox. Otto Preminger had recently signed a contract with Fox as a director-actor. He had performed as an actor in *The Pied Piper* (1942) and *Margin for Error* (1943), in addition to directing the latter, and he was looking for another property to direct. He remembered *Laura* from New York and convinced the studio to buy the book in June 1943 for $30,000, allowing the writers—Caspary and Sklar—to retain the dramatic play rights.*

Earlier in his career, in the mid 1930s, Preminger had been under contract to Fox as a director. After testing him with two relatively modest pictures, Darryl Zanuck assigned Preminger to an important and big-budgeted costume drama, *Kidnapped* (1938). However, Zanuck and Preminger had a major falling out during filming, and Preminger was replaced on the picture by Alfred Werker. He couldn't get any work in Hollywood for the next few years, so he went to New York and started to produce and direct plays.

Shortly after Pearl Harbor, while Preminger was still in New York, Zanuck was away from the studio on duty as a colonel in the Signal Corps, for which he was filming documentary and training films. When he returned to Fox in June 1943, William Goetz, who had been Zanuck's assistant and in charge of the studio during his absence, left Fox. Goetz had been responsible for the rehiring of Preminger (originally as an actor only). Eventually Preminger met with Zanuck. They had not spoken since the *Kidnapped* episode five years earlier. According to Preminger, Zanuck told him to continue working on three properties (*Laura, Army Wives*—released as *In the Meantime, Darling*—and *Ambassador Dodd's Diary*—not filmed): "You can produce them, but you will never direct again as long as I am here at Fox," Preminger quotes Zanuck as saying. *In the Meantime, Darling* (1944) went before the cameras under Preminger's direction in the middle of December 1943—some time after Zanuck's return and months before *Laura* began filming. Zanuck put Preminger under Bryan Foy, an executive in charge of relatively low budget films.

Jay Dratler, a well-educated and cultured writer from the east who had done postgraduate work at the Sorbonne before writing some novels, was selected to do the adaptation and screeenplay of *Laura* because of his sophisticated and urbane background. He had been in Hollywood only about three years, working as a free-lance writer on a few undistinguished B films

* The play was not presented in New York until June 1947. Otto Kruger played Waldo, K. T. Stevens was Laura, and Hugh Marlowe played Mark.

and routine program pictures (*La Conga Nights, Meet Boston Blackie, Fly By Night.*)

Vera Caspary says that she was asked to work on the screenplay. "But I was sick and weary of an old passion. I'd worked too hard on the abandoned first play, the novel, the second play that had been re- and rewritten, and had heard the various ideas of the directors who had hoped to do the play. 'Let Laura stay dead in the first act,' I said. 'I'm through with her.' "

By October 30, 1943, Dratler had finished his first draft. He stayed very close to the novel with regard to plot, characters, and structure, even to the device of having Waldo narrate the first portion of the novel, followed by Mark, and then, in the last third, Laura. The ending also followed the book: Waldo, the cynical columnist, returns to Laura's apartment and repeats his attempt to kill her using a walking stick that conceals a gun that fires BB-shot.

According to Preminger, Foy did not care for the script. Preminger persuaded him to let Zanuck read it. On November 1, Zanuck sent five typewritten pages of notes on the first draft to Foy and Preminger. Some of his points were as follows:

> Waldo is the only well-drawn character throughout, and even his lines can be punched up with more sarcastic humor and ironic, sadistic wise-cracks. He should speak lines like *The Man Who Comes To Dinner* . . . .
>
> Laura is a mess. She is neither interesting nor attractive, and I doubt if any first-rate actress would ever play her. As it is now, she seems terribly naive—a complete sucker. It is bad enough for her to fall in love with a glorified pimp like Shelby Carpenter, but when she tries to protect him later on I feel that she is either a very stupid person or just a puppet . . . .
>
> By curing Shelby, we will help Laura's character. By "curing" I mean by making him a more attractive personality, for instance like [actor] Reggie Gardiner. Unless he is charming and debonair, and a very cultured pimp, then we will never have any respect for Laura . . . .
>
> But you still have to work on Laura. I can understand Mark [the detective] falling for her, even falling for her picture. But it is difficult for me to accept her falling for Mark. Their relationship is so brief. She is in a hell of a jam. It seems to me that her mind would go to anything but romance . . . .
>
> Mark is generally well drawn, but I think needs work. He shows flashes of a distinct characterization such as you might

find in *The Maltese Falcon* or *The Thin Man*. But these are only brief flashes. There ought to be more of Cagney about him. He should also have humor, but his humor is entirely different from Waldo's. His is the humor of the police desk, the morgue; the humor of a guy who is used to dealing with tough people. Then when he comes up against this gorgeous creature, Laura, we see that it is something new to him . . . .

All of the people, Mark included, should seem as if they stepped out of *The Maltese Falcon*—everyone a distinct, different personality. This is what made *The Maltese Falcon*. It wasn't the plot, it was the amazing characters. The only chance this picture has of becoming a big-time success is if these characters emerge as real outstanding personalities. Otherwise it will become nothing more than a blown-up Whodunit . . . .

When he [Mark] examines her [Laura's] apartment I would like to see him look at her lingerie, among other things. He looks at her shoes, her clothes, and he keeps looking back at the picture. He tries to reconstruct her. She begins to get under his skin.

The only place that I did not like the voice [narration] at all was when Laura starts to tell her own story . . . . It was good with the other people because you had to explain what they were thinking about, but for Laura you do not need it because then it [the story] becomes straight action.

It is evident that at this stage Zanuck was no longer thinking in terms of a low-budget picture. His references in the notes to a "first-rate actress," "big-time success," "blown-up Whodunit" and his overall interest in the property indicate that it was now to be an A picture in Zanuck's domain. An examination of the first draft of the script indicates that Zanuck's points were well taken for the most part. Ex-newspaper reporter Ring Lardner, Jr., who had recently collaborated on the script for the Spencer Tracy–Katharine Hepburn film *Woman of the Year*, was then assigned to rewrite Dratler's version. He had been working with Preminger at Fox on a screenplay that dealt with the rise of Nazism (*Ambassador Dodd's Dairy*). When that project was scuttled he moved over to *Laura* and completed his revised screenplay three weeks later. Lardner retained Dratler's structure but modified the dialogue in many instances in an attempt to reflect the changes requested by Zanuck. Laura was built up, Shelby acquired more charm—and even sang and played the piano at a party. However, Laura's narration remained during the final portion of the film. Lardner did two more drafts with Dratler—or using Dratler's material—making only minor changes.

Meanwhile, Preminger needed a director, since, according to Preminger, Zanuck would not let him direct. Preminger and Dana Andrews recall that Lewis Milestone was offered *Laura* but turned it down. Vera Caspary remembers John Brahm (*The Lodger*) telling her that he rejected it; Preminger says that Walter Lang (associated primarily with musicals at Fox) also declined. Rouben Mamoulian accepted. He recently had directed the original production of *Oklahoma!* on Broadway. After reading the novel and the Dratler–Lardner script, Mamoulian suggested that Samuel Hoffenstein, who had worked on Mamoulian's film versions of *Dr. Jekyll and Mr. Hyde* (1932), *Love Me Tonight* (1932), and *Song of Songs* (1933), be put on a rewrite with Hoffenstein's current collaborator, Betty Reinhardt. Reinhardt, among other things, had written some pictures in the Maisie series at MGM. Just before beginning work on the next revised script, Zanuck held a story conference with Preminger, Mamoulian, and Hoffenstein on March 20, 1944. He then dictated notes to all of the them:

> Our main, our central character is a nonentity. On one page she is looking for a job (via the fountain pen endorsement which, incidentally, is very good), but on another page we find that she has a rich aunt who travels with the smart set and sleeps with gigolos . . . . I do not know whether she

Deleted scene from Laura: *Vincent Price as Shelby singing "You'll Never Know" at a party.* (COPYRIGHT © 1944 TWENTIETH CENTURY-FOX FILM CORP. ALL RIGHTS RESERVED.)

[Laura] was a school girl who wanted a career, or whether she was a rich girl who was trying to break away from her aunt and society by trying to get a job.

The decision about which actor would play Waldo, Zanuck noted, would, of course, influence the writing. If it was to be Laird Cregar, "you should look again at those scenes in *Blood and Sand* [the 1941 Mamoulian–Fox version] in which he was so magnificent as the sardonic super-critic." Shelby would have to be rewritten slightly to fit Reginald Gardiner. "While Vincent Price would have been good, I am sure Reggie will give it a splendid flavor":

> Starting on page 71 . . . I want to dissolve to Mark in front of a little New York newsreel theater. He glances at his watch. We feel that he is killing time. He goes into the theater and sits down in the darkness. A newsreel is on, of course, and the woman in the newsreel dissolves into Laura. Madame Chiang Kai-Shek dissolves into Laura. A girl on a surfboard dissolves into Laura. Every woman on the screen begins to dissolve into Laura, and finally the scene is filled with Laura. Mark gets up and goes out.* We then dissolve back to scene 141 on page 71, and we put in the business from scene 116 where Mark's voice comes over as he looks at her clothes, thinks about her, and begins to realize that she has really gotten under his skin . . . .
>
> On page 128, when Waldo says to Laura, "With you a lean, strong body is the measure of the man," I do not believe it for a moment. This is not Laura. She is not a woman who goes for every guy with a good physique. She is nothing like this. I think this remark hurts her character terribly . . . .
>
> I can understand a certain mothering instinct making her like the worthless Shelby. He is charming and weak, but wonderful women frequently marry likable men even though they are weak.

While the final draft of the script was being written, casting proceeded. There had been thoughts about Jennifer Jones for the title role (she had recently done *The Song of Bernadette* on loan to Fox), and, according to some sources, Hedy Lamarr. Then Gene Tierney, a Fox contract star, was agreed upon instead. Tierney liked the script, but after one reading was unenthusiastic about her role. The time on camera was less than she would

---

* This suggested sequence was not included in the next revision or in any subsequent version in the Fox files.

Wardrobe test for Laura: Note the original director's (Rouben Mamoulian) name on the slate. (COPYRIGHT © 1944 TWENTIETH CENTURY-FOX FILM CORP. ALL RIGHTS RESERVED.)

like, she noted, "and who wants to play a painting? The treatment of the story seemed unorthodox . . . . In truth, only Otto Preminger had absolute faith in the project."

Tierney had heard that Jennifer Jones had turned down the part, and she admits that it wasn't so much the part she minded as the idea of being second choice. "Anyway, it [Laura] was an escape from . . . all the half-caste girls I had played . . . . a Polynesian, a Eurasian, an Arab, and a Chinese. Strangely enough I had played highly spirited roles in New York. [Then in Hollywood] I used to look in the mirror and wonder how this Brooklyn girl ever could have gotten transplanted so far."

Apparently Zanuck had John Hodiak in mind for the role of the detective. Dana Andrews told me that one night when director Lewis Milestone and Andrews were driving home from location on *The Purple Heart* (1944), Milestone handed Andrews the script of *Laura*, which Preminger had asked Milestone to direct. Milestone had turned the picture down, but he told Andrews that the part of the detective could make him a star. Andrews read the script and set out to get the role. He met Preminger at a party at Milestone's house. Preminger told him he thought that John Hodiak was set for the part and that Zanuck thought Hodiak had considerable sex appeal in Hitchcock's *Lifeboat* (1943). Later, Andrews was able to get Hedda Hopper to put a hint in her column about "Andrews for *Laura*": "Then one day on the back lot while shooting *Wing and a Prayer* [1944]," Andrews recalls, "Virginia Zanuck, Darryl's wife, and I had a long discussion about various things while her young son Richard and a friend were playing around the Navy planes. Finally she said, 'You know, Dana, I never thought of you as a leading man, but as a character type. But I've seen a different side of your personality today.' "

Since he was usually cast as the man who loses the girl, Andrews told her, he would naturally play that role differently from the way he would play the leading man. "She looked at me and said, 'You really believe that?' and I said, 'Of course.' That was on a Saturday. On Monday morning Preminger called me up and said, 'Dana, I don't know what happened, but Zanuck says that you have the part in *Laura*.' "

It appears that Reginald Gardiner (a friend of Zanuck's) was thought of originally for Shelby. Then Vincent Price was considered, then Gardiner again, and finally Price was cast. Mamoulian apparently recommended Judith Anderson for the role of Laura's aunt.

Waldo presented special problems. Monty Woolley, under contract to Fox, was mentioned by Zanuck as early as November 1943. He was a logical choice, having played the role of Sheridan Whiteside—a take-off on Alexander Woollcott—in the original Broadway company of *The Man Who*

Came to Dinner (1939) and in the Warner Bros. film of 1941. Laird Cregar, under contract to Fox, had been considered for the role of Waldo, but Preminger did not want Cregar: "I . . . felt that the only possibility to make this a success was if people did not know from the beginning that this amusing and very urbane and civil character was the villain. You must have a man who either is unknown or has never played heavies before. A friend, Felix Féfé [Ferry], who knew everyone, knew Clifton Webb, who at that time was playing in Noel Coward's play *Blithe Spirit* downtown in Los Angeles." Preminger attended a performance and was fascinated by Clifton Webb, to whom he immediately gave a copy of the script. "He loved it and wanted to play the role. When I went to Zanuck and suggested him, the reaction was completely negative." Casting director Rufus LeMaire was present at this interview and felt immediately that Zanuck would not like Clifton Webb. According to Preminger,

> he [LeMaire] said: "You can't have Clifton Webb for this part. He flies." I said: "What do you mean?" I didn't even understand what he meant. I already knew that Clifton Webb was a little effeminate, but that didn't bother me at all. I said I would like to make a test with him.

Finally Zanuck agreed to a test, but Webb refused. According to Preminger, Webb told him that if Zanuck wanted to see him he could come to the theater and observe him in *Blithe Spirit*. "I don't know your Miss Tierney and I don't want to make a test with her." Then he agreed to test with a monologue from *Blithe Spirit*. Zanuck was adamant about having Webb do a scene from *Laura*. Besides, he wanted to see how the script would play. Preminger felt that Zanuck's belief in the script had been shaken because so many directors had turned it down. Undaunted, Preminger shot the test—a monologue from *Blithe Spirit*—without Zanuck's permission. Preminger recalls Mamoulian at the time being "out of town, or somewhere." Mamoulian declines to comment. "When it was finished," says Preminger, "I took it to Zanuck's projection room, absolutely ready to be fired, and ran it for him. It was beautifully photographed and Clifton played it very well. He knew what Zanuck's objection might be, and he avoided that completely [referring to the previously mentioned "flying"]. Zanuck looked at me, and being a professional, he liked it. He said: 'You son-of-a-bitch, I told you I don't want to see the play, but okay, he can play the part.' "

Waldo, in the novel, is described as being 52 years old, 6 feet 3 inches tall, heavy, with soft flesh, sporting a graying Van Dyke beard and a black homburg. In Jay Dratler's first draft of the screenplay he is referred to as

The above deleted scene from Laura, *directed by Rouben Mamoulian, was retaken by Otto Preminger. Judith Anderson's dress was radically different.* (COPYRIGHT © 1944 TWENTIETH CENTURY-FOX FILM CORP. ALL RIGHTS RESERVED.)

a "middle-aged, bearded, raconteur, dramatic critic, man-about-several towns, and oft-misquoted wit." Webb, in his early fifties, was tall, lean, beardless, and elegant, with a rather haughty manner. He had been a dancer and then a Broadway musical comedy star in the late 1920s and early 1930s, going on to star in such nonmusical plays as Oscar Wilde's *The Importance of Being Earnest* and the first national touring company of *The Man Who Came to Dinner* (as Whiteside-Woollcott).

Although *Laura* was announced as his film debut, actually he had played supporting roles in a few silent films, such as *Polly with a Past* (1920) with Ina Claire, *New Toys* (1925) with Richard Barthelmess, and *Heart of a Siren* (1925) with Barbara La Marr. In 1935 MGM signed him to a contract after the tremendous success of the 1933 Broadway revue, *As Thousands Cheer*, in which he starred. Webb was to be MGM's answer to RKO's Fred Astaire. His first film, *Elegance,* was to be based on the story of Maurice, the famous ballroom dancer. Joan Crawford was to play Walton, his partner. But the film was not made, and after eighteen months of inactivity the MGM contract was canceled. Webb went back to the theater.

The writing team of Samuel Hoffenstein and Betty Reinhardt completed their revision of *Laura* on April 18, 1944, and rehearsals, under Mamoulian's direction, began immediately. Mamoulian was a strong advocate of rehearsing for a week or two before the start of shooting and had done so on most, if not all, of his previous productions.

At this point, events become confusing. On May 15, after Mamoulian had shot for eighteen days, Preminger took over as director as well as producer, and Mamoulian left Fox. One version of the circumstances leading to Mamoulian's exit is that Preminger had been undermining Mamoulian, hoping all along to take over as director. According to this story, Mamoulian finally went to Zanuck and eventually resigned. Preminger's version is that Mamoulian's footage was not good and Zanuck was unhappy. "Everything was blamed on me," said Preminger. "Mamoulian was to start the picture again, but without any 'interference' from me. In the meantime Mamoulian, who didn't talk to me, who didn't permit me on the set, had also gone to Zanuck. He started again, and it was worse than before . . . . [Zanuck] took him off the picture, went back to his office, called me and said: 'You can start directing on Monday.' "

Dana Andrews recalls another version: At the party mentioned earlier, when he first talked with Preminger about playing in *Laura*, Andrews remembers Preminger discussing his (Preminger's) concept of the detective as being "a highly educated criminologist, rather than just a tough cop." According to Andrews, Mamoulian apparently was going along with this approach when rehearsals and shooting began. "So I was thinking about an intellectual type," says Andrews. "Then, after two weeks or so of filming, Zanuck returned from New York. I was told to report to his office. When I arrived, Rouben and Otto were seated on either side of Zanuck. Zanuck said to me, 'I saw the rushes. I don't think the detective should be the kind of character you're trying to play. We'll have to change that. This guy has got to be a regular cop. We have this beautiful girl—high society, and all that. We need the contrast!" Andrews remembers Preminger saying, "I told Rouben that this was wrong," and Mamoulian, incensed, retorting, "I told *you!* You talked me into it!" Then Andrews left the room. "That was Saturday," says Andrews. "On Monday we had a new director. Preminger took over." When I discussed all this with Mamoulian, he requested that he not be quoted in any way with regard to *Laura*, obviously regarding the entire experience as extremely unpleasant and, in his view, unworthy of comment.

At first there was considerable tension when Preminger began directing. Dana Andrews even called Samuel Goldwyn, who shared Andrews's contract with Fox, to see if Goldwyn could get him off the picture. That didn't work.

"Judith Anderson and Otto did not get along at all," Andrews told me. Miss Anderson recalled, "We were all on edge and very tense. Preminger's direction was Germanic in approach. He saw the picture his way. There was a change of everything, and conflicts about everything. I much preferred Mamoulian's direction. It would have been a happier experience if he had been directing."

The original portrait of Laura made for the film had been painted by Mamoulian's wife, Azadia, a popular Hollywood artist, but when Preminger took over he had a photographic portrait of Gene Tierney shot by Fox still photographer Frank Polony. It was enlarged and then painted over by the Fox Special Effects Department to make it appear to be an original painting. In the novel, the portrait was described as being done "by an imitator of [Eugene Edward] Speicher."

Bonnie Cashin was assigned as wardrobe designer. At that time she was relatively low in the Fox echelon (she was on Preminger's low-budget *In the Meantime, Darling*), but subsequently she became a famous designer of women's fashions. At least one outfit worn by Judith Anderson was changed in the retake of her first scene in the film. With regard to Gene Tierney's wardrobe, it is difficult to say if any changes were made. It is not clear how many (or, indeed, if any) scenes with her were photographed before Mamoulian left the film.

Cameraman Lucien Ballard was replaced by Joseph La Shelle after Mamoulian left. "Ballard had been close with Mamoulian," La Shelle told me. "Otto was responsible for putting me on the picture." La Shelle had been a director of photography for only a short time before *Laura*, having been promoted from camera operator. (La Shelle had photographed Clifton Webb's test for Preminger.) According to La Shelle, Preminger discussed the photographic style with him and requested a continuous camera flow from one room to another and from medium shot to closeup (rather than a cut) whenever it served a purpose.

According to Gene Tierney, La Shelle was determined to make a success of his big opportunity. "He would take ages to light a scene. Every time I heard him say, 'No, no, it's not right,' I could feel my teeth clench, and I knew there went another hour or two of waiting for the lights to be reset." She was on the set before the sun came up and not home until eight or nine in the evening. Once Oleg Cassini, Tierney's dress-designer husband, furious over the eternal delays, walked onto the set and took her by the arm. "Come on," he roared, "it's not worth it. Nothing is worth it. We're going home." And they did.

"Oleg knew better," Tierney says. "The effort was worthwhile . . . . Preminger . . . drove himself, and us, so hard! He was simply tireless. When the rest of the cast seemed ready to drop from exhaustion, Otto would still muster as much vigor as when the day began."

The question of retakes of Mamoulian's material is uncertain. Joseph La

Shelle told me that although only the bare minimum were requested by Zanuck (presumably those scenes involving Dana Andrews's interpretation and other problem areas), in actuality Preminger gradually kept sneaking in additional scenes to be retaken during the shooting schedule until almost everything was redone. "We're not going to leave any scene at all of Mamoulian's in this picture," Preminger confided to La Shelle during the course of filming, as La Shelle remembers it. Andrews does not recall how much, specifically, of Mamoulian's footage was reshot. From all accounts, apparently the opening scene in Waldo's apartment, with the various art objects, and the dialogue between Waldo (in his opulent bath) and Mark were retained from Mamoulian's direction.

At the end of May (two weeks after Preminger took over as director) and during the first two weeks of June, Samuel Hoffenstein and Betty Reinhardt revised the last part of the screenplay. Departing from the novel and previous drafts of the script, it was decided at this point to have a sawed-off shotgun hidden in a secret compartment in the large antique clock in Laura's

Filming on the Laura *set representing Waldo's apartment. Clifton Webb (Waldo) and Gene Tierney in front of the camera; producer-director Otto Preminger behind camera.* (COPYRIGHT © 1944 TWENTIETH CENTURY-FOX FILM CORP. ALL RIGHTS RESERVED.)

In the filming of Laura *under Otto Preminger's direction, Laura takes the sawed-off shotgun hidden in the antique clock in her apartment and hides it in the storage room of her apartment building. This was changed completely in the subsequent retakes ordered by Darryl F. Zanuck.* (COPYRIGHT © 1944 TWENTIETH CENTURY-FOX FILM CORP. ALL RIGHTS RESERVED.)

apartment. This weapon took the place of the concealed gun in Waldo's walking stick. Now, after realizing that Waldo is the murderer, Laura takes the gun and hides it in the storage room in her apartment building. She then goes to Waldo's apartment building to persuade him to get away before Mark arrests him. She tells him she found the gun, but not to worry; it is put away in her golf bag in the attic. Waldo promises to leave the city and Laura returns to her own apartment building.

Shortly afterward, Mark goes to Waldo's empty apartment. He walks to a clock—the twin of the one in Laura's apartment, which Waldo had tried to reclaim earlier. After discovering that the hidden recess in the clock is empty, Mark realizes what is about to happen and leaves immediately. Meanwhile, Waldo, having retrieved the gun from the storage room in Laura's apartment building, presses the front buzzer at her apartment. He is on the verge of killing her when Mark intervenes.

Vera Caspary remembers meeting Preminger on the Fox lot at about this time and being asked if she would like to read the script. She did, and then went to see Preminger in his office. Her chief complaint was (and is) the use of the baroque clock in which Waldo Lydecker hides the gun. In the novel,

Waldo's gun is hidden in his cane. This was not merely a murder story device, a shock to the reader, and a menace to the heroine, but a Freudian symbol of Waldo's impotence and destructiveness—actually the theme of the novel, according to Caspary. She contends that Preminger argued that a gun capable of destroying a woman's face could not possibly have been contained in a walking stick. Ballistics experts had been consulted, and besides, Preminger said, no one would understand the symbolism. Says Caspary, "I had done research in museums and consulted a specialist in antique weapons . . . . a drawing [had been made] of the walking stick with a diagram of the concealed weapon. I offered to show this to Mr. Preminger. He was not interested."

Dana Andrews remembers recording voice-over narration to be used in the second part of the story, but it was decided to drop all narration except for Waldo's in the first part of the film. There was even narration by Mark intended for the famous scene in which he returns to Laura's apartment, goes through her things, and stares at her portrait. During this time the audience realizes he has fallen in love with a woman who is presumed to be dead.

Also lost along the way was a scene at Ebbetts Field, where Mark questions Shelby while watching a ball game. This scene was to follow Mark's initial encounter with Shelby in Laura's aunt's apartment, and it had

Deleted scene from Laura: *Mark (Dana Andrews) questions Shelby (Vincent Price) while watching a ballgame at Ebbetts Field. The urbane Waldo (Clifton Webb) is impervious to the surroundings.* (COPYRIGHT © 1944 TWENTIETH CENTURY-FOX FILM CORP. ALL RIGHTS RESERVED.)

appeared in each version of the script. One scene, included in all previous versions of the script and originating in the novel, but excluded from the latest Hoffenstein-Reinhardt revision, took place at Laura's presumed funeral. This, of course, was before it was discovered that Laura was not the woman who was killed. In this version, curiosity seekers crashed into the funeral parlor while the eulogy was being delivered.

Following the completion of the filming and editing, a rough cut was shown to Zanuck. "He didn't like it," recounts Preminger. "The picture was over and he said: 'Well, we missed the boat on this one,' and left. That night, I remember it was raining in California, and my poor cutter, Lou Loeffler, and I were standing there, in front of my car in the parking lot. He couldn't understand it. You always know, when you run a film for the first time, the rough-cut, if there is something to it. We felt there was."

Zanuck maintained that the fault was with the last fifteen minutes, which he wanted to rewrite and retake. Zanuck dictated his thoughts to his secretary and assigned another staff writer, Jerome Cady, to write the revisions. Cady had graduated from B movies during the war to work on such films as *The Purple Heart* (1944) and *Wing and a Prayer* (1944). Toward the end of July the new scenes were being shot. The altered approach picked up with the scene in Laura's apartment just before Waldo leaves. In this version, Waldo does not leave the building, but instead waits in the shadows toward the rear of the corridor, outside the servants' entrance to Laura's apartment. Inside, Mark opens the inner door of the twin baroque clock and discovers the gun. He then describes to Laura how Waldo shot Diane Redfern, the model, thinking she was Laura. The scene continued on as we know it from the eventually released film—with the important exception of some speeches by Laura to Mark shortly after he finds the gun:

LAURA
(*referring to Waldo*)
I owe him everything I am.

MARK
(*impatiently*)
Just because he endorsed that pen five years ago, for a nice fat check—

LAURA
He told you that story, too?

MARK
It's true, isn't it?

LAURA
(*shaking her head*)

You see, Mark, you simply don't understand Waldo. He dramatizes everything. To him, I, like everything else, am only half real. The other half exists only in his own mind. The story he told you about the pen was one he had written for his column. Once he writes something, he believes it. Do you know where he *actually* first found me? In a night court. I had been picked up for vagrancy.

(*Mark reacts as from a physical blow.*)

MARK

Vagrancy?

LAURA

Oh, I wasn't guilty. It was just something that happens every day, I suppose. I came to New York, looking for a career. Highest honors in art school back home—the usual background. But I couldn't get a start. One night I found myself locked out of my room. They picked me up on a bench in Central Park.

(*she shakes her head unhappily at the memory*)

The judge wouldn't believe my "hard luck story." But Waldo believed me. He was in court, gathering material for his column. He came forward and paid my fine. Then he called Bullit and Company, and got me a job. I went to work the same day.

(*she looks up at him*)

It isn't easy to forget anything so wonderful as that.

Preminger did not like the material and says, "When I handed the new script to the actors, they too found it ridiculous. I told them we had to do it nonetheless." Dana Andrews remembers the performers thinking this one aspect of the revised scenes laughable.

Later, a screening was arranged for Zanuck of the entire film, including the insertion of the new closing scenes. The popular columnist and radio commentator Walter Winchell, an old friend of Zanuck's, was a guest at the evening showing, along with Preminger, Loeffler, and Zanuck. Apparently Winchell reacted very well to the film. According to Preminger, when the picture was over Winchell said to Zanuck: "Darryl, that was big time—big time—Great, great, great! But you are going to change the ending? What's happening at the end? I don't understand." Then Zanuck asked Preminger if he wanted to have the old ending back. "I said: 'Yes, sure.' He said: 'Okay.' I threw everything out, all the retakes, [and] put the old ending back." Preminger's memory is not entirely accurate. The dialogue reproduced above was eliminated, but the rest of the modifed scenes and retakes remained in the film.

The picture was now ready to be scored. Composer David Raksin recalls, "The word was around the studio that it was a 'hard luck picture'—from which all sensible people shy away for fear of being tainted . . . . Preminger . . . wanted the top composer [at Fox], Alfred Newman. But Al, who as chief of the music department had more films currently in work than he could handle, had heard the rumors, so he declined the honor." Next it was offered to Bernard Herrmann, who promptly turned it down. Raksin, on staff, was then assigned. "I liked the picture at once but was disheartened at a screening to hear Zanuck immediately zero in on an essential scene in which . . . the detective . . . wanders disconsolately around Laura's apartment at night. I gathered that the sequence had already been severely shortened, and now it was about to be reduced still further . . . . I was heard to interject, 'But, if you cut that scene, nobody will understand that the detective is in love with Laura . . . . This is one of those scenes,' said I, 'in which music could tip the balance—tell the audience how the man feels. And if it doesn't work, you can still trim the sequence.' Permission granted to try."

In the novel Waldo explains that "old tunes had been as much a part of Laura as her laughter . . . . A hearty and unashamed lowbrow, she had listened to Brahms but had heard Kern." Jerome Kern's *Roberta,* in the fall of 1933, was Laura's first attendance at an opening night with Waldo. "Smoke Gets in Your Eyes," from that score, is mentioned specifically in Vera Caspary's book. In all the drafts of the script, "Smoke Gets in Your Eyes" is referred to as "one of her favorites." It emanates from her phonograph, is heard being played by three musicians at the restaurant where Waldo and Mark dine, and is indicated to be used as underscoring throughout the montage depicting Laura's rise in the business world. It is not clear whether an attempt was made to acquire the rights for the use of the song or not. Both Raksin and Preminger refer to the latter's desire to use George Gershwin's "Summertime" as the key theme, but it was not available for use in this context. Raksin told me that Alfred Newman at one time was thinking of using his extremely popular and enduring theme from *Street Scene* (1931) but was talked out of it by his orchestrator, Edward Powell. Raksin met with Preminger in Newman's office. He was not aware at the time that Preminger had tried to get "Summertime" for use in the picture. Now Preminger told Raksin that he intended to use Duke Ellington's

"Sophisticated Lady" as the theme. Raksin replied that much as he admired the tune and its urbane composer he thought it wrong for this film, because of the accretion of ideas and associations that a song already so well known would evoke in the audience. Raksin also suggested that Preminger probably favored that piece as much for the coincidence of its title with his own conception of Laura as for its music. Recalls Raksin: " 'But the girl is a whore—she's a whore!' Preminger stormed. 'By whose standards, Mr. Preminger?' said I."

It was agreed that if over the weekend Raksin could come up with a melody that Preminger liked, it would be used, otherwise "Sophisticated Lady" definitely would be purchased and interpolated. Raksin says:

> All weekend I struggled with the idea . . . . I was tied up in knots, in trouble emotionally and out of touch with myself. On Saturday I had received a letter from a lady with whom I was in love and to whom I was married. All I could make of it was that it said something I didn't want to hear, so I put it in my pocket and hoped it would go away.
>
> By Sunday night I knew that my big chance was fading fast: I didn't really believe in any of the themes I had written, and I was beginning to think that a wiser man would have known it was time to end the pain and give up. From the time I was a boy, when the music wouldn't flow I would prop a book or a poem on the piano and improvise. The idea was to divert my mind from conscious awareness of music-making. I hadn't done that for a long time—and certainly didn't intend to try to outwit my sorrowing mind, but I took the letter out of my pocket, put it up on the piano and began to play. Suddenly the meaning of the words on the page became clear to me: She was saying Hail, Farewell, Better Luck Next Life and— GET LOST! Knowing that, I felt the last of my strength go, and then—without willing it—I was playing the first phrase of what you know as "Laura" . . . .
>
> I feel certain that the reason people responded as they do to that melody, in the picture and on its own, is that it is "about" love, specifically about that yearning particular to unrequited love.

After the so-called hard-luck film was released to popular and critical acclaim, the studio received an unusual amount of mail asking about the music and noting its lack of availability on sheet music and records. The interest was so great that Johnny Mercer was engaged to write a lyric, and

"Laura" was published and recorded as a popular song. It soon became number one on the Hit Parade and a phenomenal record seller. The song, of course, has become a classic.

Another film composer, Elmer Bernstein, sums up the relationship of the picture to the music: "The film portrayed a man falling in love with a ghost. The mystique was supplied by the insistence of the haunting melody. He [the detective] could not escape it. It was everywhere . . . . We may not remember what Laura was like, but we never forget that she *was* the music."

In Gene Tierney's autobiography, she speaks candidly about her role as Laura: "I never felt my own performance was much more than adequate. I am pleased that audiences still identify me with Laura, as opposed to not being identified at all. Their tributes, I believe, are for the *character*—the dreamlike Laura—rather than any gifts I brought to the role."

Laura is composed of several seemingly diverse elements, which when brought together yield an intriguing aura. The film transcends the psychological mystery-suspense and detective genres by superimposing significant portions of urbane wit and off-beat romance. In addition, *Laura* has some indirect echoes of Daphne du Maurier's *Rebecca* and the subsequent 1940 Selznick–Hitchcock film adaptation of the novel. And in a way, *Laura* is a forerunner of certain aspects of Hitchcock's superb *Vertigo* (1958).* Both Mark McPherson, the detective in *Laura,* and "Scottie" Ferguson, the detective in *Vertigo*, are fascinated by a woman whom they believe to be dead but who turns out to be alive. Vera Caspary's original idea of a woman thought to be dead becoming a murder suspect by walking into her own apartment was a good device in a well-plotted novel with at least a few characters of more than one-dimensional interest. Preminger, fortunately, felt strongly that the unusual blend would work.

Vincent Price, who had known Preminger for some time and previously had acted under his direction in the 1938 Broadway stage production of *Outward Bound*, said to me that Preminger had an implicit knowledge of the pseudo-sophisticated world. "And he had an extra ability to give each one of the characters in *Laura* an underlying sense of evil."

* Based on the novel *D'Entre les Morts* by Pierre Boileau and Thomas Narcejac.

11

WAVES OF LOVE OVER THE FOOTLIGHTS:
ALL ABOUT EVE
(1950)

Writer and director Joseph L. Mankiewicz has always been intrigued by the theater. His primary interest is in the "inhabitants of the theater—those who cause it to exist—its creative commune." Drama books of various kinds, particularly biographies, fill his bookcases. He often thought about writing and directing a film telling the story of how a great actress achieved fame, starting with her dressing preparations on the night she is to receive a major award and then flashing back into her life.

Mankiewicz also became increasingly interested in the award itself as a symbol. "Together with the conniving and soliciting and maneuvering that goes on for the acquisition of it—and, in the end, the strangely unenduring gratification it provides, award winning can often be followed, almost reactively, by a period of depression," Mankiewicz has said. But he always felt his general idea needed some additional element to make it different. Then Twentieth Century-Fox's associate story editor James Fisher reread a short story called "The Wisdom of Eve." The story deals with Eve Harrington, a stagestruck girl who plays upon the sympathies of Margola Cranston, an aging and happily married Broadway actress. Eve becomes her understudy and then ruthlessly attempts to replace her both on the

200

IT'S ALL ABOUT WOMEN---AND THEIR MEN!

"*all about eve*"

Darryl F. Zanuck presents BETTE DAVIS · ANNE BAXTER · GEORGE SANDERS · CELESTE HOLM in **ALL ABOUT EVE** with GARY MERRILL · HUGH MARLOWE · Thelma Ritter · Marilyn Monroe · Gregory Ratoff Barbara Bates · Walter Hampden · Produced by DARRYL F. ZANUCK Written for the Screen and Directed by JOSEPH L. MANKIEWICZ 20th CENTURY-FOX

stage and in her husband's affections. Margola's husband is referred to as a pompous English producer-director. Though Eve fails in this attempt, she does win the lead in a new play written by Lloyd Richards, Margola's favorite playwright, and eventually steals Richards away from his wife Karen, also an actress, who is Margola's best friend.

Actress and writer Mary Orr, the author of the story, is the wife of director-playwright Reginald Denham. As she recalls it, when Denham staged *The Two Mrs. Carrolls* on Broadway in 1943–1944, he and his wife became friendly with the show's star, Elisabeth Bergner, and her husband, Paul Czinner, the Hungarian producer-director. One night when the four had dinner together, Bergner told them about an experience she and Czinner had had with an unscrupulous young actress they had befriended.

Mary Orr, author of a short story, "The Wisdom of Eve," upon which All About Eve *was based.*

Mary Orr realized the anecdote had possibilities as a magazine short story. She wrote it, and after considerable delay it was purchased by *Cosmopolitan* and published in May 1946. Although it was offered to all the major film companies, including Fox, it could not be sold. (The fact that Eve was a completely unscrupulous and unsympathetic character who never suffered retribution evidently limited her chances of appearing on the screen.) So Mary Orr adapted the story as a radio drama, and it was done on NBC's *Radio City Playhouse* on January 24, 1949. Claudia Morgan played the established star and Marilyn Erskine was the protégée.

Mary Orr wrote to me regarding Eve's true-life prototype: "She [Elisabeth Bergner] never called her by any name except that 'awful creature,' 'that little bitch,' etc. But when I wrote 'Eve' she was a combination of many young actresses I had met, including a great deal of myself. For some reason everyone wanted to think she was based on a real girl. I suppose she was, but the girl was in the plural not the singular."

After rereading "The Wisdom of Eve" in the spring of 1949, James Fisher felt it should come to the attention of Joseph L. Mankiewicz, whose treatment of women in *A Letter to Three Wives* (1949) had charmed the public. Mankiewicz found Eve's character intriguing, and the story provided him with the vital gimmick he needed to solidify the theatrical story idea he had been mulling over.

On April 29, 1949, Mankiewicz wrote a memo to Darryl F. Zanuck, production head of Fox, where Mankiewicz was under contract as a writer-director. He recommended purchasing the property and said that "it fits in

with an original idea and can be combined. Superb starring role for Susan Hayward." According to the files at Fox, the rights were purchased a week later for $3,500—"a remarkable price," to quote another memo—and the project was given to Mankiewicz to write and direct.

Mankiewicz retained all of Mary Orr's characters except Margola's British husband; he also added several characters. Margo Channing, the Broadway star, is not married in the screen version, but she is in love with an American director, Bill Sampson, who is eight years her junior. Margo's age changed from well past forty in the original to forty in the screen version. Mankiewicz has described forty as "the single most critical chronological milestone in the life of an actress." Addison De Witt, the critic (George Sanders); Birdie Coonan, Margo's maid (Thelma Ritter); Max Fabian, the producer (Gregory Ratoff); Miss Caswell (Marilyn Monroe); and Phoebe, the girl who assumes Eve's character at the conclusion (Barbara Bates), were all inventions of Mankiewicz, having no basis in the short story.

Before doing much work on *Best Performance*, as the screen adaptation was first called, Mankiewicz was busy finishing the screenplay of *No Way Out* (1950) and directing that project. Then in the early fall of 1949 he spent six weeks at the San Ysidro guest ranch near Santa Barbara developing the treatment of *Best Performance*, which he turned in to Darryl F. Zanuck in January 1950.

Zanuck, in addition to being responsible for all A product at Fox, usually produced one or two pictures a year personally. He was generally enthusiastic about Mankiewicz's treatment and decided to make *All About Eve* (the new title, bestowed in January) a personal production. Years later Mankiewicz said that "*Eve* started out to be a picture written, directed, and produced by Joseph L. Mankiewicz . . . . I didn't want a producer."

In the material sent to him at the time, Zanuck made his usual thick pencil notes throughout the text and on the inside back cover. On page two, during Addison De Witt's voice-over narration, "No brighter light has ever dazzled the eye than Eve Harrington. Eve . . . . but more of Eve, later. All about Eve, in fact." Zanuck underscored in pencil the phrase "All about Eve," which may have been the first indication to use it as the title.

Many of Zanuck's comments had to do with his concern about revealing to the audience too early that Eve is a villain: "Beware of Birdie's jealousy as it will tip off that Eve is a heel," "Do we give it *all* away?" and so forth. Also, when Eve makes an overture to Bill Sampson in her dressing room and kisses him, Zanuck notes: "This is all wrong. She is too clever to jump in so quickly." The overture remained but the kiss was eliminated. Some long speeches were cut down to a few lines accompanied by a marginal note: "This should cover it all." And there were the usual assorted "Make clear. This can be confusing." Reacting to Karen draining the gas out of the tank of the Richardses' car to prevent Margo from getting to the theater, Zanuck scrawled: "This is difficult to swallow."

A major concern was a series of scenes depicting Eve's calculated designs on Lloyd Richards. Zanuck wanted to cut the entire four pages that showed Eve and Lloyd spending time together—in little cafes on side streets, in Lloyd's apartment with Karen present and later without Karen, Eve's little furnished room, and Lloyd going to see Eve late at night after a phone call form a friend of Eve's. Zanuck noted: "Dull, obvious, dirty . . . . This is wrong . . . . All relationships with Eve and Lloyd [should be] played off stage by suggestion . . . . We get it by one brief scene at rehearsal." The material (other than the rehearsal scene) was subsequently dropped.

After Zanuck read the first draft of the screenplay six weeks later, he praised it but sent Mankiewicz some notes detailing suggested changes and cuts. "I have tried to sincerely point out the spots that appeared dull or overdrawn. I have not let the length of the script influence me. I have tried to cut it as I am sure I would cut it if I were in the projection room." Zanuck's initial editorial judgment was always considered quite astute, and many of his suggestions were included in the final shooting script. One in particular was disregarded: "On page 32 I think the use of my name in a picture I am associated with will be considered self-aggrandizement. I believe you can cut it with no loss." The line was provoked by Bill Sampson's impatience with Margo:

BILL

The airlines have clocks, even if you haven't. I start shooting
a week from Monday—Zanuck is impatient, he wants me, he
needs me!

MARGO
(facetiously)
Zanuck, Zanuck, Zanuck! What are you two—lovers?

Remarkably few changes took place during Mankiewicz's writing of the various treatments and scripts with regard to construction, characters, or dialogue.

Next, thoughts were concentrated on the casting. Although Susan Hayward had been mentioned at the time the story was purchased and for a while afterward, it became obvious as Mankiewicz worked on his script that the part required a forty-year-old woman. Hayward was at the time thirty-one.

On the inside back cover of Zanuck's copy of the original treatment, he noted in pencil the following casting possibilities: Claudette Colbert or Barbara Stanwyck for Margo, John Garfield or Gary Merrill for Bill Sampson, William Lundigan or Hugh Marlowe for Lloyd Richards, Celeste Holm for Karen, José Ferrer for Addison, Thelma Ritter for Birdie, J. Edward Bromberg for Max Fabian, and Jeanne Crain for Eve.

Later, according to Mankiewicz, Zanuck suggested Marlene Dietrich for the role of Margo. Although Mankiewicz was an admirer of hers, he "simply could not visualize— or 'hear'—her as a possible Margo." They did agree on Claudette Colbert and she was signed in early February 1950.

Mankiewicz says that although Zanuck wanted Jeanne Crain, who was a popular Fox contract player at the time, to play Eve, Mankiewicz had not been pleased with her performance in his recent *A Letter to Three Wives* and he felt he would not be able to extract the proper degree of "bitch virtuosity" that was essential. However, Anne Baxter, who had been under contract to Fox for ten years, recalls that she was called to replace Crain after Crain became pregnant.

Gary Merrill was selected to play director Bill Sampson, Margo's lover. Under contract to Fox only for a short while, Merrill had just been seen to excellent advantage in Zanuck's fine personal production, *Twelve O'Clock High* (1949). Merrill previously had spent many years appearing in Broadway plays (*See My Lawyer*, 1939; *Winged Victory*, 1943; *Born Yesterday*, 1946) and on radio (*The Right to Happiness, Gangbusters, The Theatre Guild on the Air, Superman*).

Celeste Holm was agreed upon for Karen, the playwright's wife, as was Hugh Marlowe for Lloyd, the playwright, and Thelma Ritter for Birdie. All

Producer Darryl F. Zanuck (left) and writer-director Joseph L. Mankiewicz.

were under contract to Fox. Instead of José Ferrer, for whatever reason, former Fox contract player of long standing George Sanders was located in France and signed for the role of the cynical critic, Addison De Witt. Gregory Ratoff, an old friend and associate of Zanuck's, was also brought back from Europe to take the role of the Broadway producer, Max Fabian.

For the small but important part of Miss Caswell ("a graduate of the Copacabana school of Dramatic Arts"), Mankiewicz recommended Marilyn Monroe, who had been dropped by Fox about two years earlier as a contract starlet. "There was a breathlessness and sort of glued-on innocence about her that I found appealing—and she had done a good job for John Huston in *The Asphalt Jungle*," said Mankiewicz. Zanuck, recalling her less than impressive earlier career at the studio, was not convinced, but her agent, Johnny Hyde, persevered, and Monroe was signed for five hundred dollars a week with a one-week guarantee. Remembering Monroe during the filming, Celeste Holm says, "I confess I saw nothing special about her Betty Boop quality. I thought she was quite sweet and terribly dumb, and my natural reaction was 'whose girl is that?' "

Claudette Colbert ruptured a disc as a result of playing a scene in Fox's *Three Came Home* (1950). She told me that she was fitted with a steel brace, then put in traction, and with the picture slated to start five weeks later it was necessary to replace her. According to Mankiewicz, Gertrude Lawrence was always the second choice. She had read the script and was enthusiastic. But all scripts had to be submitted to and approved by her lawyer, Fanny Holtzman. As Mankiewicz tells it, Miss Holtzman insisted that Margo's getting drunk at Bill's party would have to be eliminated, and that during that party scene the pianist would not play "Liebestraum" but would accompany Miss Lawrence as she sang a torch song about Bill. Thoughts turned to another possibility. According to some sources, Ingrid Bergman was approached but she declined to return from Italy to do the picture. Darryl Zanuck personally called Bette Davis, who was shooting *Payment on Demand* at RKO, told her about the crisis and sent the script to her. She read it and eagerly accepted. When Davis had dinner with Mankiewicz the next night, he gave her the key to Margo's character by saying, "She is a woman who treats a mink coat like a poncho."

The filming of *Payment on Demand* was accelerated. It finished about seven days ahead of schedule, allowing Davis to be available for the revised "must-start" date of April 10. (She was signed on March 7). Other than the usual studio scheduling problems and actors' commitments for specific dates, *All About Eve* had little or no flexibility in the starting date, because of an arrangement already made to shoot for approximately ten days inside the old Curran Theater in San Francisco. Earlier, when Fox had budgeted the picture, it was determined that it would be better for various reasons to

*Claudette Colbert was set to play
Margo Channing in* All About Eve
before Bette Davis was cast.

shoot in an actual old-time New York-style theater rather than on a set, in accordance with the semidocumentary style of the time. Nothing available in Los Angeles seemed appropriate. There were some thoughts of using the Ethel Barrymore Theater in New York, but that was financially unsound and difficult to schedule. Lyle Wheeler, supervising art director, hit upon the solution of using the Curran, but it was available only during that brief period.

Before the start of shooting at the Curran with the principal players, Mankiewicz and his cameraman Milton Krasner flew to New York. There, using doubles for Bette Davis and Celeste Holm, they shot the exterior of the John Golden Theater, which would tie in with the scenes to be shot in the Curran. The exteriors of the 21 Club and Eve's Park Avenue apartment were also photographed as establishing shots for interior scenes that would be filmed later at the studio. As there was no snow in Westchester for the country road sequence (eventually photographed at the Canadian border), they moved on to New Haven for other shots. Here again exteriors of the Shubert Theater and Taft Hotel were photographed, with doubles used for Anne Baxter and George Sanders. Rear projection scenes, made at this time, would furnish the New Haven background against which Baxter and Sanders would later enact the scene.

The filming of sequences at the Curran went well enough, but Mankiewicz finished a day and a half behind the allotted time. Back at the studio, the company settled down for more than a month of solid work. Four days were spent filming the Sarah Siddons Society awards banquet, and after completing the party sequence and the supper in the Cub Room of the Stork Club, Mankiewicz concentrated on scenes between two and three people.

It was ironic that on the hottest day of spring, Bette Davis and Celeste

Holm, bundled in fur coats, had to play the scene that showed their car stalled on that snowy New York road. Projected on a process screen behind their specially prepared car was the background scenery that the second unit had photographed at the Canadian border. With the lights blazing down, the temperature inside the coupe was well over 100 degrees. Unfortunately the rushes showed that a slight jiggle in the process film had spoiled several of the scenes, so retakes were made the next day.

Saved for last was the important confrontation in the Taft Hotel suite between Eve and Addison. It was a highly emotional and difficult scene that took up thirteen pages of script. As was his custom, George Sanders usually napped in his portable dressing room between shots. (Celeste Holm says that Sanders "never spoke to anyone. He was a brilliant actor, but he wasn't much fun.") Anne Baxter in her autobiography related that Sanders's penchant for sleeping bothered her only during this climactic scene in which Addison reveals Eve's real self to her and lays down their private ground rules:

> [The scene] required a gamut of emotions, building to and culminating in hysteria and ending in acrid defeat . . . .
>
> George yawned his way through rehearsals. I was spiraling through them. That first take was an opening night. Joe took me aside.
>
> "Take it easy, Annie," he cautioned gently . . . . "He'll warm up . . . . Save yourself the first few takes." I tried, but by take five I was a rag. Understanding Joe called a short break and took George aside. Bending his heavy, handsome head, he talked with a hand on George's elegantly tailored shoulder.
>
> I walked around, taking deep breaths and trying to relax and yet maintain my emotional juices.
>
> Take six. Take seven—and George went off like a rocket. You know how you hold smoking punk to a firework? And just as you think it's a dud, it explodes into action. I felt like that punk.

Bette Davis and Gary Merrill, who had never met before filming began, fell in love during production and married in July, a month and a half after filming was completed. They were divorced ten years later.

The film had been given a forty-day shooting schedule. It ran over a few days and was brought in for $1,400,000, according to Fox records. The original estimate was $1,246,500. Mankiewicz delivered his rough cut of the entire film by the end of June, two weeks or so after shooting finished.

The on-screen romance between Gary Merrill and Bette Davis in All About Eve *precipitated their off-screen romance and marriage.*

Zanuck saw it and asked for some structural changes. The shooting script (in part) had a device reminiscent of *Citizen Kane:* Eve's story was presented from three different points of view, those of Addison, Karen, and Margo. Each of these narrators at the Sarah Siddons Society banquet (a fictional composite of the New York Player's Club and the Garrick Club in London) would complete one segment of the tale, and another would pick it up. In addition, as scripted and shot, one scene was presented from two points of view, as in *Citizen Kane* (1941) and the Japanese film *Rashomon*, released here in 1951. This was Eve's speech about the meaning of applause ("like waves of love coming over the footlights and wrapping you up . . . . Just that alone is worth anything") at Margo's party. The speech was shown as seen by Karen and by Margo. Mankiewicz strongly opposed Zanuck's plan to eliminate some of the footage that established and maintained the interrelated points of view and the two versions of Eve's applause speech, but he was overruled. Zanuck wanted to improve the pacing in what was a very long film and aksed for minor tightening in other areas (including the elimination of Eddie Fisher's role as the stage manager). Editor Barbara McLean finished working on Zanuck's revisions in three days, and the film was now down to two hours and eighteen minutes.

Then composer Alfred Newman, head of Fox's music department, began work on the score. Gradually the thematic treatment of the various characters began to take shape in his mind, but the duplicity of Eve's character seemed to defy musical interpretation, according to Newman at the time. One night, however, he hit upon just the right theme. It was the keystone, and everything else now fell into place. Forty-eight minutes of scoring were completed in a few weeks. Then it took twenty-one hours, spread over several days, on Fox's Stage One to record the score under Newman's baton. The opening title music is a true theatrical overture—majestic, glamorous, and important-sounding. Almost half of the score is source music: that is, music being played by the pianist during the party, by an off-screen group at the Stork Club, music coming from Lloyd's car radio. It consists of generous servings of such standards as "How About You?" "Manhattan," "Stormy Weather," "Blue Room," "Poinciana," "My Heart Stood Still," "Linger Awhile," and "That Old Black Magic." Debussy's "Beau Soir" and Liszt's "Liebestraum" round out the source compositions, all of which were recorded during the scoring sessions following photography.

All About Eve had its premiere at the Roxy Theater in New York on October 13, 1950. It was a huge success from every standpoint. The film, Mankiewicz, Bette Davis, and others associated with the production were the recipients of many awards, domestic and foreign. Claudette Colbert, recovering from her ruptured disc, was quoted by columnist Erskine Johnson as saying: "It's like I told Joe Mankiewicz—every time I read the beautiful notices, a knife goes through my heart. It's fate."

About two months after the premiere, Darryl Zanuck sent a confidential memo to Mankiewicz regarding their new project, *Dr. Praetorius* (*People Will Talk*, 1951). In it he announced that he would not take any screen

All About Eve: *Eve (Anne Baxter), Margo (Bette Davis), Miss Caswell (Marilyn Monroe), and Addison De Witt (George Sanders).*

credit as producer, although he would function exactly as he had in *All About Eve* and give the project as much of his time, energy and attention as he had given in the past. "My reasons for avoiding screen credit on your assignments are purely personal and selfish reasons," he noted.

> When you are both the writer and director on a film the producer is inevitably subjected to a forgotten or completely secondary role. I am experiencing this now on *All About Eve* and it is the first time I have ever experienced it. Usually I give a director a finished script to work with. That script is the result of my collaboration with the writers. It is *my* job . . . . As a matter of fact, it has always been true, including *Twelve O'Clock High, How Green Was My Valley, Grapes of Wrath*, etc . . . .
> You completely deserve all of the credit you are getting on *All About Eve*. By the same token, when I put my name on a picture as the producer I have my own conscience as well as my own reputation to consider. In *Dr. Praetorius* you will again make the major contribution and if the picture is a hit you will get the major share of the credit since you will serve in two capacities.
> On *David and Bathsheba* Phil Dunne is the writer, Henry King is the director and D.F.Z. is the producer. Both my conscience and my reputation will survive or fall on the result of my work and good or bad, I will not be lost in the shuffle.

Zanuck eventually did take producer's credit on *People Will Talk*. It received some good reviews but did only fairly well commercially. *David and Bathsheba* was a major box-office hit but did not get rave notices.

Mary Orr received no official credit on the screen or otherwise as the author of "The Wisdom of Eve." Zanuck inquired about this in a memo to Fox story editor Julian Johnson in early November 1950, shortly after the film's world premiere. Johnson replied on November 10 that "no credits are put in a contract which are not required. No author credit was demanded and none was put in the contract." There had been complications with the radio show's producer and with NBC, who contractually acquired half of the film rights when they purchased the short story for radio adaptation. As a result, it was agreed that there would be no credit given.

The overwhelming success of *All About Eve* revived Bette Davis's career when she badly needed it. Her eighteen-year contract with Warner Bros. had ended in 1949 with a major flop, *Beyond the Forest*. But most of her films made during the final years at Warners were a far cry from her first-rate vehicles produced at that studio during her (and Warners') golden years, the late 1930s and early 1940s; this was the time of *Jezebel, Dark Victory, The Letter,* and *Now, Voyager.* Davis told Anne Baxter shortly after *All About Eve* began filming that she had "thought her career was finished." *All About Eve,* of course, had the advantage of not being a vehicle for Davis, as her films at Warner Bros. had been. In addition, the Twentieth Century-Fox milieu in general was different. Most important, Mankiewicz's dialogue was first-rate and witty. Indeed, as Kenneth L. Geist says in his book *Pictures Will Talk* (1978): "What keeps *All About Eve* evergreen is the quality of its writing. Like Wilde's *Importance of Being Earnest,* the felicity of its epigrammatic style is such that it can still be relished even when the surprise of its repartee has been lost through familiarity."

This dialogue is not to be confused with that which is realistic or naturalistic, however. Mankiewicz, opposing a theory about using actual conversation as a basis for writing a script, said in 1954 that "there is no such thing as realistic dialogue! If you [simply recorded] the real conversation of any people and then played it back from the stage, it would be impossible to listen to. It would be redundant . . . . The good dialogue writer is the one who can give you the *impression* of real speech."

Anne Baxter revealed in 1977 that "I patterned my performance after my first understudy on Broadway at 13 who was nice to everybody but me and would always be in the wings watching me like a hawk. In the movie I tried to follow Bette around with my eyes to get that feeling across."

Apparently the subtle hints of Eve's lesbian tendencies were missed at the time of the film's initial release, but years later mail reflecting awareness of Mankiewicz's clues began to be delivered to the writer-director. Most important, to justify Eve's falling for her own tactics, Eve suggests that Phoebe, her younger counterpart, stay the night rather than make the long subway trip home. Twenty years later Anne Baxter had the unique opportunity of playing the role of Margo in the stage musical version of *All About Eve,* retitled *Applause* (1970). She took over from Lauren Bacall after the show's first year on Broadway.

Many people have always assumed that the interpretation of Margo Channing for the film was based on Tallulah Bankhead. There were rumors that Mankiewicz patterned his script on incidents in Bankhead's life when she starred on Broadway in *The Skin of Our Teeth* (1942). Davis's performance—and particularly her uncharacteristically husky voice—were said to be based on Bankhead. Davis comments on this in Whitney Stine's book, *Mother Goddam* (1974):

> Tallulah herself, more than anyone else, accused me of imitating her as Margo Channing. The problem was that I had

no voice at all when I started filming *All About Eve* due to emotional stress as a result of [my] . . . divorce [from William Grant Sherry]. A doctor gave me oil treatments three times a day for the first two weeks so that I could talk at all.* This gave me the famous husky Bankhead voice. Otherwise, I don't think the similarity to Bankhead in my performance would ever have been thought of.

According to Mankiewicz, it never crossed his mind that there was any particular Bankhead quality about Margo. Tallulah commented on this in her autobiography: "For comedy reasons this charge was fanned into a feud on my radio show [*The Big Show*]. I was supposed to be seething with rage over the alleged larceny. In superficial aspects Miss Davis may have suggested a boiling Bankhead, but her overall performance was her own."

Mary Orr related an amusing anecdote to me: After the film was a success, *The Theatre Guild on the Air* presented a second radio adaptation. Bankhead played Margo and Orr was Karen. "During the course of the rehearsals Tallulah said to me, 'Of course, I was the prototype of Margo, wasn't I?' I assured her that she wasn't, and that I had Elisabeth Bergner in mind only. This made her so angry, she never spoke to me again, except on the air."

When writer Gary Carey asked Mankiewicz if he had Bankhead in mind when he revamped Margo for the film, he replied, "I've always told the truth about that, and nobody has ever quite believed me . . . . The archetype for [my] Margo Channing . . . had been none other than Peg Woffington."

Peg Woffington was a beautiful English actress who became the idol of the London and Dublin stages in the mid-eighteenth century. She had vivacity and wit but was temperamental. She was also notorious for her love affairs and a feud with her arch-rival, Mrs. Bellamy. "Woffington was/is Margo Channing," continued Mankiewicz, "from her talents and triumphs on stage to her personal and private torments off. She was also . . . . every woman for whom acting was identical with existence . . . . Woffington, to me, was their prototype, all of them. And all of them in part are Margo Channing, I hope."

Bill Sampson, apparently, had no specific prototype. He was intended to be typical of the relatively young, dynamic, no-nonsense school of directors. In some ways he was similar to Mankiewicz's good friend and colleague, director Elia Kazan (and in his occasional sounding-offs, he was not unlike the loquacious Mankiewicz).

---

* Davis had to re-record her early dialogue after filming was completed. Other cast members also were postsynchronized in part from the San Francisco shooting because of disruptive street noises, including the clatter of street cars on Geary Street outside the Curran Theater.

Regarding the supercilious and caustic Addison De Witt, there were some surface resemblances to that major critic of the first half of this century, George Jean Nathan. "In his mannerisms and posturings, I suppose Addison reflects some of those of George Jean Nathan—but not to the exclusion of many others on the periphery of the creative community," said Mankiewicz. Mankiewicz revealed that to a certain extent Addison represented himself: "His comments on the nature of the actor, for instance, and also those on the pontifications of the elder statesmen of stage and screen."

Whereas Karen, the playwright's wife, was a rather sharp-spoken actress in the original short story, and, according to Mary Orr, somewhat autobiographical, she emerged as a charming and warm nonprofessional in the screenplay. Mankiewicz has said that he intended Lloyd Richards, the playwright, to be representative of the talented, responsible craftsman, partial to the good life—someone on the order of Philip Barry, Robert E. Sherwood, Moss Hart, or S. N. Behrman.

As for Eve, her nature transcends the theater, and apparently Mankiewicz had no specific prototype in mind. "There are Eves afoot in every competitive stratum of our society," says Mankiewicz. "That goal—toward which Eve is frantically and forever in full charge—is no less than all of whatever there is to be had."

12

THE RAVISHMENT OF THE TENDER:
A STREETCAR NAMED DESIRE
(1951)

When it opened on Broadway in December 1947, Tennessee Williams's play *A Streetcar Named Desire* was generally regarded as a major theatrical event. But for more than a year and a half not one Hollywood studio or independent producer made a bid to produce the play as a film. It was accepted as a foregone conclusion that a film version could not clear the relatively rigorous censorship of the time—the Production Code Administration and the Catholic Legion of Decency. Certain intrinsic elements of the play—rape, homosexuality, the sordid recent past of one of the play's leading characters—were forbidden subjects in the late 1940s.

Tennessee Williams had done most of his work on *A Streetcar Named Desire* after the Broadway opening of his first successful theatrical venture, *The Glass Menagerie* (1945). However, he has said that he "worked on *Streetcar* on and off for three years or more. I thought it was too *big* for the theater. Its subject had not been dealt with before. It was Blanche, this lascivious, demonic woman, who possessed me."

While recuperating from an eye operation in 1945 Williams began to recall the time he had spent in the 1930s in New Orleans as a waiter in the French Quarter. He had lived on Royal Street, along which ran two streetcars, marked "Desire" and "Cemeteries". "Their indiscourageable progress up and down Royal," the playwright says, "struck me as having some symbolic bearing of a broad nature on the life in the *Vieux Carré*— and everywhere else, for that matter."

Part of the catalyst for his play came from an isolated scene he had written some time earlier. "The plot was murky, but I seem to see a woman sitting in a chair, waiting in vain for something. Maybe love. Moon rays were streaming through the window and that suggested lunacy. I wrote the scene and titled it 'Blanche's Chair in the Moon.' My longer plays emerged out of earlier one-acters or short stories I may have written years ago."

Blanche DuBois's further development can be traced to two early one-act plays. The first, written in 1939, is "The Lady of Larkspur Lotion," which tells the story of a crumbling Southern ex-belle who vainly attempts to cling to respectability with her delusions in a shabby New Orleans rooming house. The second, "Portrait of a Madonna" (c. 1941), is a sympathetic study of the mental deterioration of an over-refined and repressed Southern spinster— another lady lost in the world of her own delusions.

Williams has said that "Blanche is certainly an aspect of my own personality . . . . [and] my mother is in all my plays, I would guess . . . . Her forms of expression, for example. And that underlying hysteria gave her great eloquence." Blanche also contained portions of Williams's delicate and sensitive sister, Rose (who was the prototype for Laura in *The Glass Menagerie*). But apparently the primary inspiration was Williams's Aunt Belle, his father's sister. "She was a Sunday School teacher in the south," says Williams. "But I have based Blanche on her personality, not on her life. She talked like Blanche: hysterically, with great eloquence." Williams's mother wrote in her autobiography that "perhaps Tom [Tennessee] stood a little in awe of her. She was very intelligent and beautiful but also very rigid, insisting everything be done her way."

Williams has stated that "there is very little autobiography in my plays, except that they reflect somehow the particular psychological turmoil I was going through when I wrote them . . . . I think *Streetcar* was a germinal play. It contains almost every theme I've ever tackled. I wrote several plays in that period of my life because I thought I was going to die of pancreatic cancer. A doctor told me."

Streetcar started out as a play called *The Poker Night*, but this material gradually was merged with other scenes and developed. In the play's final form, Blanche, the Southern gentlewoman, the last representative of a dying culture, is confronted with the primitive Stanley Kowalski, who in the end destroys her. It is a study of a final descent into madness, with all its implied comment about two opposing codes and views of life.

A Streetcar Named Desire had a tremendously successful two-year run on Broadway and has become one of the best-known plays of the modern theater. This can be attributed to its originality but also to the endless debates over morality and art that it has provoked. In August 1949 it was announced that producer-director William Wyler was having discussions with the play's producer, Irene Mayer Selznick, regarding making a film version with Bette Davis at Paramount. At one time it was announced that Irene Selznick had considered producing the film herself. Then agent-packager-producer Charles Feldman became involved and in October purchased the screen rights for $350,000. Feldman engaged Tennessee Williams to do the screenplay for $50,000 and offered Elia Kazan, who had directed the play, a percentage to direct the film. But Kazan turned down the percentage in favor of a flat fee of $175,000.

With the basic package set, Feldman had trouble interesting any studio in the production because of the censorship problems. There was one exception—Warner Bros. Earlier in 1949, Feldman had made a deal with Jack L. Warner for the production and distribution of a film version of *The Glass Menagerie*. In December an agreement between Charles K. Feldman's Group Productions and Warner Bros. was reached regarding *A Streetcar Named Desire*. Warner then put up half of the purchase price and screenwriter Oscar Saul was sent to work on the screen adaptation with Tennessee Williams at the latter's home in Key West, Florida.

It had taken quite some time for Feldman to convince Elia Kazan to do the film. "It's very hard", Kazan says, "to become involved in something a second time. I did it for an extremely personal reason, which is that I feel closer to Williams personally than to any other playwright I've worked with. Possibly it's the nature of his talent—it's so vulnerable, so naked—it's more naked than anyone else's. I wanted to protect him, to look after him. Not that he's a weak man—he's an extremely strong man, very strong minded. But when he asked me repeatedly to make the film of *Streetcar*, I finally said I'd do it."

Kazan's first approach to the screen adaptation was "to find visual equivalents for the verbal poetry that it [the play] has." This involved opening up the play and including scenes from Blanche's past in order to show the circumstances under which she left her home community and came to New Orleans, where the play begins. But eventually, after months of work, Kazan decided that the approach was wrong. "It had lost the best qualities of Williams's work. Even as story telling it was bad, because the strength of *Streetcar* is its compression. And I suddenly made a very radical decision . . . I'm going to just shoot the play."

A script was ready in April 1950 and sent to the Production Code office for approval. At this stage, relatively few of the problem areas of the drama had been modified to meet the Production Code requirements.

Feldman and Warner knew that a year earlier a number of studios had shown interest in making the film but had been fearful that the material would have to be altered so drastically to win the required seal of approval that *Streetcar* would emerge as a different work. Joseph Breen, head of the Production Code office, had told Paramount in no uncertain terms that the homosexuality and rape would have to be eliminated. He had written Irene Selznick "that the provisions of the Production Code are quite patently set down in the knowledge that motion pictures, unlike stage plays, appeal to mass audiences, to the mature and the immature; the young and the not-so-young." The subject itself was censorable, regardless of style, beauty, artistry, or sensitivity. The concept of the nonfamily adult movie for sophisticated tastes was not acknowledged by the Production Code officials in 1950.

In a memo to Warner Bros. confirming points discussed and agreed to by Production Code staff members, Feldman, and Warner executives, it was stated that Mr. Shurlock and Mr. Vizzard (from the Breen office) set forth the following three points as representing the three principal problems posed by this material under the Code:

> NUMBER 1: The script contains an inference of sex perversion. This principally has reference to the character of Blanche's young husband, Allan Grey. There seems little doubt that this young man was a homosexual.

> NUMBER 2: There seems to be an inference of a type of nymphomania with regards to the character of Blanche herself. Her peculair and neurotic attitude towards sex and particularly to a sex attraction for young boys has about it an erotic flavor that seems to verge on perversion of a sort.

> NUMBER 3: The third problem has reference to the rape which is [presented as] both justified and unpunished.

With reference to the first point, the memo stated that the solution would lie in affirmatively establishing some reason other than homosexuality for the suicide of Blanche's young husband. Regarding the second problem, it was felt from the standpoint of the Code that Blanche's difficulty should be one of an emotional nature and not one of sexual promiscuity. It had been suggested that in her approaches to the various men referred to in the course of the story she should seem to be searching for romance and security, not for "gross sex."

In dealing with the problem of the rape, the following suggestion had been made: The scene of the assault on Blanche by Stanley would be kept relatively intact as written. In the sequences that followed, in which Blanche was found to be demented, she would hint that Stanley actually raped her. But Stanley, when this accusation came to his attention, would violently deny this and prove positively that he did not rape her. The device by which he proves this was yet to be invented. The point of this suggestion seemed to be that Blanche in her pitiable state was making one last effort to assault the security and well-being of her sister, Stella, of whom she was envious.

An alternate suggestion was made: that it would be clearly established to the audience during the course of the rape scene that Blanche is, at the time, demented. She would call Stanley by the name of her husband, Allan; she would imagine the rape; the rape would not actually take place, and this would be known by the audience. Another suggestion was that the scene would be told from Stanley's point of view and that although he would contemplate rape he would not go through with the act, but would leave the room when he realized that Blanche was demented. It was agreed by Shurlock and Vizzard from the Breen office that this would be the most satisfactory solution to the difficult problem.

Points one and two were relatively easy to fix. In the play Blanche tells Mitch about her homosexual young husband:

> There was something different about the boy, a nervousness, a softness and tenderness which wasn't like a man's, although he wasn't the least bit effeminate looking—still—that thing was there . . . . Then I found out. In the worst of all possible ways. By coming suddenly into a room that I thought was empty—which wasn't empty, but had two people in it . . . the boy I had married and an older man who had been his friend for years. Afterwards we pretended that nothing had been discovered . . . . [Later] on the dance-floor—unable to stop myself—I'd suddenly said—"I saw! I know! You disgust me."

Tennessee Williams was asked to revise this long speech—only part of which is reproduced above—and some other spots in the text referring to Blanche's husband. Feldman wrote Williams in September that a new version had been submitted by Kazan to the Breen office but had not been approved. A line that Kazan inserted about the husband was: "He couldn't face the realities of life." In addition to asking Williams to cut down the speech as much as possible without hurting the content, Feldman asked "for any suggestion to meet the Breen office requirement that we be as affirmative as possible about the fact that the boy was *not* homosexual. Gadge [Kazan's nickname] assured Breen that it was not his intent to play up the homosexual angle in this scene but, on the contrary, to eliminate it or any suggestion of same."

Kazan, apparently, was sincere about eliminating the homosexuality aspect. In a later letter to Breen he wrote: "I wouldn't put the homosexuality back in the picture if the Code had been revised last night and it was now permissible. I don't want it. I prefer debility and weakness over any kind of suggestion of perversion." The key speech was pruned and modified considerably, and included one rather oblique addition: "He wasn't like other men."

The nymphomania problem was taken care of by some reworking and cuts in the dialogue. But although the blatant facts in Blanche's past were glossed over, edited, or merely suggested, what she had been up to in the past several years was fairly clear from the remaining hints.

The rape problem remained the major stumbling block. A revised script was sent to the Breen office on July 11, 1950. In their acknowledgment it was agreed that great strides had been made toward rendering the script acceptable screen material under the Code. But the rape scene was still unacceptable: a clear-cut case of a heinous rape which was allowed to go unpunished. A solution that was suggested and subscribed to by Feldman was that the indication of rape be eliminated and that in its place it be indicated that Stanley struck Blanche quite violently and that this blow caused her mental collapse. In the scenes that follow Blanche would implicitly accuse Stanley of having violated her, but he would, in some dialogue still to be written, strongly and convincingly deny that he had raped her and would protest that she was merely brokenly seeking to get revenge on him.

On August 24, reacting to another revised script, Breen wrote Jack L. Warner: "The rape scene . . . which we have repeatedly informed you was unacceptable under the Code, still remains unchanged." Williams and Kazan were adamant about keeping the rape scene in the film. Williams wrote to Breen that *Streetcar* was "an extremely and peculiarly moral play, in the deepest and truest sense of the term."

> The rape of Blanche by Stanley is a pivotal, integral truth in the play, without which the play loses its meaning, which is the ravishment of the tender, the sensitive, the delicate, by the savage and brutal forces of modern society. It is a poetic plea for comprehension . . . .
>
> Please remember, also, that we have already made great concessions which we felt were dangerous, to attitudes which we thought were narrow. In the middle of preparations for a new play, I came out to Hollywood to rewrite certain sequences to suit the demands of your office. No one involved in this screen production has failed to show you the cooperation, even the deference that has been called for.
>
> But now we are fighting for what we think is the heart of the play, and when we have our backs against the wall—if we are forced into that position—none of us is going to throw in the towel! We will use every legitimate means that any of us

has at his or her disposal to protect the things in this film which we think cannot be sacrificed, since we feel that it contains some very important truths about the world we live in.

Kazan, in a memo to Jack Warner on October 19, 1950, made a reference to his position:

> May I recall to you the conversation we all had in your trophy room, after lunch, several months ago. That was the occasion when Joe [Breen] said that the "rape" could not be in the picture—and I withdrew from the project. If you remember, Charlie Feldman asked me directly, "You mean to say that if the 'rape' is not in, you will not do the picture?" Whereupon, I said he was absolutely right and to count me out. You were there and will remember this. You will also remember that later we got together on a basis that I suggested. And this, too, was very clearly put. It consisted of (1) the rape would be in, but done by suggestion and delicacy; (2) Stanley would be "punished" and that the punishment would be in terms of his loss of his wife's love. In other words, there would be a strong indication that she would leave him.
>
> On this understanding, I embarked on the project . . . .
>
> We can have a perfectly clear conscience about the "sensationalism" in the picture—for absolutely none of it is for its own sake. And, I really think the picture's theme is deeply moral.

Kazan's approach to the rape problem was finally accepted. In both the play and the film Blanche is destroyed by the rape. At the play's conclusion Blanche is led off to an institution by a doctor and matron. In the theatrical version, after they have left, Stanley comforts his sobbing Stella and starts to unbutton her blouse to fondle her breasts. The poker game with Stanley's cronies continues as one of the men speaks the curtain line: "The game is seven-card stud." But the film ends with the possibility that Stella has rejected Stanley. She says to him, "Don't you ever touch me again!" and assures her small baby that "I'm not going back in there again. Not this time. I'm never going back. Never!" The play's ending showed life being sustained by a lie. In the film the truth is not kept secret but is confronted, and, we presume, acted upon.

Certainly *Streetcar* is a major landmark in the evolution of screen censorship. After World War II particularly, when the box office had lost

Vivien Leigh, playwright Tennessee Williams, and director Elia Kazan on the set of the film version of A Streetcar Named Desire.

its draw and film makers were desperately searching for ways to introduce more mature, challenging material, active disenchantment with the out-moded Production Code was widespread. Producer Jerry Wald sent a memo to the executives at Warner Bros. in November 1947 as a result of problems with the censors regarding his proposed production of *Key Largo* that is typical of the frustrations of that time:

> To my way of thinking, the Breen Office is narrowing our range of properties down to where we can either make a musical or a comedy . . . .
>
> The Breen Office today goes by a production code that was written in 1930. Many important events have taken place since the Code was written. Is it possible that the Code is dated? Certainly a re-examination is due . . . .
>
> The industry is continually being ridiculed . . . .
>
> Censorship is what is making all our pictures empty, and running along with a competent mediocrity.

A Streetcar Named Desire was the most important film in forcing censors to broaden their interpretation of the Code and to consider the realities of American behavior.

Geoffrey Shurlock, later director of the Production Code Administration, said years afterward: "For the first time we were confronted with a picture that was obviously not family entertainment. Before that we had considered *Anna Karenina* a big deal. *Streetcar* broke the barrier . . . [and] made us think things through . . . . Now we know that a good deal of what we decide in censoring movies is not morality but taste. It began with *Streetcar*."

With the censorship problem temporarily out of the way it was time to concentrate on the casting. Kazan recalls: "I urged that we use the original cast, and he [producer Feldman] would not go for it. Finally, after much hassling, we came to an agreement that we would have one movie star in it. Brando was not a star in those days, his first picture had not come out yet [*The Men*] . . . . Feldman wanted Vivien Leigh, and finally I agreed, with the understanding that I could have all the rest of the cast I had had in New York, which was in the spirit of sticking as much as possible to the original stage production."

Of course, almost every actress in the world coveted the pyrotechnical role of Blanche. Jessica Tandy, who created the role on Broadway, was anxious to do the screen version, and in the preliminary stages there was talk about Olivia de Havilland. Initially neither Tennessee Williams nor Kazan was sold on Vivien Leigh, according to a telegram at the time from Jack L. Warner, but they later changed their minds. Miss Leigh had played the role for nine months under the direction of her husband, Laurence Olivier, on the London stage in 1949–1950. She had been fascinated by the character of Blanche ever since she had read *Streetcar* early in 1948. About the time she was reading the play, Tennessee Williams saw her in repertory at the Old Vic in London. He wrote to his friend Donald Windham in January 1948: "Vivien Leigh is not really good in *Antigone* but I have a feeling, now, that she might make a good Blanche, more from her off-stage personality than what she does in the repertory, though she is quite good in *School for Scandal*. She has great charm."

When the offer came to do the film version, Miss Leigh was reluctant to accept because the play had taken a great deal out of her emotionally, and after nine months she felt she had played it long enough. In addition, she did not want to be separated from Olivier. But when in the spring of 1950 Olivier was asked to play the costarring role of Hurstwood in William Wyler's *Carrie*, at a time when he needed more money to support his own British theatrical ventures, they both decided to accept their Hollywood offers.

Jack Warner wanted to use in the supporting roles performers other than Karl Malden and Kim Hunter from the stage cast, but Kazan was still holding out for the New York company. Warner wired Feldman in New

York on June 9, 1950: "Ran the two tests we made of Kim Hunter which have been air expressed to New York. Personally I am adverse to her playing [Stella, Blanche's sister] in *Streetcar* as she has a negative screen personality. I know she is good on the stage but stage and screen are two different mediums and we want to be extremely careful casting this role . . . . There must be others we can get for this part." Then, in a letter from Kazan in Connecticut to Warner a week later, Kazan said, "I'll test [Ruth] Roman this week. I'll test anyone else whom you think a strong personality. I still think Anne Baxter is our best bet—but—there's time yet on this."

Warner wrote back: "I trust the test of Ruth Roman will come off okay. This girl has developed not only into a good actress but a good draw at the box office. I am putting in an extra plug for Miss Roman because of her good work in the last couple of pictures she did for us and hope you see eye to eye with me on her." However, eventually Kazan got his way and all the members of the original cast were used in the film, with the exception of the boy who played the young collector, a few bit parts, and, of course, Jessica Tandy.

Kazan says, "One of the best things I did for the play was to cast Brando in it—Brando has the vulgarity, the cruelty, the sadism—and at the same time he has something terribly attractive about him. So you can understand a woman *playing* affectionately with an animal that's going to kill her. So she at once wants him to rape her, and knows he will kill her. She protests how vulgar and corrupted he is, but she also finds that vulgarity and corruption attractive." Brando, Kazan noted, was as close to an acting genius as he had ever met. "He has everything. He has terrific feeling and violence, he has great intelligence, he's extremely intuitive. He is bisexual in the way an artist should be: He sees things both as a man and as a woman. He's strong in his sympathies to people, to all small people on the set." A very honest man who spoke plainly, Brando was also "a very devious man, in that he conceals his processes and reactions; they're none of your business. He even surprises the other actors."

John Garfield was originally set to play Stanley on the stage, but there were disagreements, and he left just before rehearsals were to start. Brando had played a relatively small role in *Truckline Cafe*, a play that Kazan had produced a year earlier. Kazan had been impressed with the young actor, who had done only one New York play before that—a small part in *I Remember Mama* (1944)—and now decided that he was right for *Streetcar*. Brando's performance was so electrifying in the stage production of *Streetcar* that many people tended to blend and confuse the real Brando and the role of Stanley Kowalski. The actor said in 1950 that Stanley is "aggressive, unpremeditated, overt, and completely without doubt about himself. The

direct antithesis of what I am." He has also said, "I detest the character."
He was, of course, referring not to his playing of the character but what
Stanley represented.

Kazan thought he might be able to use the wardrobe that Vivien Leigh
had used in the London stage production, but after Leigh sent him a
complete set of photographs from the play he quickly changed his mind. In
a letter to Jack Warner, he said, "to put it in one word: they were 'English.'
I mean stuffy, dull, ultra conservative and—'English.' They have to be
completely redesigned, in order to get the best out of Leigh." Kazan then
requested Lucinda Ballard, who had worked on the Broadway play, to do
the costumes for the film. Williams had indicated in the play's text that
there was something about Blanche "that suggests a moth." Using that as
a key, Ballard designed light chiffons and faded flowered organdies to allow
Blanche her delicate and fragile mothlike flutterings. A blonde wig was
designed to help add a faded look to her beauty.

Karl Malden told me that Kazan gathered the acting company together
before Vivien Leigh arrived and told them that the actress "was returning
to Hollywood after ten years [her last film produced in Hollywood was *That
Hamilton Woman* (1941)], and since we have been together for so long and
know each other so well, let's go out of our way to be friendly and make her
feel welcome." And, according to Malden, there were no tensions or flaring
temperaments. He recalls everyone working extremely well together. "And
Vivien," says Malden, "worked twice as hard as the rest of us because of the
demands of her role."

Shooting started on August 14, 1950, after almost two weeks of rehearsal
on the actual sets and two days of camera rehearsal. The two days were, to
quote cameraman Harry Stradling, "a method of experiment, to try out
effects and set a definite style. As a result, shooting went much faster.
'Gadge' Kazan kept telling us all to be bold." The photographic style that
evolved captured "a mood of sordidness softened by the romance of fantasy
as visualized through the dream-shrouded eyes of the main characters."

Art director Richard Day had been borrowed from Samuel Goldwyn to
design the sets. The exterior Elysian Fields street in the Old Quarter of
New Orleans was constructed on Stage One at Warners' studio in Burbank,
and the interior of Stella's flat was on Stage Fifteen. As in the play, most
of the action took place in the flat. But some shifting and opening up was
felt necessary. A long scene between Blanche and Mitch (Karl Malden) that
had been played in the flat for the theatrical version was moved to a set
representing an open pavilion on Lake Pontchartrain. A brief scene took
place in the upstairs flat, another brief scene at the shop where Stanley and
Mitch work, and the bowling alley scene near the opening of the film,

covering dialogue that in the play took place in the flat, was photographed in an actual bowling alley on Pico Boulevard in Los Angeles.

Vivien Leigh and Kazan apparently were not entirely in synchronization regarding the interpretation of Blanche. Leigh had not seen the New York production and Kazan had not seen the London production. Kazan told me that "Vivien's experience with the role had to be adjusted to my own intentions." Leigh was remembering Olivier's direction. "She kept telling me, the first week, 'when Larry and I did it in London—'and I had to keep saying, 'but you aren't doing it with Larry now, you're doing it with me' . . . . Then somewhere around the second or third reel [the film was shot in sequence for the most part], she and I got together, got an understanding; and she became enthusiastic about what I was saying to her. And we became very close—and I really loved her."

However, Vivien Leigh told critic John Gruen sometime afterward:

> I'm absolutely convinced that my screen performance turned out well more through Larry's remembered direction than through Elia Kazan's film direction. I recall having had a bit

Between scenes of the film version of A Streetcar Named Desire: *Marlon Brando and Vivien Leigh.*

of a row with Gadge over Blanche's characterization. He didn't really like the character—preferred Kowalski, the Brando part. He kept robbing Blanche of her poignancy and vulnerability, thus making her more and more unsympathetic. Finally we had a *very* serious talk—and luckily I won out on a good many points.

As for the experience in general, she told David Lewin "I loved every second. I couldn't wait to get to the studio every morning and I hated to leave at night." Regarding Marlon Brando, she told Lewin: "I thought he was terribly affected . . . . I got to understand him much better as he went on with the filming. He is such a good actor."

Kazan feels that Leigh eventually came to admire Brando, although she knew that their techniques were quite different. "They respected each other and certainly worked well together, and still there was this difference that was valuable and which I used—that she came from another civilization, from another way of life, and somehow that fitted in to the way the characters were."

Of course Brando had great respect for Kazan. He said recently, "Kazan is the best actor's director you could ever want, because he was an actor himself, but a special kind of actor. He understands things that other directors do not. He also inspired me." Karl Malden described to me some aspects of Kazan's approach:

He is alone in his style of direction. With Kazan you first go through a period of what I call wining, dining, and walking. He'll call you up and say "let's have lunch or dinner." During the meal, he'll find out all he can about you and your background. He's a great walker, so then you'll walk six or seven miles—talking all the way. He's probing, asking, and deliberately not talking about the play. Now you come to rehearsal. He knows more about you than you know about yourself. He'll use it. With most directors you come to rehearsal and *you* make the adjustment to his concept. With Kazan he sees first what you bring to the role. You may contribute something better than what he had in mind. If you don't, he always has his ideas. With Marlon on *Streetcar* Kazan just let him go; he guided him very little.

When we filmed *Streetcar* each one of the cast members were at the studio every day, because Kazan never knew which scene he might rehearse on the other end of the stage. Kazan felt that the actor loses some momentum while the lighting of a particular camera setup is being done, so often during that time we would work on a scene that was going to be filmed the next day. Kazan had tremendous energy. He was constantly saying "let's try this; let's try that."

Principal photography was completed on October 17. Two weeks later Kazan, Vivien Leigh, cameraman Stradling, and a relatively small crew went to New Orleans for three days to shoot the opening of the film. Working all night, they photographed scenes at the L and N train station at the foot of Canal Street. Although the original streetcar named Desire had been replaced by a bus named Desire, the city revived one of the retired trams and put it into service for one night of shooting. Kazan told me that much of what was shot in New Orleans was later eliminated.

As he did with every other key person assigned to the film, Kazan had his way when it came to selecting a film editor. In an undated letter sent to Jack Warner before shooting commenced he said: "Please don't forget about [Warner staff editor] Dave Weisbart. I really need a good cutter, since this is the one side of the business that I am still unsure about." Kazan also wanted Alex North to score the film. North, a talented composer for New York modern dance companies, the theater, and industrial and government film projects, had known Kazan for many years but had worked with him only on the New York stage presentation of *Death of a Salesman* (1949), for which North wrote the incidental music. North had had nothing to do with *Streetcar* in New York. The music for the stage production consisted of a small New Orleans jazz combo playing mood and locale-setting music in the background. North had been set to score Kazan's *Viva Zapata!* (1952) as his first feature, but *Streetcar* interceded and *Zapata* followed.

North told me that he and Kazan had many long talks about the approach to the music for the film version of *Streetcar*. A jazz-oriented score was logical. North always had an interest in jazz as an important ingredient in American music, and he felt strongly about using jazz in this film. Kazan sent North to New Orleans to sop up atmosphere. While the film was being photographed, North was writing thematic ideas in his New York apartment on the basis of the script. Later, in Hollywood, when he saw a rough cut of the film, North scored music that was related to the characters at all times, but not necessarily the action. "Instead of 'themes' for the specific characters," says North, "there were mental statements, so to speak, for Stanley vs. Blanche, Mitch vs. Blanche, and Stanley vs. Stella . . . . I think you will find some of the scoring running counter to the scene because of the attempt to reflect the inner feeling of the personalities rather than the situation."

Streetcar was the first major jazz-oriented film score, and its impact on film music was considerable. However, sixty percent of the score was actually nonjazz and symphonic in approach. The subtle and inobtrusive interweaving of New Orleans source music, jazz-influenced incidental music—not improvised—and distintive and contemporary symphonic scoring was most effective. Occasionally North brought in a series of mournful descending figures in the orchestra ("to sound like the wailing of the women of the world," says North). This was accomplished without the aid of any electronic devices.

Since the mid-1930s, Warners' music had always been explicit and somewhat in the foreground of the sound track, but North and Ray Heindorf, the head of Warners' music department and the conductor of the *Streetcar* score, both recall being extremely depressed about the volume level of the music after attending the previews and first being confronted with the final mix and balance of dialogue and music. For the most part, *Streetcar*'s music was subdued in level.

The picture was previewed in Santa Barbara in mid-February 1951. Although well-received, it was trimmed here and there after the preview to move things along more rapidly. The cutting notes included:

> Speed up entrance of Leigh into bowling alley . . . . Speed up argument between couple upstairs . . . . Speed up scene between Leigh and the young boy collecting for the newspaper . . . . Take out several shots of Brando during scene of him eating cake on account of interference with Leigh's lines . . . . Try to speed up last poker game . . . . Dupe down Leigh's animal cries when she goes mad.

The picture was previewed again in Huntington Park toward the end of February. Feldman wrote to Warner: "Picture went quite well at Huntington Park. Preview cards were 70% excellent, 30% fair to good with a few bad ones. Despite what Kazan told you in the projection room the other day the audience was very restless and felt the picture was too long, particularly the last sequence. There is still work to be done on the newspaper-boy sequence and a lot of work to be done in the last reel."

More trims were made:

> When Leigh arrives at her sister's home, do not have her go into house. Go from courtyard to her asking policeman for directions to entrance to bowling alley . . . . Do not have Mitch come back after the fight and talk to Leigh . . . . When

everyone is waiting for the sanitarium people to get Leigh, try to speed up poker game and scene between Leigh and Hunter and Eunice discussing what Leigh will wear.

Kazan agreed to some of the cuts but argued for retaining certain things:

> About cutting the little Mitch–Blanche scene at the end of the poker night, I don't know—a little later on . . . she is talking about Mitch, and even as it is some of the audience doesn't know whom she is talking about . . . . However, I won't be precious about this judgment and will watch it at the [next] preview.

Warner wrote back to Kazan saying that he understood what the director meant about the scene between Mitch and Blanche.

Another preview was held in New Jersey and eventually all concerned agreed on the trims. The Breen office gave their final approval and Kazan began his next film, *Viva Zapata!* for Twentieth Century-Fox. *Streetcar*'s budget originally was projected at $1,570,000, but the final negative cost came in at about $1,800,000.

In July, Warners learned that the Legion of Decency, established by Catholic churchmen and lay members in 1933 to impose standards of morality and to implement the new Production Code, was about to give the picture a "C" or condemned rating. This would mean that members of the Roman Catholic faith would be instructed not to see it. The studio not only feared the effect of this on the box office but also worried that theaters showing the film might be threatened with boycotts, and the "C" rating might be interpreted as an invitation for every local censor board in the country to make further cuts in the film or to ban it altogether.

Kazan was concerned. No one was telling him what was going on. He wrote Steve Trilling, Jack Warner's executive assistant:

> What disturbs me is the silence. The fact that something is being done to my picture—I don't know what! . . . You said that the Legion had seen it once and had asked for certain deletions. You were not sure what these were, but you felt they were minor, and to quote Charlie [Feldman], "nothing to worry about." You know very well, Steve, that as far as I am concerned they are plenty to worry about. I don't want any meddling by these people into the guts of my picture, or of your picture either. If the deletions really are minor, they might be o.k. with me. And they might not . . . .

> I may be sore as hell about what the hell is done to please the Legion and if I'm sore as hell nothing in this wide world will keep me silent. To quote an old Jewish proverb, if someone spits in my face, I will not say it's raining . . . .

Kazan then discovered that David Weisbart, the editor, had been sent to New York to run the film for the Legion and to make certain changes. Weisbart soon returned with a revised print, which received a desired "B" rating (which meant "objectionable in part for all"). Kazan was then allowed to see this version, after which he decided to go immediately to New York. There he was introduced to a prominent Catholic layman, Martin Quigley, who informed him that he, Quigley, having given time and thought and great care to the matter, had suggested the cuts in *Streetcar*. He was present at the invitation of Warner Bros., and he had striven to establish a bridge between the picture's artistic achievement—which he praised highly—and "the primacy of the moral order" as interpreted by himself, in conformity with the Legion's standards. There had been no overt involvement of the Legion, who did not want to be considered censors. They simply viewed finished work and pronounced their verdict. The Legion then passed the cut version. "And that was that," said Kazan. "There was no recourse, as I discovered when I tried to reopen the matter."

There were twelve cuts altogether, and they removed some three or four minutes from the film. They range from a deletion of three words, "—on the mouth" (following the words "I would like to kiss you softly and sweetly—"), to a recutting of a wordless scene in which Stella comes down the staircase to Stanley after a quarrel. Kazan recalls that the scene was carefully worked out, in an alternation of close and medium shots, to show Stella's conflicting revulsion and attraction to her husband, and that Kim Hunter played it beautifully. "The censored version protects the audience from the close shots and substitutes a long shot of her descent. It also, by explicit instruction, omits a wonderful piece of music. It was explained to me that both the close shots and the music made the girl's relation to her husband 'too carnal.' " Alex North told me that the original music used to underscore this scene featured a sensuous solo saxophone against growling cup-muted trombones ("early Duke Ellington," as North describes it). He substituted another piece of music that was orchestrated for French horn, strings, and woodwinds to suggest a mournful quality.

Kazan describes further deletions:

> Another cut comes directly before Stanley attacks Blanche. It takes out his line, "You know, you might not be bad to

interfere with." Apart from forcing a rather jerky transition, this removes the clear implication that only here, for the first time, does Stanley have any idea of harming the girl. This obviously changes the interpretation of the character, but how it serves the cause of morality is obscure to me, though I have given it much thought.

The other cuts are of like nature. Certain of them were interpreted to me as stemming from the thought that if one character—Stella was the candidate—could be shown as "good," the film would be redeemed. Such a thought, of course, is directly opposed to Tennessee Williams' thought. All his characters are a mixture of the qualities we label "good" and "bad," and that is their humanity . . . .

The cut version was the one that was finally released in the fall of 1951. Despite the censorship problems, we are fortunate to have preserved on film an exceptional theatrical piece of its time, one that is representative of Tennessee Williams at his best. And Kazan, the number one American theater director of that time, for the only time transferred one of his biggest successes to the screen. The Kazan style is a synthesis of various revolutionary influences—Chekhov, Stanislavsky, Freud, the Group Theater of the 1930s, and later the Actors' Studio. The play and film of *Streetcar* reflect all of these, and the film contains extraordinary and timeless performances by Marlon Brando and Vivien Leigh. Brando was to a large degree professionally shaped by Kazan's influences, while Vivien Leigh's technique, for the most part, developed from a different tradition. The resulting interplay of these two artists is certainly memorable.

13

"REMEMBER ELEANOR ROOSEVELT'S SERENE SMILE":
THE AFRICAN QUEEN
(1951)

Shooting a fictional film on location in Africa with Hollywood stars was a most unusual undertaking in 1951 when *The African Queen* was being photographed in the Belgian Congo and Uganda. Although travelogues and documentaries had been around for years, only two previous feature films with a story and actors had been made by an American production company in Africa. MGM sent a unit in 1929 to photograph *Trader Horn* at various locales in Africa. The four Hollywood performers who made the journey were Harry Carey, his wife Olive Golden, Duncan Renaldo, and Edwina Booth. The trials and tribulations encountered while making this epic have been recorded in many books and periodicals. *Trader Horn* was a huge success, but although innumerable African adventure feature films followed, none was made in Africa. Even Twentieth Century-Fox, while preparing their generously budgeted major production of 1939, *Stanley and Livingstone*, sent only a second unit to Africa with doubles for Spencer Tracy, Cedric Hardwicke, and Walter Brennan. And the jungles of the popular Tarzan films were to be found in Southern California until the mid 1950s.

234

Following World War II it became desirable and fashionable to shoot different kinds of films on location all over the globe. At that time MGM producer Sam Zimbalist wanted to film H. Rider Haggard's Victorian adventure novel, *King Solomon's Mines*, using the Technicolor process for the first time in an American feature film made in Africa.* Finally, in 1949, following extensive investigation and preparation, MGM began production at many of the same locations—among others—used in its *Trader Horn* twenty years earlier. Stewart Granger, Deborah Kerr, and Richard Carlson were the only actors sent to Africa.

The problems encountered were, as usual, overwhelming, and in many ways a familiar reprise of those encountered during the making of *Trader Horn*. A cablegram sent on December 4, 1949, from codirector Compton Bennett to producer Zimbalist at MGM (from the studio files), said in part: "Still at Murchison Falls. Conditions and heat unbearable. Shooting yesterday 150 degree heat. Deborah collapsed. Unable to finish scene. Also sound crew and others of unit out of action [due to] exhaustion and stomach trouble." Cameraman Robert Surtees cabled Zimbalist three weeks later: "Still worried [about] health of crew. One third now indisposed." A month later Bennett wired: "Must request studio allow us return next week as nearly all suffering extreme tiredness and exhaustion . . . . Nearing point of complete breakdown."

Excerpts from director W. S. Van Dyke's African diary of 1929, written during the filming of *Trader Horn*, told the same story. May 23: "My illness reaches crisis . . . . May 30: [script supervisor] Miss Chippo knocked out with sun. Also has slight touch of fever . . . . June 6: [cameraman Bob] Roberts suffering terribly from tsetse fly bites. Neck swollen terribly. Miss Booth hit with sun . . . . June 8: Carey hit with sun . . . . June 26: Miss Gordon, Miss Booth's hair dresser, has desperate case of malaria. Rushing her into Kampala . . . . August 16: Mrs. Carey very ill and sent to hospital in Kampala. About fifty natives in bed with fever," and so on.

While *King Solomon's Mines* was being completed at the MGM studios in the spring of 1950, director John Huston, who was on the lot working on *The Red Badge of Courage*, and producer Sam Spiegel, his partner in the independent production company Horizon Pictures, bought the screen rights to C. S. Forester's 1935 novel, *The African Queen*. Warner Bros. had intended to film the novel back in 1947. Forester, an English author and authority on naval warfare of the nineteenth and twentieth centuries, wrote *The African Queen* two years before he introduced his most popular creation,

---

* The 1939 British production of *The Four Feathers* was photographed in Technicolor partially in the Sudan.

Horatio Hornblower, in the first of a long series of books about the British naval officer.

Included in the sale of *The African Queen* to Spiegel and Huston was a 130-page temporary screenplay by John Collier, which was completed in April 1947 while the writer was under contract to Warners. Collier, an English-born American short-story writer and novelist whose works are witty, satiric, and often macabre, had finished a screenplay for *Deception*, a Bette Davis vehicle of 1946. At that time his agent, who was also Forester's agent, sent Collier a copy of *The African Queen*. In an interview with Tom Milne in 1976, Collier said:

> I wrote an enthusiastic note to Jack Warner and persuaded him to buy the novel [April 1946] and let me write the screenplay. All that was necessary was to transpose the book into the conventional script form. But when I had done the first draft, Warner, who had neglected to read the book, was told that it was concerned with two people all alone on a little riverboat, and that it would cost nearly $3,000,000 to make. Some ill-disposed person whispered to him that the script had been written with Bette Davis in mind, and that she was disposed to play the part. I'm told that he was reminded also that Miss Davis had the right to preempt the feminine lead in any property produced by the studio. Choler prompted him to get rid of me, an impulse he responded to with such alacrity that Reason had not the time to get a word in edgeways. When at last its small still voice could make itself heard, it advised him to get rid of the script also, lest Miss Davis exercise her right.

In his book *Bring on the Empty Horses* (1975), David Niven remembers being borrowed from Samuel Goldwyn by Warners producer Henry Blanke to play Allnutt opposite Bette Davis as Rose:

> The deal was signed, and bemused by my glorious opportunity, I had spent four weeks polishing up a Cockney accent. I even grew a beard which made me look like a diseased yak, but at the last minute, Bette Davis fell out with Blanke and told him she refused to be photographed out-of-doors (a likely story), so the picture was cancelled.

When I questioned John Collier about this, he had no knowledge of Niven being set or even discussed for the role, and to the best of his knowledge Bette Davis was enthusiastic about the project.

Shortly afterward, in July 1947, the script was submitted by MCA in behalf of Warner Bros. to Twentieth Century-Fox. Phyllis Rogers, a Fox story analyst, said in her comments that the screenplay "has been suggested as a vehicle for [Fox contract star] Rex Harrison. The script, now owned by Warners, was originally prepared for Bette Davis in the role of the missionary's sister, but Warners do not intend to make it now . . . . The screenplay is exceptionally well written . . . . While the picture might be costly, it certainly is worth considering . . . . *African Queen*, which in this reader's opinion far surpasses Hemingway's 'Short Happy Life of Francis Macomber' [filmed in 1946 as *The Macomber Affair*], should be fine box office." The studio passed. It was submitted again in March 1948, this time by another agency, Famous Artists, through the interest of Fox director Jean Negulesco. Again Fox declined. John Collier told me that in May 1949 he was allowed to purchase an option to buy his script from Warner Bros. for a relatively small price.

Enter Sam Spiegel (whose screen credits at that time read "S. P. Eagle") and John Huston. Spiegel, who was literally without funds, borrowed $25,000 from Charles A. Medcraft, who took a mortgage on Spiegel's home, to join with Huston in forming a corporation called Horizon Pictures. Spiegel borrowed another $50,000 to purchase from Collier the option to buy from Warners the rights to *The African Queen*, which included Collier's script. Collier says that he received a 6.25 percent interest in the eventual profits. (Medcraft was promised five percent of the profits.) *Daily Variety* on November 4, 1949, stated that the picture was "planned for production next year, with possibility that Bette Davis will star . . . . Other stars reportedly interested in the property . . . are Olivia de Havilland and Ida Lupino." Lupino's name was mentioned in a Warners publicity release of October 1946, which stated that the book had been purchased by the studio and Ida Lupino was scheduled to star. But by April 1947 it was Davis whom producer Henry Blanke and Collier wanted for the role, according to some studio correspondence of the time and what Collier told me. (Collier's notion at the time was to get British actor John Mills for Allnutt.) Blanke, who had produced two John Huston films, *The Maltese Falcon* (1941) and *The Treasure of the Sierra Madre* (1948), while they were at Warners, had talked over the project with Huston when they worked on *Treasure*. Huston was intrigued, but Jack Warner, in the final analysis, was not.

Reports vary on how Bogart and Hepburn became involved. Bogart and Huston were good friends and had worked together on various projects in the past. Bogart had done the first film directed by Huston—*The Maltese Falcon*—ten years earlier. Convinced that she was perfect for the part of the missionary's sister, they both went to see Katharine Hepburn. Hepburn was immediately intrigued with the idea and the trip to Africa. She was promised $65,000 in cash, a like amount in deferred payments, and ten percent of the film's profits. Bogart was to be given $35,000 in cash, a deferred payment of $125,000, and a twenty-five percent interest in the profits. He eventually agreed to forget about the $35,000 in return for a new contract giving him thirty percent of the profits. Huston originally had a fifty percent interest in Horizon Pictures and was promised $87,000 for his services as director.

Spiegel arranged for funds to be borrowed from a Chicago corporation. Then John and James Wolf, of Britain's Romulus Films, entered the scene. Sir John Wolf in a letter to me said:

> My brother and I became involved in the project as we started our company Romulus Films with the intention of producing Anglo/American films at a time when there was some dissatisfaction in Hollywood, on the part of the major stars, with the studios. My brother was in California and heard about [The African Queen] . . . and we made a partnership agreement with Sam Spiegel . . . . The negative cost, I believe, was between £4/500,000 sterling and something under $1,000,000. My company, Romulus Films, provided the sterling costs and Sam Spiegel formed a syndicate to cover the American costs.

To further compound the complex financing, United Artists put up some additional funds in exchange for the western hemisphere distribution rights to the film. This was at a time when international coproduction was just getting under way. The major studios were in a period of decline, because of the poor post-World War II market, the forced divestiture of the studios' theaters, the introduction of television, and changing recreational patterns of the public. Independent production (with stars increasingly getting a percentage of the profits) and the desire to film in actual locales were part of the background, conception, and execution of The African Queen project. Polish-born Spiegel was a master promoter who knew all the angles. He also had taste and a desire to produce quality films for a primarily adult audience. An independent producer in Europe during the 1930s, he came to America and produced Tales of Manhattan (1942) and The Stranger (1945) before his association with Huston.

In the fall of 1950, shortly after Huston finished directing The Red Badge of Courage for MGM, he began working on a new script of The African Queen with writer-critic James Agee. They started the script in Horizon's office on the old California Studio lot at Melrose and Bronson in Hollywood and finished it in Carmel. From late 1941 to the middle of 1948, Agee had been the movie reviewer for *Time*, and from the fall of 1942 to 1948 he also wrote the film column for *The Nation*. Agee was a great admirer of Huston, and spent a considerable amount of time with him while preparing a special lengthy *Life* magazine essay about him called "Undirectable Director" (1950). Huston told author Gerald Pratley that "Jim wanted to stop reviewing. He wanted to get out of that, and I suggested that he work on the script with me. He fell in with that instantly."

In a letter from Los Angeles to his long-time friend Father James Flye, Agee said in early December 1950:

> I'll be staying out till middle or late January, working on a script with John Huston . . . . If everything works out right, it could be a wonderful movie. If much works out wrong, it can be lousier than most . . . . The work is a great deal of fun: treating it fundamentally as high comedy with deeply ribald undertones, and trying to blend extraordinary things—poetry, mysticism, realism, romance, tragedy, with the comedy.

In January 1951, at the time he was working on the screenplay, Agee collapsed while playing tennis with Huston and suffered a heart attack. His hospitalization and recuperation prevented him from going with Huston to England and Africa, where presumably more work on the script would have taken place.

As to their method of collaboration, Agee wrote to David Bradley in 1953 that "*African Queen*, first draft, was 160 pages. The first hundred were mine and brought it through almost half the story. The last sixty, except a few scenes and interpolations, were Huston's; but the playing time worked that his sixty and my hundred amounted to about the same."

Huston had gone to England in February for a series of meetings with Sam Spiegel, the Wolf brothers, and key staff people regarding the production details of *The African Queen*. Among other things, there were arguments about whether or not color film should be used. Although it is now difficult to imagine that there could have been any question regarding the matter, since this was to be a relatively modest independent production and color added a considerable amount to the budget—to say nothing of the complications of shooting on location in Africa with the old, cumbersome three-strip Technicolor camera—there were legitimate concerns. At that time most feature films were still photographed in black and white. Finally it was decided in favor of Technicolor, for which cinematographer Jack Cardiff was ideally suited. His previous outstanding Technicolor films

The African Queen *had some
similarities to* The Beachcomber
*(1938), based on Somerset
Maugham's "The Vessel of
Wrath," with Charles Laughton
and Elsa Lanchester.*

included *Black Narcissus,* (1947) *The Red Shoes,* (1948), *Scott of the
Antarctic* (1948), and *The Black Rose* (1950)—an interesting combination of
controlled studio color treatment and difficult location shooting.

Writer Peter Viertel, who had worked with Huston on the scripts of *We
Were Strangers* (1949) and *Reminiscences of a Cowboy*—the latter eventually
rewritten and directed by others as *Cowboy* (1958)—was employed by Sam
Spiegel in London to work with Huston on another draft of the script. Viertel
wrote to me:

> This final draft, which underwent a few changes during
> shooting, was based on the book, as well as Agee's script. It
> incorporated, however, a great many new scenes, or revised
> scenes that were only suggested in the book and the previous
> script.

Forester's novel—set during World War I—and Collier's script start after
the Germans devastate a native village in which Rose and her missionary
brother reside and work. The missionary is dying of malaria and a broken
heart. In the Agee-Huston-Viertel scripts there is a prologue that introduces
the missionary, his sister, and Allnutt (the dissolute skipper of the river
launch *African Queen*) before the Germans invade the peaceful community.
After delivering the mail, Allnutt ritualistically has tea with Rose and her
brother. Immediately the comedic aspects of the character relationship is

established by the persistent gurgling sounds emanating from Allnutt's stomach during the strained and somewhat formal tea. Huston and Agee had made Allnutt a Canadian, to better accommodate Bogart, rather than the Cockney he was in the novel and Collier's script.

Forester's novel, along with the subsequent scripts and film, are reminiscent to a degree of an earlier Somerset Maugham short story, "The Vessel of Wrath," and even more so its film adaptation, called *The Beachcomber* (1938) in America. That narrative deals with the repressed and bitterly intolerant sister of an English missionary, played by Elsa Lanchester in the film, who becomes involved with a disreputable, drunken hedonist (Charles Laughton) in the Dutch East Indies. Circumstances that throw them together cause them both to modify their deficiencies and fall in love. The primary interest is in the humorous and incongruous relationship between two such opposite people, who at the beginning of the story thoroughly detest each other.

Says Viertel of *The African Queen:*

> I worked with Huston on several endings, which were supposed to please the Breen office, as well as ourselves. As the characters had slept together without being married, the Code required they end badly, if not unhappily. But as the material was essentially comic and romantic, neither Huston nor I felt a tragic ending was in keeping with the rest of the piece.
>
> Therefore the bogus wedding ceremony was devised on board the German ship. Prior to that we had various other endings: one that I recall was to have the film end with the couple arguing in the water, once they had lost the *African Queen.*

The original endings of Forester's novel, Collier's script, and the eventually filmed Huston-Agee-Viertel version were all different. Forester's novel had two endings. The author stated in 1940:

> I do not know what novel it was that I was writing by the time the typed script of *The African Queen* reached [publishers] Messrs. Little, Brown and Company . . . . However, I could not work up any interest when they told me that they did not like the end of the book and had thought of a simple way of changing the end without calling for any effort from me. The fact that no effort was called for was sufficient inducement. I wrote blithely and agreed, and it was only when my complimentary copies reached me in England that I really appreciated what had happened to the book when it had been docked of its last two chapters.

For the Modern Library edition of 1940 and subsequent editions the last two chapters were restored. As in the film, Rose and Allnutt are preparing to ram the German ship with their improvised torpedoes on the *African Queen* when a storm upsets the craft. Later, Rose and Allnutt are tried in a court martial by the Germans, and because of their deteriorated physical condition and the miracle of their river journey, it is decided to turn them over to the British. The British in turn interrogate the couple and then go after the German gunboat, which is no match for two British fighting ships. The German vessel is sunk. Rose and Allnut are sent with an escort to the British consul at Matadi on the cosat. Before embarking on the journey, Rose tells Charlie that they must get married by the consul. Charlie says, "Righto, Rosie. Let's," and they begin the long journey. The book ends with the line: "Whether or not they lived happily ever after is not easily decided." Although this leaves the plot unresolved, the subsequent deletion of the last two chapters abruptly ended the narrative with the British lieutenant-commander planning to lead his ships into action against the German gunboat.

In John Collier's script, after the *African Queen* sinks, the German gunboat spots Allnutt and Rose in the water and heads toward them. Then the ship, as Allnutt had hoped, hits the partly submerged *African Queen* and explodes. Rose and Allnutt struggle to the beach. For mile after mile the lake shore is scalloped with beaches leading down to the open country held by the British. Rose and Allnutt happily start off to let them know the way is now open.

The ending eventually used in the film also has the *African Queen* swamped in a gale. Rose and Allnutt are hauled aboard the German gunboat and sentenced to be hanged. Allnutt asks the German captain to marry them before they die, and just as the ceremony ends, the ship runs into the derelict *African Queen* with its torpedos intact and blows up. Thrown into the water together, Allnutt and Rose set out to swim for shore.

Other than the ending, the narrative line of John Collier's script and the Agee-Huston-Viertel versions are the same as Forester's. The differences are in tone, dialogue, and detail. The novel was regarded as romantic adventure, and Collier's adaptation remained faithful to this approach. He added an entirely new sequence that had no counterpart in the novel or subsequent drafts of the screenplay: In the early part of the voyage, Rose goes ashore to gather some firewood for the boiler. Allnutt, in a sudden rush of homesickness, decides to run away. He gathers some canned goods and other necessities for a long trek. But as he slips off to take a last look at Rose, he sees her frozen in terror. On a high spot above her sits a huge Kivu gorilla. This is the turning point in Allnutt's life. Dropping his knapsack, he rescues Rose. Together they run back to the safety of the boat, hoist anchor, and push off. Rose, aware that Allnutt was planning to leave her stranded, is grateful to him for saving her. Accidentally, as they haul in branches for firewood, their arms touch and they gaze at each other self-consciously.

Peter Viertel wrote me:

> Work [on *The African Queen* script] was to be done in London and in Africa . . . . Not much was accomplished in London. Once in Entebbe, Huston and I wrote the final draft . . . .
>
> Katharine Hepburn arrived with Spiegel and the Bogarts [Lauren Bacall accompanied her husband] in Stanleyville three to two weeks before major photography was to begin. Hepburn read the script, and went over it with me in Stanleyville. She had a great many small suggestions which were improvements on the whole. I suggested she speak to Huston about them. He was at the main location at the time, and not in Stanleyville. Later, he approved of most of her small changes. They were, on the whole, comic inventions and transpositions of dialogue inside certain scenes.

Filming The African Queen *on the Ruiki River in the Congo.*

Huston and his art director, Wilfred Shingleton, had previously scouted the African locations by air, covering about 25,000 flying miles. They would set down on emergency strips built during World War II when the British were transporting planes across Africa. "It was looking for locations in the grandest way one could imagine. Africa was a revelation. The whole trip was just an earth-shaking experience," Huston told Gerald Pratley.

The first location was on the Ruiki River in the Congo. The water was almost jet black because of decaying vegetation in the water and was surrounded by lush and verdant jungle. A camp had been built by eighty-five natives in eight days; bungalows were made from bamboo and palm leaves. There was one large building with a dining room, an adjoining bar, and outdoor privies and showers. The showers consisted of overhead tin barrels filled with water.

Shooting was ready to begin, but the rains came and lasted for almost a week. Finally the weather cleared and work commenced. Cameraman Ted Scaife recalled that "the unit used to set sail down river each morning in Sam Spiegel's 'fleet,' which consisted of a towing vessel pulling the *Africa Queen*, followed by a generator, lights and reflectors, a camera raft, another raft with props and sound equipment, and finally Kate's loo—a floatable toilet she insisted on."

Producer Spiegel says that "the water was infested with tiny worms carrying a disease called bilharziasis. The worms penetrate the skin and stay with the victim for up to thirty years. The disease affects the liver and weakens you, and can eventually kill you. It's said to be the most agonizing way to die. At one time or another, practically everyone fell into the water. We would quickly fish them out, dry them down, spray them with disinfectant and pray. The cast and crew uncomplainingly put up with more danger and discomfort than any other group I've ever worked with. I got bitten on the back of the neck by a tarantula spider. Penicillin saved my life, but I was sick for six weeks."

John Huston wrote in 1952:

> Certain additions to the original story also developed in the course of making the film. Chief among these is an element of comedy, absent from both the novel and the screenplay, which grew out of the relationship between Hepburn and Bogart. This situation has never happened to me before, although I had worked with Bogie on four other films. Katie and he were just funny together, one calling forth that quality in the other, and the combination of their two characterizations brought out the humor of dramatic situations which, originally, none of us thought existed. Basically, the humor underlies

Director John Huston and Katharine Hepburn in Africa during filming of The African Queen.

the story, for it's a case of the little worm of a man who turns or the prim spinster suddenly becoming the captain of the ship. But it doesn't come out of the printed page. It was the surprising combination of Hepburn and Bogart which enabled the comedy to emerge.

It is true that the element of comedy is not as obvious in the book or t various screenplays, but apparently James Agee, at least, as noted in letter to Father Flye, was thinking of "treating it fundamentally as h comedy with deeply ribald undertones."

In her autobiography, Lauren Bacall recalled:

> The work was very slow, the sun very hot. Tempers flared once between Bogie and John. When it rained, John would go off hunting, but Bogie wanted him to pay attention, God damn it—be practical and figure out what to do if the weather proved insurmountable. John really became a white hunter in Africa—he believed he *was* one—and he adored it; he didn't care how long he stayed. That was John. Bogie was different—he wanted to be back in civilization. He had a life that he'd built, nurtured, cared about. John seemed to be wherever he was with whatever film he was making. He liked moving about. So they complemented each other, and the resulting work was always their best. John was fantasy—Bogie reality.

Huston said in 1952 that the idea of making *The African Queen* on location was not based on capturing the African flora and fauna in Technicolor. He wanted to put the accent on the people; the animals, he felt, had been covered more than adequately in earlier African films. "The point about location filming is that if the actors are living in a certain way, it will come out in their performances. Their very hardships give character to the finished film . . . . When you go on a location of this kind, where the going is more than a bit difficult, it is very important to have people that like it." He noted that Katharine Hepburn, whom some people had described as being "very dainty," turned out to be anything but. "She took to Africa like a duck to water."

Huston told Hepburn shortly after filming began that her mouth drooped and her faced turned hard whenever she was in solemn thought. He advised her to remember Eleanor Roosevelt's serene smile whenever she became pensive, and she used that as part of her acting process in the film.

At one point the *African Queen* sank during the night. Filming was carried on with the mock-up while the craft was pulled out of the river and repaired at the location. The propeller was removed and hammered into shape with the help of a native bellows made of wood. Palm leaves fanned the flame. (A case of reality imitating art: In the script, Allnutt, with Rose's aid, repairs the propeller and shaft in a similar manner.)

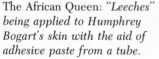

The African Queen: *"Leeches" being applied to Humphrey Bogart's skin with the aid of adhesive paste from a tube.*

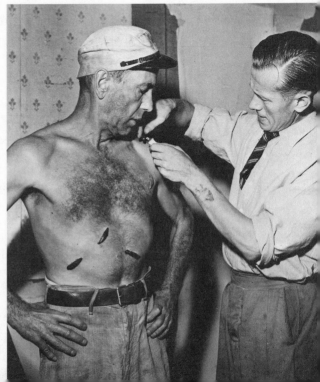

Then, after the *Queen* was afloat again and work in the Congo was almost finished, an army of thousands of soldier ants in a column a foot and a half wide invaded the camp. Only fire could head off their relentless march; otherwise they would continue their advance, consuming everything in their path. The ants could quickly strip an animal or human to the bone. Driven back by torches, they returned the next day and again were repulsed. But everyone knew that the ants eventually would win. In a short while the camp almost certainly would disappear into the jungle without a trace, so the company—not quite finished with the shooting—left the location and headed for Entebbe in Uganda (then a British protectorate).

The Congo had been damp and stifling; Uganda was cool and invigorating. The second location was on Lake Victoria. At Butiaba a grass-hut village had been built by the natives to be burned down for the scenes near the opening of the film. The company stayed on a 125-foot sidewheel paddle steamer for the next five weeks. Then another deluge of rain slowed down the proceedings. After finishing the burning of the village, the company moved up the Nile to the spectacular Murchison Falls and surrounding area, where there were plenty of crocodiles and hippos. Things were getting even more difficult. Again the rains came. Assistant director Guy Hamilton had a nervous collapse from overwork and had to be flown back to London. Then several of the crew members came down with dysentery. According to Lauren Bacall (1952):

> One day the two sound men were ill with dysentery and then the four members of the camera crew were struck. Kate was also miserable with the dysentery but trying to carry on. Huston had to stop production . . . . Huston said that the shutdown would last four days. If a crew could not be mustered by that time we would pack up and go back to London. At this point there were more sick members of the company than well. After four days, enough of the crew staggered back to their posts for shooting to resume. Kate reported to work bravely, but she still wasn't well. I would watch her in a scene while her face turned from red to yellow to green to blue. "I've got to go back," she would say, gently but firmly. Production managed to stagger along, carrying the decimated crew with it.

Katharine Hepburn told author Charles Higham in 1973 that temperance was the cause of her dysentery. To shame Bogart and Huston out of drinking hard liquor, she began drinking water in their presence at mealtime. "Well,

The African Queen: *Filming on the backlot of Worton Hall Studios near London. Katharine Hepburn at the tiller.*

the water was full of germs! They never got sick, and I had the Mexican trots and was in bed every day for weeks! I thought I was going to die."

There were continued meetings between the camera crew and Huston, searching for ways to simplify the remaining work. Then nine members of the British crew had to be sent home. Finally, with only two days of shooting to go, Huston asked for three additional days. "Bogie was in such a fury at his [Huston's] lack of foresight—and at Katie, who he thought was aiding and abetting John—that I thought he'd explode," according to Lauren Bacall. A compromise was made, and some more filming was accomplished, but everyone managed to make the plane at Entebbe as scheduled.

Peter Viertel says that producer Spiegel's "contribution to the production was a big one—especially pulling loose ends together once he had landed in Africa. He was like a good Service of Supply general landing on a disputed beachhead." Later Spiegel was to exercise these attributes on a larger scale as producer of *The Bridge on the River Kwai* and *Lawrence of Arabia*, both filmed on remote locations.

In 1953, Peter Viertel published a novel called *White Hunter, Black Heart*. Although fictitious names were used for all of the characters, they were in fact based to a greater or lesser degree on the principal people involved in the filming of *The African Queen*—indeed, the novel told of the production of a feature film in Africa. I questioned Viertel about how much his book had to do with the real people and events behind the making of *The African Queen* and he responded that his "novel does . . . lean heavily on the actual happenings, although the talk and the confrontations were eighty percent invention."

When the company finally arrived in London after eight weeks of filming in Africa there was to be another six weeks of work at Worton Hall Studios near London. As with *Trader Horn* and *King Solomon's Mines*, the studio material comprised much more of the footage than generally was known. Obviously, it was better for promotion, publicity, and advertising purposes to stress the "photographed in Africa" angle. Therefore, all studio and back-lot shooting was underplayed and, for the most part, not publicized.

The first scenes to be shot in England were those with Robert Morley, in the role of Rose's missionary brother, who was involved only in the opening sequences. (Morley did not go to Africa, although he was doubled in some of the long shots photographed there.) Huston had met Morley when the director was at MGM in 1950 contemplating a proposed production of *Quo Vadis* (which Mervyn LeRoy eventually did instead). Huston thought of Morley as Nero, but the actor was unable to do it because of a play commitment in New York.

Morley writes of *The African Queen* in his autobiography that since he had only a small part he had felt that there would be time for learning it as the film progressed. On the first day he fluffed and stammered his way through a scene with the two stars, and then rushing back to the theater sat up that night memorizing his role. "Huston never said anything to me about the incident, but I learned from a friend that that night he had been at a party and someone had asked how he had fared with me on my first day. 'Not well,' he replied, 'not well at all. To tell you the truth, Morley sent down his substitute.' "

All of the scenes involving the German gunboat at the end of the film were then filmed (Peter Bull, Theodore Bikel, and the other actors playing the ship's officers did not go to Africa). Next, the scenes requiring Bogart or Hepburn to be in the water were photographed at Worton Hall, for safety and health reasons. These included shots of the two bathing, each keeping to his or her own end of the old river steamer, Allnutt removing and putting back the propeller and shaft under water, and his pulling the *African Queen* through the thick reeds and sludge—chest deep in water— and then getting back on board only to discover that he was covered with leeches. The German-occupied fort at Shona was constructed with plaster over tubular scaffolding at the studio-built lake (Worton Hall) for the sequence in which Rose and Allnutt manage to take the *African Queen* safely through gunfire. Scenes involving the pair caught in deluges of torrential rain, and relatively close shots of them going through the rapids, were all photographed on the back lot with special apparatus. Many shots of Bogart and Hepburn were photographed against a blue backing, which later was matted optically against actual African footage. A small model of the *African Queen* was constructed and used for some scenes, including a few involving rapid shooting, with mannequins standing in for the principal players.

Bogart made an interesting comment at the time in an interview for *The New York Times*. After praising Huston's ability, he said, "But he's murder to work with during the last three weeks of shooting. Always restless, wanting to quit for some new idea."

All editing was done by Ralph Kemplen in England, after which composer Allan Gray completed work on the score there. Gray had a varied career in all types of music in Europe. His most well known British films before *The African Queen* include *The Life and Death of Colonel Blimp* (1943), *I Know Where I'm Going* (1945), and *Stairway to Heaven* (1946). Gray composed two primary themes for *The African Queen*, and they were reiterated with variations throughout the film. For the little steamer he wrote a quaint, whimsical piece of music that utilized the familiar devices of syncopated piccolos and bassoons. The second theme served the relationship of Rose and Allnutt and is essentially sentimental. *Trader Horn* and *King Solomon's Mines* had effectively dispensed with an orchestral background score and instead used natural sounds in conjunction with the chanting and primitive instruments of various African tribes (although *Trader Horn* did use a composed piece of "jungle music" behind the opening titles).

The African Queen succeeds not in spite of changing the mood of C. S. Forester's novel but because of the evolution on film of what is primarily

A model of The African Queen *was used for some shots.*

a distinctive comedy of character. Hepburn and Bogart are superb together, with each presenting new and interesting aspects of their acting reserves as well as extensions and variations of their personalities. Perhaps Huston's point regarding location filming ("If the actors are living in a certain way it will come out in their performances. Their very hardships give character to the finished film") is valid. Bogart's Allnutt in *The African Queen* bore little relationship to Sam Spade in *The Maltese Falcon* (1941) or Rick in *Casablanca* (1943), although there is a slight parallel with his Fred C. Dobbs in *The Treasure of the Sierra Madre* (1948). And Hepburn's Rose is a far cry from her characters in *Little Women* (1933), *The Philadelphia Story* (1940), or her roles in the many vehicles with Spencer Tracy, although one could find some parallels in the offbeat interplay of Hepburn–Tracy and Hepburn–Bogart.

As for director John Huston, Peter Viertel told me:

> Huston's imprint and view of and on the story were decisive. As with most of his movies, his was the biggest creative force involved . . . . His method [was that] he used the writer or writers as creative mules which were guided by him; checked and reversed, and occasionally led by hand on foot through the bad passages.

14

ALL TALKING! ALL SINGING! ALL DANCING!: SINGIN' IN THE RAIN (1952)

By 1949 Arthur Freed had been making musicals at MGM for ten years. He was generally regarded as the best and most knowledgeable of the musical producers, and one who had a keen eye for developing fresh talent in front of and behind the camera. Before becoming a full producer with *Babes in Arms* in 1939, Freed wrote the lyrics for a considerable number of songs in collaboration with composer Nacio Herb Brown, both having been under contract to MGM since 1928 when they contributed the songs to the original *Broadway Melody*. Irving Thalberg, production head at Metro, following the success of *Broadway Melody*, immediately put Freed and Brown on another musical, *The Hollywood Revue of 1929*, and it was for this film that the team supplied their most successful song, "Singin' in the Rain."

By the middle and late 1940s, two major trends in musical pictures had evolved: the feature built around the life of a famous composer of popular songs, in which his most durable numbers were presented (Gershwin, Cole Porter, Jerome Kern, Rodgers and Hart, etc.); and the feature based on the trials and tribulations of a married vaudeville team, as in *Mother Wore Tights* (1947). In these, one partner inevitably went to Hollywood and made it big while the other hit the skids.

Freed was not interested in doing a biographical musical film about himself, but he did decide to do a musical to be called *Singin' in the Rain*, the score of which was to be derived from his catalog of songs. Freed had recently had considerable success with Irving Berlin's *Easter Parade* (1948) and was planning George Gershwin's *An American in Paris* (1951). Neither film was biographical, but each contained proven songs from the composers' lists. On March 28, 1949, Freed had a story outline of *Singin' in the Rain* made up from an old MGM silent feature called *Excess Baggage* (1928), which had been based on a play of the period by John McGowan dealing with a vaudeville acrobat and a dancer who marry, separate when she becomes a success in films, and later reunite. A Dan Dailey musical utilizing many of the same elements and called *You're My Everything* was being filmed at Fox in 1949.

On March 15, 1949, *The Hollywood Reporter* announced that Freed had started preparations on *Singin' in the Rain*, which would use several Freed songs and "a large cast of top studio personalities." Then, on March 31, Howard Strickling, MGM publicity director on the West Coast, sent a wire

Songwriters Nacio Herb Brown and Arthur Freed on the set of Going Hollywood *(1933) with Bing Crosby and Marion Davies.*

to Howard Dietz, MGM director of advertising and publicity in New York, in which he said, "Ann Miller to star in *Singin' in the Rain*, to be produced by Arthur Freed." At this point the plan was still to use *Excess Baggage* as the plot springboard, but no writers were as yet assigned.

Fourteen months elapsed before the team of Betty Comden and Adolph Green arrived from New York to begin work on the project. Comden and Green had been alternating between writing for Broadway and Hollywood. After the stage success of *On the Town* (1944), for which they did the book and lyrics in addition to playing leading roles, and of *Billion Dollar Baby* (1945), Freed brought them to Hollywood to work on an adaptation of the old Broadway college musical *Good News* (1947), followed by an original screen story that reunited Fred Astaire and Ginger Rogers, *The Barkleys of Broadway* (1949), and an adaptation of *On the Town* (1949) for Gene Kelly and Frank Sinatra.

This time all Comden and Green knew was that the title of the film was to be *Singin' in the Rain* and that Freed's songs would be featured. Stanley Donen, who eventually was to codirect the picture, recalls screening at MGM with the team several old MGM pictures such as Jean Harlow's 1933 Hollywood farce *Bombshell*, to see if one could be converted into a musical.

Comden and Green remember listening to Freed and Brown's extensive inventory of songs played on the piano at MGM by Roger Edens, Freed's associate producer, vocal arranger, music supervisor, and songwriter. Many of these songs had been written for the earliest musical films during the transition from silent films to talkies, and it seemed to Comden and Green that those years—the late 1920s—would work to the advantage of the script. The writing team knew the period well (*Billion Dollar Baby* and *Good News* were both set in the 1920s) and were amateur authorities on silent movies and early talkies. During that time of the big changeover, the studios had all kinds of problems, not the least of which was the public acceptance of certain stars' voices. What individual members of an audience imagined their favorite silent hero or heroine sounded like was one thing, but what the actors sounded like in actuality was often quite another. Many a career was finished because of audience disenchantment with a star's recorded voice in just one talkie.

Comden and Green remembered particularly the downfall of John Gilbert and decided that their leading character would be just such a star. The trick, they felt, was to make the stuff of tragedy fit into a lighthearted satirical comedy. "Our silent star would have to survive his downfall and make good as a musical star, and to give *that* story point a faint air of credibility, we had better establish our hero as someone who had had a song-and-dance vaudeville background before he entered pictures . . . . We spent an agonizing month trying to get a grip on ourselves and our screenplay."

During this period, and before it, according to the files at MGM, Freed was being asked by various people at the studio if the story was going to be an adaptation of an existing property, such as *Excess Baggage,* or new material. Freed stalled, but on June 19 he wrote that there is "every possibility it will be an entirely original story."

Comden and Green later recalled that "we finally had what seemed to be three possible opening sequences of a picture: a big silent movie premiere in New York; a magazine interview with the star in Hollywood telling a phony life story; a sequence from the silent movie being premiered in New York, the star meeting the girl in New York, losing her, and going back to Hollywood . . . . Our depression deepened as our story refused to move."

It was Betty Comden's husband, Steven Kyle, who suggested they use a composite of all their openings. Comden and Green said that "this led to the eureka moment of realizing that maybe it could work if the action never went to New York, but all took place in Hollywood . . . . From here on, the gates were open and the writing of the screenplay gushed in a relatively exuberant flow. We tapped the roots of our memories and experiences without editing ourselves when our ideas got wild, satirical, and extravagantly nonsensical."

When it was decided that the silent screen actor with a vaudeville background would become a film musical star, the logical choice for the role was MGM's Gene Kelly, who was then preparing *An American in Paris* (1951). Kelly had worked with Comden and Green on the film version of *On the Town* (1949) and was an old friend from New York. Before he came to Hollywood he used to go down to the Village Vanguard, a little club in a Greenwich Village basement, to watch a small group called The Revuers, who wrote and performed satirical sketches and songs. Comden and Green were members in their pre-Broadway days, and so was Judy Holliday.

Betty Comden and Adolph Green, who wrote the screenplays for Singin' in the Rain, On the Town, The Bandwagon, The Berkleys of Broadway, Good News, *etc.*

The first *Singin' in the Rain* script in the MGM files is dated August 10, 1950. The structure and characters are reasonably close to the final script and film, but there are some interesting differences. Arthur Freed had suggested that the role of Cosmo, close friend and former vaudeville partner of Don Lockwood (Kelly), be tailored for Freed's friend, pianist and wit Oscar Levant. Levant was at the time working in *An American in Paris* with Kelly and the year before had appeared in Freed's *The Barkleys of Broadway*. This initial version of the script was clearly written with Levant's presence in mind. His big number was to be a scene labeled "The Piano Playing Pioneer." In the script, Cosmo describes this to the head of the studio as a possible musical picture vehicle for him. He verbally sets the scene: "There is a dissolve to Cosmo in a Daniel Boone outfit staving off an attack on a wagon train by charming the Indians with a concert selection played on a piano dragged out of a covered wagon."

In this early screenplay there is no reference to Don singing "You Were Meant for Me" to Kathy on an empty sound stage, but instead a number to be done on a studio backlot street made up of different sets with various locales—Paris, London, Venice, Mandalay, a jungle. Don and Kathy would move from one set to another. Suggested songs for this sequence were

"Would You?" "Chant of the Jungle," and "Broadway Melody." "You Are My Lucky Star" was designated the number Kathy would do during the party at the studio head's residence after the opening premiere (this was later changed to "All I Do Is Dream of You"). The "Good Morning" number at Don's home was still to come; indeed, that scene, which followed the disastrous preview of *The Dancing Cavalier*, takes place in a restaurant in this version. The script indicates that the unnamed song and dance "would be impromptu fun . . . . They [Don and Cosmo] do something perhaps from their old acts . . . . [Later] as they leave the cafe, all three [Don, Cosmo and Kathy] do 'Singin' in the Rain' on the street."

There is no ballet indicated, but there was to be "a big musical number finale" after the plot had been resolved. This finish is somewhat different from the one that evolved. In the early version, following the successful premiere of *The Dancing Cavalier*, there is a party at Don Lockwood's home. It is here that Lina Lamont mouths the song "Singin' in the Rain" to Kathy's singing voice and reveals to the guests—rather than to the theater audience—the voice-substitution trick. Then there is a sequence at the premiere of Don's next film, *Broadway Rhythm*, in which Mr. and Mrs. Lockwood (Don and Kathy), who are the stars of this attraction, and Cosmo and his wife—Lina—arrive. It is stated that Lina is currently appearing in *Jungle Princess*, in which "she doesn't say a word—just grunts!"

There was as yet no provision for the montage of early musicals, "Beautiful Girl," the fashion tableaux, "Moses," and Donald O'Connor's specialty number "Make 'Em Laugh." At the place in the script where the latter number occurs there is instead another Levant piano solo, the Paderewski Minuet, performed to cheer up Don on the set of *The Dueling Cavalier*.

Freed was enthusiastic about Comden and Green's first draft of the script and so were codirectors Gene Kelly and Stanley Donen. "So much of it was based on early material they had written for themselves when they were The Revuers," said Kelly. The script writers, after making some revisions, then checked off the lot in October, returning to New York to work on a new theatrical revue, *Two on the Aisle* (1951), while Kelly immersed himself in *An American in Paris* until early January. He then took a long vacation before starting preproduction work on *Singin' in the Rain* in March 1951. Comden and Green were brought back that month for three weeks of further script revisions.

As a matter of routine, the April 11 revised script was sent for approval to the Production Code Administration. Joseph Breen then wrote and cautioned the studio on some aspects of the screenplay: "Pages 24 and 25: None of the showgirls in the process of changing their clothes should be shown in their underwear . . . . Pages 27 and 28: This dialogue between

Cosmo and the girl must be delivered without any offensive sex suggestion flavor:

> GIRL: Oh, Mr. Brown—could you really get me into the movies?
>
> COSMO: I should think so—
>
> GIRL: Really?
>
> COSMO: There are ways—
>
> GIRL: Oh, what would I have to do?

Page 65: Don's line, 'What are you doing later?' approaches the element of sex perversion and we ask that it be eliminated." [The line was said in jest to Cosmo after Cosmo lip synchronizes to Kathy's singing as a demonstration of vocal substitution on the sound track.]

By now it had been decided that the role of Cosmo should be played by an actor who could dance well, thereby giving Kelly a partner in the many tap numbers. Donald O'Connor was born into a circus and vaudeville family and was trained from childhood to sing and dance and be part of the family act. He had been in films since 1938, but he had never had a truly outstanding vehicle in which to strut his stuff. But O'Connor was under contract to Universal. A loan-out figure of $50,000 was agreed to by MGM. O'Connor told John Mariani that he was in London playing the Palladium

Co-directors and co-choreographers Gene Kelly and Stanley Donen on the set of Singin' in the Rain.

at the time. "I got the call as I was lying in bed writing a short story. And although I was flattered, I said no, because in those days, under the terms of the contract, I wouldn't have seen a penny of that $50,000. Finally, Universal agreed to give me the money, so I said okay."

O'Connor proved to be a revelation with his dancing contributions. He worked well with Kelly in "Fit as a Fiddle" and "Moses" (the only song in the film that does not contain Freed's lyrics. It was written especially for the scene in the diction coach's office by Comden, Green, and Roger Edens). O'Connor's other number (besides the famous "Make 'Em Laugh"), "Good Morning," was performed with Kelly and Debbie Reynolds.

An MGM contract player, nineteen-year-old Debbie Reynolds was the antithesis of Kelly and O'Connor in song-and-dance experience. Coming to films after having been elected Miss Burbank 1948, she had appeared in only five pictures—in bit or supporting roles—before *Singin' in the Rain*. As Jane Powell's younger sister in an MGM musical of 1950 called *Two Weeks with Love*, she did a rendition of "Aba Daba Honeymoon" with Carleton Carpenter that stole the picture and made studio executives sit up and take notice. It was decided to take the big step and cast her as Gene Kelly's costar in *Singin' in the Rain* as part of the studio's policy of grooming young talent for star status. Her dancing experience was almost nil. Debbie Reynolds says that "Gene would put me in a rehearsal studio with either Carol Haney or Jeannie Coyne, his assistants, and a tap teacher called Ernie Flatt, and he wouldn't let me leave until I was step perfect . . . . But I wanted to prove to him that I could do it, so I just worked and worked. He makes you feel you're capable of more than you are, and I didn't want to let him down."

Kelly says that "fortunately Debbie was as strong as an ox . . . . Also she was a great copyist, and could pick up the most complicated routines without too much difficulty."

For the key role of Lina Lamont, the silent film star who is visually the epitome of glamour, decorum, and charm but who has a shrill, nasal, and flat voice, the ideal choice at the time the script was being written was Judy Holliday. The character in the script was modeled on the rendition of the classic dumb blonde that she had experimented with while working with Comden and Green in The Revuers years before and developed in the stage version of *Born Yesterday* (1946). But by the time *Singin' in the Rain* was being cast, Judy Holliday had become a major film star following the release of the movie version of *Born Yesterday* in late 1950. Other players were tested, including Nina Foch; then MGM contract player Jean Hagen, who had played Judy Holliday's role in *Born Yesterday* on the road, was found to be perfect.

Donald O'Connor and Gene Kelly between scenes of Singin' in the Rain *chat with visiting Fred Astaire, who was filming* The Belle of New York (1952) *on a nearby stage at MGM.*

One featured part to be cast was the film columnist, Dora Bailey, who addresses the crowd and interviews Don Lockwood at the entrance to Grauman's Chinese Theater, where the opening scene of the picture takes place. The lady was to be a gentle spoof of syndicated columnist Louella Parsons. Miss Parsons's agent, Wynn Rocamora, wrote a letter to Freed suggesting that "you consider Louella Parsons for the part of the commentator . . . . She, I know, would be interested in doing this." Madge Blake was later cast in the role.

Meanwhile, the numbers were being finalized and put into rehearsal. Obviously, the Levant material, "The Piano Playing Pioneer" and the Minuet, was out, and in place of the latter was to be "The Wedding of the Painted Doll," featuring O'Connor and Kelly. This was changed at the last minute to O'Connor's solo number. Kelly recalls that "Donald O'Connor was always making us laugh so I said, 'Let's do a number called 'Make 'Em Laugh.' " Stanley Donen then went to see Freed and asked for a new song. When Freed asked what kind of song, Donen said, "Well, it should be kind of a 'Be a Clown' type number from *The Pirate* [MGM musical of 1948 with a Cole Porter score], because he's trying to cheer Gene up." Freed later came back with "Make 'Em Laugh." He and Nacio Herb Brown had whipped this up to specification and it was perfect. But to the amazement of everyone, the melody was virtually "Be a Clown." No one has ever discovered whether this was an amazing coincidence, a private joke between songwriters, or an innocent and amusing pastiche. Everyone in the unit preferred, apparently, not to bring up the subject to Freed.

Gene Kelly says that the execution of "Make 'Em Laugh" was all based on improvisation. As a spontaneous artist and comedian, O'Connor could never do anything the same way twice. "And so to put it on the same beat, my assistants, Carol Haney and Jeannie Coyne, and I would sit there with a note pad, and he would just do tricks, and we'd put them on one beat. We'd say, 'Do it again' or 'No, you did that on the first beat,' and so he would adjust for the first beat." O'Connor was so funny that he cracked the trio up. The number was his own and nothing was imposed on him, except for the finish. "I wanted him to do the trick that he had done as a little boy in vaudeville. So we got his brother over to rehearse him with a rope to get his confidence back and then to break through the wall at the end. The rest was all his, and it was unbelievable."

O'Connor adds that he ad-libbed all sorts of stunts. He had done the somersault off a wall before in two other pictures. Kelly gave him the bit where he scrunched up his face after running into the door. "We began to rehearse the number and I'd get very tired. I was smoking four packs of cigarettes a day then and getting up those walls was murder. I'd roll around the floor and get carpet burns. They had to bank one wall so I could make it up and then through another wall. My body just had to absorb this tremendous shock."

The Don and Kathy number on the streets of the backlot was now to be "Should I?" but in the middle of June, after the film started shooting, it was changed to "You Were Meant for Me" and the locale was moved to an empty sound stage. "Broadway Melody," listed for Kelly, was not scheduled to shoot until last.

As the title number "Singin' in the Rain" evolved, it became a solo for Kelly, but it remained in the same position in the script as in the original draft. Kelly recalled to biographer Clive Hirschhorn:

> [I was] running through the lyrics of the song to see if they suggested anything other than the obvious when, at the end of the first chorus, I suddenly added the word "dancing" to the lyric—so that it now ran "I'm singin' and *dancin'* in the rain." Instead of just singing the number, I'd dance it as well

. . . . Roger Edens began the number using an expanded introductory "vamp," and all that was left for me to do was to provide a routine that expressed the good mood I was in. And to help me with this I thought of the fun children have splashing about in rain puddles and decided to become a kid again during the number. Having decided that, the rest of the choreography was simple. What wasn't so simple was coordinating my umbrella with the beats of the music, and not falling down in the water and breaking every bone in my body. I was also a bit concerned that I'd catch pneumonia with all the water pouring down on me, particularly as the day we began to shoot the number I had a very bad cold.

This famous number was shot on MGM's backlot Number Two in a day and a half. Special rain pipes were rigged all over the area, and a black tarpaulin covered the exterior street, allowing the company to shoot a controlled night scene during the day.

Although the song "Singin' in the Rain" was used for the first time in films in *The Hollywood Revue*, it was introduced earlier, in a Los Angeles stage presentation called *The Hollywood Music Box Revue* (the 1927 edition). Arthur Freed recalled its origin: "I had the title for some time before writing the song . . . . He [Nacio Herb Brown] came to me one afternoon with the news that he'd just written a great tune for a coloratura soprano. He sat down and played it with all the classic trills. All I could think of was that a vamp in the bass and a few minor changes would give it the zip for some lyrics I'd written." Brown played it again Freed's way and that was it. Some of the lyrics were derived from an earlier Freed song, "The Sun's in My Heart," written in collaboration with Abel Baer.

Here are the other primary songs used in *Singin' in the Rain* and their original sources:

"Broadway Melody" and "You Were Meant for Me," from *The Broadway Melody* (1929).

"Fit as a Fiddle," from the stage revue, George White's *Music Hall Varieties* (1932).

"Beautiful Girl," from *Stage Mother* (1933) and *Going Hollywood* (1933).

"All I Do Is Dream of You," from *Sadie McKee* (1934).

"You Are My Lucky Star" and "Broadway Rhythm," from *Broadway Melody of 1936*.

"Would You?" from *San Francisco* (1936).

"Good Morning," from the film version of *Babes in Arms* (1939).

The heritage of MGM provided the basis for research into the transition from silent to sound in the late 1920s. Still photos of the studio from the period were used as guides by art director Randall Duell and set decorator Jacques Mapes in re-creating portions of an authentic movie lot. Designs of old microphones, cameras, and lighting equipment—and sometimes the genuine articles—were unearthed. For Don Lockwood's Hollywood mansion, the furniture was resurrected that had been seen in the Greta Garbo–John Gilbert vehicle of 1927, *Flesh and the Devil*.

Kelly told me that everybody involved in making the picture went around the studio talking to the veterans of the various departments to get their recollections. More material than could be used was gathered, but what was used was based on actual happenings. "We spent a lot of time with the sound people talking about the problems of recording in those days, when they had to hide microphones all over the set to pick up the actors . . . . Almost everything in *Singin' in the Rain* springs from the truth. It's a conglomeration of bits of movie lore. Douglas Fowley's director is a little bit of Busby Berkeley, and Millard Mitchell's producer has a touch of Arthur Freed in him."

When Walter Plunkett's costumes were shown to the creative group, everyone was so excited that they decided to interpolate a fashion musical sequence reminiscent of the many "Girl on the Magazine Cover" and "Calendar Girl" numbers from previous musicals, to work in conjunction with the song "Beautiful Girl." "We all got together on that," says Plunkett. "We tossed around different ideas; what are camp things of the period?— like pearls with tweed, and I said, 'monkey fur as trimming, for instance' . . . . I entered the business at the height of the flapper's reign. Many of Jean Hagen's costumes are, as nearly as I can remember, duplicates of some I did in all seriousness for Lilyan Tashman. And she was the epitome of chic at that time."

Kelly and Donen, in addition to codirecting, also cochoreographed all the numbers. Donen had been associated with Kelly for years (he was a dancer in the original Broadway production of *Pal Joey* [1940] in which Kelly played the leading role). Later, he became Kelly's assistant choreographer in Hollywood, moving to cochoreographer and then codirector with *On the Town*. Sometimes during rehearsal and shooting they worked together, while at other times they divided their work. "I'd tell Stanley to go over there and direct that scene," says Kelly, "and I'd see that *my* number gets done. That was a marvelous kind of interdependence and independence we had with each other." They often rehearsed in two adjacent rehearsal halls, going back and forth to show each other how things were progressing. But, Kelly emphasizes, they always discussed in detail in advance what they were going to do and how they were going to do it.

Kelly and Donen had extraordinary dedication, energy, and drive. Roger Edens said that "Kelly is a worker—he loves to work." Debbie Reynolds remembers toiling on the "Good Morning" number:

> It was eleven at night and Gene was shouting, "Dance harder! More energy!" Finally Stanley gave the signal that it looked all right and I got up off the floor, only to faint dead away. I was carried to my dressing room and they called my family doctor. He looked at my feet and saw the blood vessels had burst. "What are you doing to this girl?" he asked. And Gene said, "We're making a movie." The doctor forbade me to come to the set for at least three days, but I was back after one day in bed.

After approximately fifty-two days of shooting, the picture—with the exception of the "Broadway Melody" number—was completed in mid-August. *An American in Paris*, which had an extended balletic climax, was about to be released. The advance word was good; the previews were successful. It had been decided to make the "Broadway Melody" number a large-scale ballet follow-up with a vast array of dancers and many sets. (The success of *The Red Shoes* in 1948 ushered in the cycle of film musicals with extended balletic sequences.) The original plan for "Broadway Melody," although nebulous, was to feature Kelly and possibly O'Connor. But O'Connor had a previous commitment to star in his first "Colgate Comedy Hour" for television in early October and had to begin work on the project soon, so he would not be available.

Kelly started to devise the story for the ballet, which now would combine "Broadway Melody" with another of Freed and Brown's songs, "Broadway Rhythm." He needed a girl dancing partner, but the requirements were beyond the ability of Debbie Reynolds. Cyd Charisse, a contract player at MGM since 1945, had been trained from childhood in classical dance and had toured Europe and America with the Ballet Russe de Monte Carlo. She recalls in her and her husband Tony Martin's joint autobiography that "Arthur Freed wanted one big production number . . . . The picture was all finished, but he felt it needed something else . . . . At the time, Carol Haney was Gene's assistant and the assumption was that Carol would be Gene's partner for the big number. Freed tested her . . . . Gene wanted her, but Arthur asked me if I'd do it. I was, at that time, completely unaware that Gene wanted Carol and that Freed wanted me . . . . I told Arthur I'd be delighted . . . . I'll always remember Carol Haney fondly for the way she helped me, when her heart must have been breaking."

At first, according to Kelly, Charisse had difficulty adapting herself to Kelly's particular style ("strong, wide-open, bravura"), but finally she came

Cyd Charisse is taller than Gene Kelly, but the ballet in Singin' in the Rain *was worked out in such a way that this is not noticeable.*

off splendidly in all respects. Interestingly, Charisse is taller than Kelly but the dance was worked out in such a way that this is not noticeable; whenever they are dancing close together they are always bending toward each other, or one or the other is not standing erect.

The resulting thirteen-and-a-half-minute production number—the ballet in *American in Paris* ran seventeen minutes—was a purposely designed kaleidoscope of show-business clichés, particularly those relating to early sound pictures. Charisse was made up and coiffed to look like a combination of silent screen star Pola Negri and vintage flapper Louise Brooks; there was a George Raft gangster type who continually flipped a coin (as in *Scarface*); Kelly's hoofer, with tuxedo, straw hat, and cane, suggested Broadway musical star Harry Richman; the scene in which dancers rush toward the camera waving their arms was a throwback to King Vidor's *Hallelujah* (1929), and so on.

The ballet, which cost $605,960 (the one in *American in Paris* ran $542,000), rehearsed for one month and took two weeks to shoot. *Singin' in the Rain* in its entirety cost $2,540,800—over its original budget by $620,996. Prior to any of the film going into production, the estimate for the "Broadway Melody" number was $85,000. This, of course, was long before the decision to make it a major production in length and scope.

By the time the ballet was finished, the rest of the picture had been edited. As was customary, Kelly and O'Connor then recorded all the tap sounds for their numbers, working to the projected picture on the screen and tapping while watching. Kelly recorded Debbie Reynolds's tap sounds in this manner for the "Good Morning" number as well. Some of Reynolds's singing and dialogue dubbing for Jean Hagen's character was later replaced by the voices of singer Betty Noyes and of Jean Hagen herself. So what we have in the final film is a scene showing Debbie as Kathy supposedly replacing the strident nasal utterances of the character played by Hagen, and in an earlier scene substituting her singing for the song, "Would You?" whereas in actuality Debbie's voice was replaced by the real speaking voice of Jean Hagen and the singing voice of Betty Noyes. There are test records from Roger Edens's special collection at the University of Southern California that include Debbie Reynolds doing her own singing for an earlier version of "Would You?" For the rest of the numbers, her vocalizing did stay in the final film. Finally, some swordplay and acrobatic derring-do footage from

This scene with Debbie Reynolds (left) was cut from Singin' in the Rain.

MGM's *The Three Musketeers* (1948) with Kelly was spliced into *The Royal Rascal* movie-within-a-movie sequence near the beginning of the film.

There were at least three previews: at the De Anza Theater in Riverside, California, on December 21, 1951; at the Bay Theater in Pacific Palisades on December 27, 1951; and at Loew's 72nd Street Theater in New York on March 11, 1952. Some time after the second or third preview, because of the long running time, Freed decided to cut two numbers from the film. The first, Kelly's reprise of "All I Do Is Dream of You," took place after the party at the head of the studio's mansion. Don had become entranced with Kathy the first night they met. Then he goes home and in his pajamas sings and dances around his bedroom a ballad version of the song that Kathy and the girl dancers had done in an up-tempo Charlestonlike manner at the party. The number, four minutes in length, although well done, apparently slowed the picture down at this point. Kelly regarded it as one of his best. A somewhat similar number in a somewhat similar situation, "I've Got a Crush on You," featuring Kelly, was removed from *An American in Paris* after a preview. Kelly says that in "every picture that I've ever done, we've had to cut one ballad, and sometimes two." He was certainly not alone in having this happen to him. Virtually every musical at every studio had at least one song or dance deleted before release.

The other number cut in its entirety was Debbie Reynolds's rendition of "You Are My Lucky Star," played to a large billboard of Kelly at the studio. This was arranged by Roger Edens in a manner similar to the treatment he had devised for Judy Garland's version of "You Made Me Love You" ("Dear Mr. Gable"), which had been used in *Broadway Melody of 1938*. Edens wrote a special introduction and a recitation section between choruses of "You Are My Lucky Star," as he did for "You Made Me Love You." Running a little over four minutes and placed almost immediately after the necessary-to-the-plot "You Were Meant for Me" duet and just before the energetic "Moses," the number suffered from crowded programming and was a logical target for elimination. Two minutes from "Beautiful Girl" were also deleted, in addition to other bits and pieces totaling eighteen minutes.

Singin' in the Rain at the time of its initial release in the spring of 1952 did not do quite as well commercially as *An American in Paris*, but over the years it has transcended by far the somewhat fleeting glory of its predecessor. With the possible exception of the "Broadway Melody" ballet, which, while marvelous in spots, is overly long and forced into a format that was then in fashion, the picture actually improves with age. Since it was a period piece in 1952 and a good-natured spoof, relatively little of the material is dated. The story is more than serviceable, the numbers are joyous, and the comedic invention is still very funny.

DO NOT FORSAKE ME, OH MY DARLIN':
HIGH NOON
(1952)

"I'd always been terribly concerned with Theme," said writer-producer-director Carl Foreman in 1958. "All writers approach their films and stories in different ways. Some begin with character or incident; with me the theme has always been the essence. So the theme had to be one that was important to me emotionally and intellectually and otherwise."

In 1949, *Champion*, a film that Foreman wrote for producer Stanley Kramer's small independent company, drew a parallel between the prizefight business and contemporary society. It was a surprise hit. In 1948, while Foreman was working on the script, Kramer's organization was approached by a representative of the United Nations who was seeking to induce companies to make a film about it. Foreman, who believed in the United Nations, was intrigued and tried to find an approach to the subject. Rather than tell a direct story as outright propaganda he decided to tell it elliptically, as in *Champion*, this time with a background of the old West. "I also wanted to do a Western because I never had. And the time-for-time thing interested me—a film that ran an hour and a half and took place over an hour and a half." Although not common, over the years some films had been made whose running time covered the elapsed dramatic time exactly. For example,

269

The Set-Up, a prizefight story produced in 1948, was structured in that manner.

Foreman did a three-page outline in 1948 titled "High Noon." It was the bare bones of the eventually realized 1952 film. The only thing of primary importance missing was the character of Helen Ramirez, the marshal's half-Mexican ex-mistress, who had also been the mistress of his enemy—the murderer he sent to prison four years earlier. At the beginning of the story the murderer is coming back on the noon train, presumably to seek vengeance. In this outline, the murderer has two cohorts rather than three, and they are both brothers of the released convict, here called Clyde Doyle (later changed to Frank Miller). The marshal's name is Will Tyler, later to become Will Kane.

Foreman discussed the outline and its theme of fear and how it affected a community with Kramer and his other associate, George Glass. According to Foreman, they "were reasonably enthusiastic; not particularly, but they thought it was possible." He then told the story to his agent, E. Henry Lewis. Lewis liked the idea but thought it sounded familiar. He vaguely recalled reading something like it in a magazine in the past year or so. This puzzled Foreman; he instituted a search and eventually found a short story, "The Tin Star," by John Cunningham, in the December 6, 1947, issue of *Collier's*. "Now whether I had read this back in 1947 or not is very hard to say," says Foreman. "it's quite likely that I did, and that what I was guilty of was unconscious plagiarism . . . . So we bought the story."

"The Tin Star" dealt with an aging, arthritic marshal called Doane who decides to face the four men who are coming back to town to kill him. The arrival of the train in the short story is scheduled for 4:10 P.M. rather than noon. Instead of getting married at the beginning of the narrative, as he does in Foreman's version, Doane is a widower. There are very few characters; no Helen Ramirez or justice of the peace. At the end of the story, the murderer he had sent to prison kills Doane, who intercepts a bullet meant for his young deputy.

Other projects were begun at Kramer's company—*Home of the Brave* (1949), *The Men* (1950), *Cyrano de Bergerac* (1951)—and "the Western" kept being postponed. Because of the controversial nature of *Home of the Brave*'s subject matter, *High Noon* was used temporarily as a working title for that forerunner of a series of films dealing with racial bigotry.

Then in January 1951 *High Noon* was reactivated. Foreman worked on a fifteen-page outline that sets up most of the characters and situations as we know them. "The time is 1880. The place is Hadleyville, population 650, somewhere in the territory of New Mexico . . . . Will Doane is in his middle thirties . . . . He is direct, practical, not too articulate . . . . Amy Doane

[Doane's bride] is, without knowing it, one of the new women of the period, women who are beginning to rebel against the limitations and restrictions of the Victorian epoch. Young, attractive, intelligent, strong-willed, Amy is determined not to be a sheltered toy-wife but a full partner in her marriage." Helen Ramirez is included, as is Harvey Pell, Doane's deputy and Helen's lover after her affair with Doane. John G. Cawelti in *The Six-Gun Mystique* (1970) discusses the presence of two different kinds of women in the Western:

> This feminine duality shows up in the contrast between the schoolmarm and the dance-hall girl, or between the hero's Mexican or Indian mistress and the WASP girl he may ultimately marry. The dark girl is a feminine embodiment of the hero's savage, spontaneous side. She understands his deep passions, his savage code of honor and his need to use personal violence. The schoolmarm's civilized code of behavior rejects the passionate urges and the freedom of aggression which mark this side of the hero's character. When the hero becomes involved with the schoolmarm, the dark lady must be destroyed or abandoned.

The murderer's name in the January outline is now Guy Jordan and his men consist of a brother and two others.

During the period Foreman was working on his new expanded outline, the Kramer organization contracted to make thirty films over a five-year period for release through Columbia Pictures. The group was preparing to move to the Columbia lot, where it was to retain complete self-operation. United Artists, the organization that had released all of Kramer's independent films since 1948, still had one picture owed them to complete the contract. It was decided that *High Noon* would be the last film for United Artists and that Foreman would stay behind and function as associate producer under Kramer, who was moving to the Columbia lot from offices at Motion Picture Center on Cahuenga Boulevard in Hollywood.

By now Foreman was much more concerned about the climate in Hollywood regarding the House Un-American Activities Committee (HUAC) than he was about his original United Nations parallel. Since the first 1947 government investigations regarding communist infiltration into the motion-picture industry, the attitude toward these hearings by the people in Hollywood had changed radically. The film colony reacted to news of another impending investigation in 1951 with something close to panic. Hollywood people were frightened, and a good many were unwilling to become involved or to take a stand on the issues. As John Cogley stated in his *Report on Blacklisting* (1956), "Whether or not the Committee was interested in

WHEN THESE HANDS POINT STRAIGHT UP...
the excitement starts!

"HIGH NOON"

STARRING

GARY COOPER

"No one puts his hands on me unless I want him to!"

STANLEY KRAMER PRODUCTIONS
presents
GARY COOPER in "HIGH NOON"
with THOMAS MITCHELL · LLOYD BRIDGES
KATY JURADO · GRACE KELLY · OTTO KRUGER
Lon Chaney · Henry Morgan · DIRECTED BY FRED
ZINNEMANN · Screen Play by Carl Foreman
Music Composed and Directed by Dimitri Tiomkin
Director of Photography Floyd Crosby, A.S.C.
RELEASED THRU UNITED ARTISTS

'establishing blacklists,' it is now beyond question that many who testified (or refused to testify) found themselves 'unemployable' after they appeared as uncooperative witnesses before the Committee. During the scattered movie hearings of 1951, ninety Hollywood figures, almost all well-established in their careers, appeared on the witness stand. They took a variety of positions."

Loyalty oaths were required by guilds and organizations; secret testimonies were held. Foreman says, "These events made me think of a story about Hollywood under the political gun, as it were, and its reaction to the situation. I began to think of using the Western town for a parallel situation . . . . Hollywood has always had its own kind of isolation from the rest of the world anyway, and the idea of a Western town out in the middle of nowhere in the late nineteenth century seemed to work." In February 1951, when HUAC began its next major set of Hollywood hearings, "the town was in a turmoil of fear on the one hand and excitement and gratification on the other. I was writing the screenplay while all this was happening, and writing it with a pretty strong hunch that sooner or later I was going to be subpoenaed and was going to have to appear before the committee. I did get subpoenaed in April 1951 for a hearing that was scheduled for June; so in a way it was almost a relief, because the waiting for it was very unpleasant . . . . I had no intention of being what was called a cooperative witness."

Originally, Foreman wanted to direct *High Noon*, but after he and Kramer showed the script to Fred Zinnemann, who reacted with enthusiasm, Foreman, Kramer, and the other members of the company agreed that it would be better to use Zinnemann as director and let Foreman function as associate producer. In this case, that meant that Foreman would be on the set and on location for all of the filming. Kramer, Foreman, and Zinnemann had collaborated earlier on *The Men* (1950), Marlon Brando's first film.

Although advised against doing *High Noon* by friends who said he was a sensitive European director and wrong for the subject, Zinnemann nevertheless accepted the assignment because he was intrigued by the theme and story. "It was essentially about courage: the victory of a man overcoming his own fear; a theme that is timeless," Zinnemann told me. The story dealt with Zinnemann's favorite character, one who would crop up with many variations in different time periods and locales in the director's films over the years: an individual inherently honor-bound to obey the dictates of his conscience who is compelled to rise to a major test and prove himself.

Kramer was able to secure primary financing from Bruce Church, a wealthy California lettuce grower who had backed two previous Kramer films, *The Men* (1950) and *Cyrano de Bergerac* (1950). The budgets on Kramer's films were relatively modest, but the finished work appeared to be expensive. Kramer's procedures in producing his films were somewhat unusual at that time, but they were designed so that money spent would show on the screen. Because he had no stars—and indeed no actors—under contract, it was necessary to use free-lance people. Spending large sums of money for big names was out of the question. There were three ways of coping with this without sacrificing quality. One was to lure an established star with a good script, pay a small salary, and give the performer a percentage of the profits. The second policy was to use solid supporting characters at their regular rate, but for a short period of time rather than a long shooting schedule. The third approach was to flesh out the cast with relatively unknown faces who, though talented and experienced on the stage and television, had not yet made any impact in films and therefore could not demand high fees.

In the case of *High Noon*, the original concept of the marshal was a man about thirty-five years old. But no one had anyone specific in mind, although Foreman told me he thought vaguely of Henry Fonda. There was an item that appeared in the *Los Angeles Times* and *The Hollywood Reporter* in March and April 1949, stating that Kramer's company was planning to produce *High Noon*, "Western suspense yarn by Carl Foreman to star Kirk Douglas." Douglas had just become a star with the release of *Champion*. Since *High Noon* was stalled, Douglas went on to other things, although neither Foreman nor Kramer recalls Douglas's being considered for the film; they suggest that it may have been a publicity release or a very brief flirtation between the actor and the project. Of course, at that time there was only a three-page outline. Douglas declined to answer my written inquiry regarding this.

Two years later, a copy of the script was sent to Gary Cooper. Cooper was not faring particularly well in films at that time. He had a nonexclusive contract with Warner Bros. and had done some films elsewhere, but none of these was noteworthy and some were poor. Cooper had just finished *Distant Drums* (1951) and was looking for a good script—something different. He liked *High Noon* and agreed to cut his price of $275,000 per picture to approximately $60,000 plus a percentage of the profits. For the role of the marshal's young Quaker bride, an MCA agent, Jay Kantor, brought around still photographs of twenty-two-year-old Grace Kelly, who had appeared in plays in New York and elsewhere and done TV shows and commercials.

Director Fred Zinnemann (seated), cameraman Floyd Crosby (with glasses and without cap), and Gary Cooper filming High Noon *on the Western street of the Columbia Ranch in Burbank.*

Kelly had appeared in only one feature film, *Fourteen Hours* (1951), playing a small role. Kramer met her in New York and later her scene from the feature was run for Kramer, Zinnemann, and Foreman in Hollywood. She was signed for a few hundred dollars a week without a test. There was concern that Cooper might come across as too old opposite Kelly, but then it was felt that perhaps this might work to advantage.

Stanley Kramer's uncle, Earl Kramer, a talent agent, represented Katy Jurado, a Mexican actress who had appeared in many Mexican feature films but only one American film, *The Bullfighter and the Lady* (1951). Kramer and his associates ran the bullfighting film, in which Jurado had a supporting role, and signed her for a small salary. Carl Foreman recalls that $35,000 was allocated to cast the entire picture, aside from Cooper. According to Foreman, Thomas Mitchell was signed for one week at $5,000 rather than his usual rate of $3500 per week when the assignment generally ran at least a few weeks.

In early 1951, while Foreman was still working on the script, location sites were being scouted in California for the town of "Hadleyville, somewhere in the territory of New Mexico" and other sites. The area around Sonora, 335 miles northeast of Los Angeles, seemed perfect for several reasons. The old gold-rush town of Columbia, kept intact and for years a state monument, would serve for Hadleyville's main street, back alleys, fire house, and residential streets. A livery stable where the marshal and his deputy (Lloyd Bridges) brawl was found near Tuolumne City, and an old church there was ideal for one sequence. The Hadleyville railroad station could be re-created near the water tower at Warnerville—one of the last key stops of the historic narrow-gauge Sierra Railroad. The ancient wood-burning train had been modified and kept up for use in motion pictures for many years. Now it was to be the noon train that carries Frank Miller back to Hadleyville. All of these sites were within a few miles of Sonora in the historic Mother Lode country.

Foreman was working on his final draft of the script from the time he was subpoenaed by HUAC in April for a June hearing, which later was postponed until September 21. His friends and associates knew he was planning to be a so-called uncooperative witness—meaning that he would refuse to answer the question about whether he had ever been a member of the Communist Party. Being a "friendly" or "cooperative" witness automatically meant that one must give names, dates, and particulars of other persons' involvement in the party at any time. Says Foreman: "The fact is I was not a Communist." As he was writing the screenplay he began to feel that life was mirroring art and art was mirroring life. Much that was in the script seemed comparable

to what was happening to him. Friends dropped him, and as he walked
down the street people would turn the other way:

> My associates were afraid for themselves—I don't blame
> them—and tried to get me off the film, unsuccessfully. They
> went to Gary Cooper and he refused [to go along with them].
> Fred Zinnemann, too, was very staunch and very loyal, and
> so was our backer, Bruce Church.
>
> There are scenes in the film that are taken from life. The
> scene in the church is a distillation of meetings I had with
> partners, associates, and lawyers. And there's the scene with
> the man who offers to help and comes back with his gun and
> asks, where are the others? Cooper says there are no others
> . . . . I became the Gary Cooper character.

Foreman told me that no one knew about the background of the script:
the political elements, the parallels with his situation, and the Hollywood
syndrome of the time. He deliberately kept all of that to himself. Zinnemann
was drawn to the subject by elements that had nothing to do with politics
and has insisted that the film's meaning is not bound by a narrow

*Director Fred Zinnemann (left), writer-associate producer Carl Foreman, and
supporting player Thomas Mitchell (right) during the filming of* High Noon.

contemporaneity. "I don't believe in ever making a movie to prove anything to anybody or to prove anything to myself," Zinnemann has said, "The only reason I like to make a movie is because it moves me; the material one way or another excites me, and then I hope to be able to transmit that emotion to the audience."

On July 12, 1951, Zinnemann and members of Kramer's company went to the area around Sonora to nail down specific locations and make final arrangements for the filming, which was to begin on September 5. It was discovered that the many trees on the main street of the historic town of Columbia were now in full leaf and therefore blocked a good deal of the view from any vantage point along the street. This was a major photographic problem with regard to the way the story was to be told visually, and it also jeopardized the mood. When the town had been scouted, in the late winter, the trees were stark and not obstructive. All the other locations were fine, so when the crew returned to Motion Picture Center, arrangements were made to rent the standing Western street on Columbia Pictures' ranch in Burbank for the scenes involving the main street and some of the interiors— such as the marshal's office and the saloon—that looked directly out on the street.

One of Kramer's policies that had been in effect since the inception of the company was a rehearsal period with key members of the cast, director, cameraman, and some crew. This was considered unusual at the time— particularly on a relatively inexpensive film. In the case of *High Noon*, approximately one week was allotted, part of which was scheduled for the Western street at the Columbia Studio ranch, and the remainder of which was scheduled for a stage at Motion Picture Center (Helen Ramirez's rooms, and so forth). Naturally, in a picture of this kind, it would be impractical to allow time to rehearse all of the script because of the number of scenes that were primarily action without dialogue. But the majority of the dialogue scenes were rehearsed. A week before, Grace Kelly arrived from Denver, where she had been featured at the Elitch Gardens Theater.

Foreman told me that everyone had thought that Cooper would not choose to take part in the rehearsals, since it was not in his agreement. After a day or two of rehearsals, Cooper called the studio and asked why he had not been asked to participate. After that he was there every day and apparently found stimulation in what was surely a new experience for him.

During the rehearsal period, Katy Jurado was having difficulty pronouncing "Doane," the name of Cooper's character. To alleviate the problem the name was change to Kane.

The filming began on September 6 at the Columbia ranch and then moved to Motion Picture Center before going to Sonora for ten days of location work. In a letter to Louis Giannetti, Zinnemann comments on his exploitation of the concept of time as the principal foil to his protagonist:

> I visualized the threat as a *static* piece of film showing nothing but the railroad tracks running all the way to the horizon. Against it, in almost perpetual motion, the figure of the marshal *moving* hither and yon in his search for help which fails to arrive as people abdicate their conscience for various reasons. Against this, the element of *TIME*, as exemplified by the clocks, moving more and more slowly and becoming larger and larger on the screen until a state of almost suspended animation is reached, just before the clock strikes the first bell of noon.* To accomplish this we over-cranked [photographed in slow motion] the pendulums more and more so movement became almost dream-like in the end. We also over-cranked the shot of the horses and wagon carrying the two women to the station, so that it almost floated by the marshal who was standing still, watching them disappear into the distance. The resolution of the sequence was a big close-up of the marshal with the camera on a boom receding into an enormous high long shot showing the entire village, empty of life, holding its breath, all windows and doors closed, not a soul, not even dogs to be seen, waiting for the impending gunfight.

Zinnemann and cameraman Floyd Crosby discussed a style of photography that would be appropriate for *High Noon*. Zinnemann felt that the black and white should be reminiscent of a newsreel. Crosby relates that "before starting the picture, we agreed that we would do nothing to make the photography pretty. We wanted the feeling of a hot, stark, small Western town. To achieve this, I did not filter the skies as we felt that white skies would add to the feeling of heat." Crosby and Zinnemann recall studying Matthew Brady's photographs of the Civil War. "We deliberately used flat lighting for Cooper to make him look as tired and as old as we could, which was a great departure for a Western hero," says Zinnemann. "And we got a lot of complaints while we were shooting. The front office said this is ghastly photography, get another cameraman!"

Cooper was not feeling well during the filming. Shortly after the completion of the picture, he learned that he had a duodenal ulcer. Lloyd Bridges, who played his deputy, recalls that Cooper was having trouble

---

* *The Set-Up* (1949) contained clocks of varying kinds that repeatedly appeared in the frame. The principal character was a man whose time was running out. His wife wants him to quit the boxing ring, but in the end he demonstrates courage and overcomes his own fear.

with his back and was reluctant to do the fight in the stable with Bridges. But he finally did do it, with very little doubling. Also, during this period Cooper was having personal problems. In any case, it all worked for the character he was playing. Cooper's deliberately unflattering closeups, reflecting perhaps his own stress as well as his effective performance, yielded an extra dimension of credibility to the drama.

High Noon's opening scenes, played under the credit titles, depicted the gathering of the three men who are to meet the noon train. The scenes were shot at Iverson Ranch, a location near Chatsworth used in countless Westerns over the years. As with so many aspects of *High Noon*'s structure and techniques, this handling of the opening titles became a cliché, but it was fresh at the time and had been pioneered by Kramer's company with particular effectiveness in *Champion*. In the March 19, 1951, first rough draft of *High Noon*, the picture was to open with scenes of Hadleyville, empty and desolate—a ghost town. Various views of the long-dead town were to be seen under the credit titles. Then, following the titles, the scene of the ghost town dissolves to Hadleyville as it was. It is Sunday, a little before eleven o'clock. At the conclusion of the film, after the marshal and Amy are seen riding out of town, there was to be a dissolve to the ghost-town street as it was seen in the opening. "In the foreground, a lizard sunning itself on a tilted board, flicks its forked tongue. The End title comes up. Fade Out." Although Hadleyville is fictitious, Foreman drew upon his recollection of Mark Twain's classic 1900 short story, "The Man That Corrupted Hadleyburg" for the name. That story was a slashing attack on the smugness, hypocrisy, and venality of a small town.

The filming reflected Zinnemann's characteristically efficient and thorough planning. Cameraman Crosby has said that Zinnemann was the kind of director who generally lined up his own shots and knew exactly what he wanted. There was a dramatic moment during the filming of the low-angle shot looking down the railway tracks to infinity. Near the climax of the story Zinnemann wanted to use this same shot to show the approach of the noon train, first seen as a wisp of smoke in the distance, then gradually approaching and stopping in front of the camera, which was positioned on the ground between the tracks. On the first take, the engineer stopped the train too soon. He was told to stop later. As the train approached closer and closer during the second take, the camera operator realized at the last second that the train would not stop soon enough. He got out of the way just in time, but the camera was crushed.

The time-honored shoot-out and the woman's attempt to talk her man out of it was popularized in Owen Wister's book, *The Virginian* (1902), and its subsequent stage and film versions—to say nothing of any number of variations in other books, stories, and films over the years. In *High Noon*, Kane's bride lays it on the line:

AMY

Will, I'm begging you—please! . . . . Let's go!

WILL

I can't.

AMY

Don't try to be a hero! You don't have to be a hero—not for me!

WILL

I'm not trying to be a hero! If you think I like this, you're crazy!

AMY

If you won't go with me now—I'll be on that train when it leaves here—

WILL

I've got to stay, Amy.

In *Stagecoach*, Dallas (Claire Trevor) pleads with Ringo (John Wayne):

DALLAS

It'll be three against one in Lordsburg.

RINGO

There's some things a man just can't run away from.

DALLAS

How can you talk about your life and my life when you're throwing 'em away?

RINGO

What do you want me to do?

DALLAS

Would it make us any happier if Luke Plummer was dead? One of his brothers would be after you with a gun. We'd never be safe. I don't want that kind of life, Ringo.

RINGO

I don't see what else I can do.

DALLAS

Go now . . . . Get away . . . forget Lordsburg . . . forget the
Plummers.

And in *The Virginian* (1929) Molly (Mary Brian) confronts The Virginian
(Gary Cooper):

MOLLY

We can go away—I'll go with you—anywhere.

THE VIRGINIAN

You mean *run* away? Where could a man go? You can't run
away from yourself. I got to stay.

MOLLY

But you can't stay just to kill—or be killed.

THE VIRGINIAN

You don't think I want to do this?

MOLLY

Everybody knows you're not a coward.

THE VIRGINIAN

No, Molly, there's more to it than that.

MOLLY

It's just your pride. Because you've got some idea about your
personal honor.

THE VIRGINIAN

I don't know what you call it—but it's somethin' in the feelin's
of a man—deep down inside. Something a man can't go back
on.

In discussing the Western hero's ideal of honor, Robert Warshow says
that "he fights not for advantage and not for the right, but to state what he
is, and he must live in a world which permits that statement. The Westerner
is the last gentleman and the movies which over and over tell his story are
probably the last art form in which the concept of honor retains its strength."
The climax of *High Noon* is lengthy and played for maximum suspense in
the back alleys, a stable, and offices of Hadleyville. It bears similarities to
the manner in which the climax of the 1929 film version of *The Virginian*
was executed—with a young Gary Cooper stalking his enemy, played by

AMY: Will, I'm begging
you—please! Let's go!
WILL: I've got to stay,
Amy.
High Noon. Gary Cooper
and Grace Kelly

Walter Huston. In *High Noon*, Frank Miller and his cohorts pursue the marshal in a relentless and complex game of hide-and-seek. Zinnemann's elaborate choreography of this mixture of cunning and confusion is handled in a relatively realistic manner. John Cunningham, the author of the short story on which *High Noon* was based, has said that the old situation of the climactic shoot out was undertaken in his story mostly as an exercise—the problem being to represent the showdown as it might actually happen, within the limits of strict plausibility.

As filming progressed, Foreman began to worry about how the traditional shoot out should end. He felt that the odds against the marshal were perhaps too great and that to be properly realistic he should go down in defeat bravely and die, as he did in the short story. Foreman discussed this with Zinnemann on different occasions. "And then I underwent a change of feeling," Foreman recalls, "perhaps out of my own needs. 'We're going to wear the audience out. If we're successful they're going to be completely identified with the marshal and they're going to want him to survive even though everybody in town is telling him to give in. If we let him go, if he dies, what we'll be saying is that you just can't win, so give in. And I don't think we should do that because maybe he has a chance to survive.' He [Zinnemann] agreed, so we kept the happy ending."

   With another week or so left of filming, Carl Foreman finally appeared
before the House Un-American Activities Committee on September 24,
1951. Foreman invoked a variation of the Fifth Amendment that later
became known as the "diminished Fifth." Foreman denied that he was a
Communist Party member at the time he was testifying but would not state
whether he had been a member at some previous date. But the "diminished
Fifth" proved to be of no help to the basically uncooperative witnesses.
Later, following considerable unpleasantness, a settlement was reached
between Foreman and his associates at Stanley Kramer Productions, Inc.,
and Foreman was not involved with the film after shooting was completed.
Before *High Noon* was released, he had moved to England, where for five
years he was able to get only sub rosa film assignments; for example, working
without credit on the script for *The Bridge on the River Kwai* (1957).
Foreman has said that, "When the political thing blew up, it was decided
that it would save the picture [*High Noon*] at the box office to eliminate my
identification with it." Actually, Foreman's name was removed as associate
producer, although he still received credit for writing the script.
   High Noon's shooting schedule was thirty-two days, including location
filming but excluding the rehearsal period. The negative cost was approxi-

MOLLY: We can go away . . .
THE VIRGINIAN: You can't
run away from yourself. I got
to stay.
The Virginian (1929). Mary
Brian and Gary Cooper

mately $750,000. Zinnemann worked with editor Elmo Williams for about a week or ten days after filming was over. Contrary to some accounts, Williams had been on the picture since the beginning of filming. Then Stanley Kramer looked at the rough cut and was not pleased. According to Williams, Kramer did not have any specific complaints at that time; he was just disappointed. He told Williams that he was going to Palm Springs for a few days and would discuss changes when he returned, after having a chance to think about the film. Williams had the feeling that his changes probably would include bringing in a new editor. Williams told me:

> I asked Stanley if I could work on the picture while he was away. He answered that it needed a lot more work than could be done over a long weekend. But I persisted by asking him what did he have to lose? He agreed, and I worked day and night recutting the film. I felt the emphasis should be on Cooper and his problem, and anything that didn't contribute to this should be eliminated—including some of the material between Grace Kelly and Katy Jurado as well as a scene between Jurado and Lloyd Bridges.

Williams knew that the picture needed tightening; the suspense was not working—as reflected in the relatively long initial cut. This is fairly standard for a first cut.

The first thing to go was a good deal of material involving another deputy and his prisoner that took place a considerable distance from the town. In the script there were three scenes with the second deputy (James Brown) and his prisoner (stunt man John Dayheim), who were heading back to Hadleyville. The first scene, about a third of the way into the script, establishes the situation and the fact that the deputy wants to get back to town in time for the marshal's wedding. The second scene, not quite two-thirds into the screenplay, involved a fight between the deputy and his prisoner at a water hole on the way. The last scene, taking place just before the arrival of the noon train in Hadleyville, is at a ranch house serving as an old stagecoach station where the deputy stops for a cold beer and to have the horses attended. Since he is already late, the deputy decides to linger a while with a pretty young Mexican girl (Roberta Haynes) who lives at the ranch house. Carl Foreman in describing the stopping-off place in his script states, "It is not a fancy place. For a good picturization of this kind of establishment, you should see *Stagecoach* [1939]." Actor James Brown said shortly after the film was released that "Fred Zinnemann and Carl Foreman told me that the scenes I had . . . were written in case they needed more suspense."

Foreman recalls that his worry as the writer was that it would become too claustrophobic never to leave the town and the railway station. Because of this he had written in the business about the other deputy, trying to make a virtue out of it, a reason to cut away from town for sequences that could be used at almost any point in the film. Since it was insurance, the material had been saved for the last two days of location shooting around Sonora. "Then, after having marvelous weather all the time we were up there at Sonora, the weather closed in on us those last two days. We were rushed; we had trouble staging the fight scene at the waterhole, and the whole sequence didn't turn out so good."

Elmo Williams eliminated the insurance material with the second deputy. Other sequences were broken up or rearranged. Williams cut for maximum tension whenever possible, and the picture was shortened by at least twenty minutes, according to Kramer and Williams.

Kramer returned from Palm Springs and a screening was set up in his home. Williams decided to set the mood of the film by putting in some temporary music over the prologue, where the main titles would be placed. This material, showing the gathering of the outlaws, had been shot without sound, as it was designed to be used in conjunction with music and titles. Since no music had been scored at this pint, Williams, who "wanted the feeling of a kind of folk tale," used over the prologue a Burl Ives commercial recording of "Riders in the Sky," which he felt had the proper mood and rhythmic pattern in the use of the guitar, which suggested horses' hooves. Kramer was delighted with Williams's re-editing and felt considerably better about the film. Later, however, Williams recalls, he "had to go back and stretch the film" somewhat by reinstating some of the material he had cut involving Kelly, Jurado, and Bridges in order for the picture to have a longer running time than a B movie. The final cut ran eighty-five minutes.

Kramer then discussed the music with Dimitri Tiomkin, who had done the scores for all of his films. Kramer wanted Tiomkin to pick up the idea of the opening Western ballad, compose one specifically for *High Noon*, and continue to use it throughout the film. It is possible that Kramer or Tiomkin, or even Williams, although they recall nothing about it, had heard at Columbia Studios a title song rendered by Tennessee Ernie Ford and used during *Man in the Saddle*, a Randolph Scott Western that was being readied for Columbia release while *High Noon* was finishing shooting and in the editorial stage. Although it did not attract major attention, the title song treatment as used in that film served as a forerunner to the ballad treatment in *High Noon*. But the real precursor of the theme ballad was *A Walk in the Sun* (1945), a World War II drama that used a simple narrative ballad rendered in a deep, unidentified solo voice for the purpose of setting the

The time-honored shoot-out: High Noon.

mood and telling part of the story. It was sung about a half dozen times throughout the film.*

Tex Ritter, the popular singer of cowboy songs and star of over fifty B westerns in the 1930s and 1940s, was engaged to sing the ballad for *High Noon*. The plaintive lyric, by Ned Washington, that starts with "Do not forsake me, oh my darlin' on this our wedding day" was expressed as the film began. It was then used as connective tissue throughout. As the picture progressed, Ritter's unique interpretation and low, husky voice took on a ghostlike echo quality made possible in the final sound mixing. Herbert Taylor's orchestration made use of three accordians, full woodwind and brass sections, violas, cellos, and three double basses, but not a single violin. In Tiomkin's autobiography, *Please Don't Hate Me* (1959), he says that "a final touch for the orchestration was provided by the pianist Ray Turner, who played in the orchestra. We were rehearsing a passage with strong rhythmic effects when he suggested a novel trick on a newfangled electronic instrument with a piano keyboard [the Novachord]. He struck it with his elbow, hitting several keys. It had a curious percussive effect, and we used it." The unique sound was used to simulate and exaggerate horses' hooves beating out rhythm.

Williams and Tiomkin disagreed over the placement of music during the gunfight at the end of the film. Williams wanted the sequence "to play between silence—no music—and sudden bursts of gunfire, whereas Tiomkin insisted there be background scoring all through the scene. We took our argument to Kramer, and Tiomkin wore him down and got his way. I still think the use of music hurt the effectiveness of the climax."

* For *Smoky* (1946), over the opening titles Burl Ives sang new lyrics to "On Top of Old Smoky," accompanying himself on the guitar.

Kramer told me that it was decided to use portions of the ballad being sung about nine times during the film, mostly over each of the marshal's walks from one place to another in the town to seek aid against Frank Miller. "At the preview," recalls Kramer, "after the fourth rendition of the ballad, the audience began to laugh, and I'm sitting there knowing there are about five more renditions coming up. The whole preview was a disaster. When we came out of the theater my associates told me to get rid of the song. There was also renewed concern that Cooper was too old and Grace Kelly too young, and so on."

The number of instances in which the ballad was sung was then cut down, and the length of the lyric references was abbreviated in some of the remaining renditions. Elmo Williams recalls no major changes between the first preview in Pomona and the second in Long Beach, which took place a week or so later. All involved agreed that the second screening was also a disappointment.

After witnessing the poor previews, composer Dimitri Tiomkin secured publication rights to the ballad. "Now I would see if I could make anything on the song on phonograph records. A flop song from a film fiasco didn't look very promising, but there was no harm trying."

Harry Cohn, head of Columbia Pictures, curious to see what Kramer's last film for United Artists was like, had arranged for a screening before the previews, unknown to Kramer. He thought that if the film had any value, it might be arranged for Columbia to handle the release. He was unimpressed and told Kramer that the movie was a turkey.

No one is quite sure why the film eventually became a success and won four Academy Awards. George J. Schaefer, who at one time had been

The time-honored shoot-out: The Virginian *(1929).*

president of RKO Radio Pictures and was now with Kramer, saw the film and was convinced that with special handling, promotion, and distribution it would do exceptionally well. Then trade screenings yielded particularly fine reviews. As a result, United Artists, recently reorganized and desperately looking for a good product, decided to get behind the picture and use every strategy to promote and guide it. Taking their clue from the reviews, the campaign for the picture emphasized the suspense, the adult Western slant, the idea that this picture was different, unusual, and nonformulaic. Certainly it was not to be put into the same category as the routine action Western, but neither was it to be categorized as being too adult or too different or dry (a problem Fox's well-done *The Gunfighter*, released two years earlier, had encountered, thereby producing low commercial returns).

Then there was the amazing popularity of the "High Noon" ballad. Before the film was released, Dimitri Tiomkin was trying to get his song recorded. In his autobiography he says: "The record company that handled Tex Ritter [Capitol] wasn't interested, at least not at first; they came along with a Tex Ritter record later. I persuaded another company [Columbia Records] to issue the song with the popular singer Frankie Laine. The record was an immediate success, one of the hits of the year . . . . The success of the record promoted [the film]. Why had *High Noon* got such an unfavorable reception at the preview? Picture business is full of such puzzles."

SELECTED
CHAPTER BIBLIOGRAPHIES

Books, articles, and oral histories that were of particular importance in tracing the origin and evolution of the films and the materials upon which they were based are included below. In certain cases, books—and particularly articles—dealing with the background and career of some of the key people in front of and behind the camera are also listed. Works that are primarily evaluative and interpretive have for the most part been excluded from the list.

In addition, the following individuals directly involved with the films discussed in this book, or the works upon which they were based, were interviewed by me in person or on the telephone or answered questions submitted in correspondence. I am grateful for their time and interest in this project.

Others not interviewed had either contributed information for previously published material, were not available, or were deceased.

Dana Andrews	William Keighley	Herbert Taylor
Pandro S. Berman	Gene Kelly	Frank Thomas
Henry Blanke	Stanley Kramer	Peter Viertel
Frank Capra	Joseph La Shelle	Elmo Williams
Vera Caspary	Karl Malden	Sir John Woolf
Albert Cavens	Rouben Mamoulian	Jane Wyatt
Claudette Colbert	Andrew Marton	Fred Zinnemann
John Collier	Seton I. Miller	
Merian C. Cooper	Alex North	
Adolph Deutsch	Mary Orr	
Robert Florey	George Parrish	
Carl Foreman	Vincent Price	
Harry Goulding	David Raksin	
Ray Heindorf	Irving Rapper	
Sam Jaffe	Irene Mayer Selznick	
Elia Kazan	Murray Spivack	

1. IN HIS OWN IMAGE: FRANKENSTEIN (1931)

BOOKS

Anobile, Richard J., ed. *Frankenstein*. New York: Universe Books, 1974.
Curtis, James. *James Whale*. Metuchen, N.J.: The Scarecrow Press, 1982.
Florescu, Radu. *In Search of Frankenstein*. New York: New York Graphic Society, 1975.
Glut, Donald F. *The Frankenstein Legend*. Metuchen, N.J.: The Scarecrow Press, 1973.
Jensen, Paul M. *Boris Karloff and His Films*. South Brunswick and New York: A. S. Barnes, 1974.
Levine, George, and Knoepflmacher, U. C., eds. *The Endurance of Frankenstein*. Berkeley: University of California Press, 1979.
Mank, Gregory William. *It's Alive! The Classic Cinema Saga of Frankenstein*. San Diego: A. S. Barnes, 1981.
Shelley, Mary Wollstonecraft. *Frankenstein, or the Modern Prometheus*. The 1818 text. Ed. James Rieger. Indianapolis and New York: Bobbs-Merrill, 1974.

PERIODICALS

"Oh, You Beautiful Monster." *New York Times*, January 29, 1939.

STUDIO AND ARCHIVAL COLLECTIONS

Universal Studios (Universal City): Central Files.
British Library (London, Great Russell Street): Lord Chamberlain's Collection of Licensed Plays.

2. A DREAM AND A VISION: LOST HORIZON (1937)

BOOKS

Capra, Frank. *The Name above the Title*. New York: Macmillan, 1971.
Hilton, James. *Lost Horizon*. New York: William Morrow, 1975.
Kreuger, Miles, ed. *Souvenir Programs of Twelve Classic Movies, 1927–1941*. New York: Dover, 1977.
Scherle, Victor, and Levy, William Turner. *The Films of Frank Capra*. Secaucus, N.J.: The Citadel Press, 1977.

PERIODICALS

Connor, Edward. "Revisiting *Lost Horizon*." *Screen Facts*, January–February 1963.
Dooley, Roger B. "Jane Wyatt." *Films in Review*, January 1972.
Rosar, William H. "*Lost Horizon*: An Account of the Composition of the Score." *Film Music Notebook*, Vol. 4, 1978.

ORAL HISTORY

D'Antonio, Joanne. *Bundy: An Oral History of Andrew Marton*. Hollywood: A Directors Guild of America Oral History, 1980.

STUDIO AND ARCHIVAL COLLECTIONS

Columbia Pictures (Burbank): Story Files.

3. THEY CALLED IT DISNEY'S FOLLY: SNOW WHITE AND THE SEVEN DWARFS (1937)

BOOKS

Feild, Robert D. *The Art of Walt Disney.* London: Collins, 1944.

Finch, Christopher. *The Art of Walt Disney.* New York: Harry N. Abrams, 1973.

Grimm, Jacob, and Grimm, Wilhelm. *Grimms' Tales for Young and Old.* Translated by Ralph Manheim. New York: Doubleday, 1977.

Maltin, Leonard. *The Disney Films.* New York: Crown, 1973.

Opie, Iona, and Opie, Peter, eds. *The Classic Fairy Tales.* New York: Oxford University Press, 1974.

Thomas, Bob. *Walt Disney.* New York: Simon & Schuster, 1976.

Vreeland, Frank. *Foremost Films of 1938: A Yearbook of the American Screen.* New York: Pitman, 1939.

Wagner, Walter. *You Must Remember This.* New York: Putnam's, 1975.

Walt Disney's Snow White and the Seven Dwarfs. New York: Harper, 1937.

PERIODICALS

Canemaker, John. "Art Babbitt: The Animator as Firebrand." *Millimeter,* September 1975.

Canemaker, John. "Disney Design 1928–1979." *Millimeter,* September 1979.

Canemaker, John. "Grim Natwick." *Film Comment,* January–February 1975.

Canemaker, John. "Sincerely Yours, Frank Thomas." *Millimeter,* January 1975.

Smith, David R. "Ben Sharpsteen: 33 Years with Disney." *Millimeter,* April 1975.

STUDIO AND ARCHIVAL COLLECTIONS

Walt Disney Studio Archives (Burbank): *Snow White* Files.

4. "WELCOME TO SHERWOOD!": THE ADVENTURES OF ROBIN HOOD (1938)

BOOKS

Appleby, John T. *England without Richard: 1189–1199.* London: G. Bell, 1965.

Behlmer, Rudy, ed. *The Adventures of Robin Hood* (includes screenplay). Madison: The University of Wisconsin Press, 1979.

Dobson, R. B., and Taylor, J. *Rymes of Robyn Hood: An Introduction to the English Outlaw.* Pittsburgh: University of Pittsburgh Press, 1976.

Pyle, Howard. *The Merry Adventures of Robin Hood of Great Reknown in Nottinghamshire.* New York: Scribner's, 1883.

Richards, Jeffrey. *Swordsmen of the Screen: From Douglas Fairbanks to Michael York.* London: Routledge and Kegan Paul, 1977.

Ritson, Joseph, ed. *Robin Hood: A Collection of Poems, Songs, and Ballads.* London: George Routledge, 1884. Originally published 1795.
Scott, Sir Walter. *Ivanhoe.* London: Adam and Charles Black, 1893. Originally published 1819.
Smith, Harry B., and De Koven, Reginald. *Robin Hood: A Comic Opera.* Chicago: Slason Thompson, 1890.

PERIODICALS

Geltzer, George. "William Keighley." *Films in Review*, October 1974.
Nolan, Jack Edmund. "Michael Curtiz." *Films in Review*, November 1970.
"Warner Brothers," *Fortune*, December 1937.

STUDIO AND ARCHIVAL COLLECTIONS

University of Southern California (Los Angeles): Warner Bros. Archives.
Wisconsin Center for Film and Theater Research (Madison): United Artists Collection.

5. THE ROVER BOYS IN INDIA: GUNGA DIN (1939)

BOOKS

Richards, Jeffrey. *Visions of Yesterday.* London: Routledge and Kegan Paul, 1973.

PERIODICALS

Abbas, Khwaja Ahmad. "*Gunga Din* Another Scandalously Anti-Indian Picture!" *Filmindia*, February 1940.
Law, Frederick H. "A Guide to the Appreciation of the Photoplay Based on Kipling's 'Gunga Din.' " *Photoplay Studies*, Vol. 5, No. 2 (1939).
Reed, Rochelle, ed. "George Stevens." *Dialogue on Film* (The American Film Institute), Vol. 4, No. 8. May–June 1975.

ORAL HISTORY

Steen, Mike. *Pandro S. Berman.* Beverly Hills: American Film Institute Oral History Project, 1972.

STUDIO AND ARCHIVAL COLLECTIONS

RKO Radio Pictures (Los Angeles): Files.
Academy of Motion Picture Arts and Sciences Library (Beverly Hills): George Stevens Collection.

6. BRET HARTE IN MONUMENT VALLEY: STAGECOACH (1939)

BOOKS

Balio, Tino. *United Artists: The Company Built by the Stars.* Madison: The University of Wisconsin Press, 1976.

Canutt, Yakima, and Drake, Oliver. *Stunt Man.* New York: Walker, 1979.
Cawelti, John G. *The Six-Gun Mystique.* Bowling Green, Oh.: Bowling Green Popular Press, 1970.
Gassner, John, and Nichols, Dudley, eds. *Great Film Plays.* New York: Crown, 1959.
Gassner, John, and Nichols, Dudley, eds. *Twenty Best Screenplays.* New York: Crown, 1943.
Klinck, Richard E. *Land of Room Enough and Time Enough.* Albequerque: University of New Mexico Press, 1953.
Nichols, Dudley. *Stagecoach: A Film by John Ford and Dudley Nichols.* (Includes "Stage to Lordsburg" short story.) New York: Frederick Ungar, 1982.
Tuska, John, ed. *Close Up: The Contract Director.* Metuchen, N.J.: The Scarecrow Press, 1976.
Warshow, Robert. *The Immediate Experience.* Garden City, N.Y.: Doubleday, 1962.
Wister, Owen. *The Virginian.* New York: Macmillan, 1902.
Zolotow, Maurice. *Shooting Star: A Biography of John Wayne.* New York: Simon & Schuster, 1974.

PERIODICALS

Eyman, Scott. "Looking Back: John Wayne Talking to Scott Eyman." *Focus on Film,* Spring 1975.
Haycox, Ernest. "Stage to Lordsburg." *Collier's,* April 10, 1937.
McCarthy, Todd. "John Ford and Monument Valley." *American Film,* May 1978.
Thomas, Bob, ed. "John Ford and *Stagecoach.*" *Action: Directors Guild of America* (special issue), September–October 1971.
Warfield, Nancy D. "The Structure of John Ford's *Stagecoach.*" *The Little Film Gazette of N.D.W.,* Vol. 5, No. 1, 1974.

ORAL HISTORY

McMahon, Louis. *Yakima Canutt.* Hollywood: A Directors Guild of America Oral History, 1979.

STUDIO AND/OR ARCHIVAL COLLECTIONS

Wisconsin Center for Film and Theater Research (Madison): United Artists Collection.
Paramount Studios (Hollywood): Music Library.
University of Texas at Austin: David O. Selznick Collection.

7. "WE'RE THE PEOPLE": THE GRAPES OF WRATH (1940)

BOOKS

Bluestone, George. *Novels into Film.* Berkeley: University of California Press, 1957.
French, Warren. Film guide to *The Grapes of Wrath.* Bloomington: Indiana University Press, 1973.
Gassner, John, and Nichols, Dudley, eds. *Twenty Best Screenplays.* New York: Crown, 1943.

Steen, Mike. *Hollywood Speaks: An Oral History*. New York: Putnam's, 1974.
Steinbeck, John. *The Grapes of Wrath*. New York: Viking, 1939.
Steinbeck, Elaine, and Wallsten, Robert, eds. *Steinbeck: A Life in Letters*. New York: Viking, 1975.

PERIODICALS

Pulliam, Rebecca. "*The Grapes of Wrath*." *The Velvet Light Trap*, No. 2, August 1971.
Quigley, Martin. "*Grapes of Wrath:* An Editorial Viewpoint." *Motion Picture Herald*, January 27, 1940.
Slocombe, Douglas. "The Work of Gregg Toland." *Sequence*, Summer 1949.

ORAL HISTORY

Stempel, Thomas R. *Nunnally Johnson*. Beverly Hills: University of California at Los Angeles/American Film Institute Oral History Project, 1969.

STUDIO AND ARCHIVAL COLLECTIONS

Twentieth Century-Fox Studios (Beverly Hills): Story Files.
University of Southern California (Los Angeles): Twentieth Century-Fox Script Collection.

8. THE STUFF THAT DREAMS ARE MADE OF: THE MALTESE FALCON (1941)

BOOKS

Anobile, Richard J., ed. *The Maltese Falcon*. New York: Universe, 1974.
Astor, Mary. *A Life on Film*. New York: Delacorte Press, 1971.
Hammett, Dashiell. *The Maltese Falcon*. New York: The Modern Library (Random House), 1934.
Nolan, William F. *Dashiell Hammett: A Casebook*. Santa Barbara: McNally and Loftin, 1969.
Pratley, Gerald. *The Cinema of John Huston*. South Brunswick and New York: A. S. Barnes, 1977.

PERIODICALS

Hammett, Dashiell. "*The Maltese Falcon*." *Black Mask*, September, October, November, December 1929; January 1930.
Hinckle, Warren, ed. "Dashiell Hammett's San Francisco." *City of San Francisco*, November 4, 1975.
Naremore, James. "John Huston and *The Maltese Falcon*." *Literature/Film Quarterly*, July 1973.

ORAL HISTORY

Steinberg, Barry. *Henry Blanke*. Beverly Hills: A University of California at Los Angeles/American Film Institute Oral History Project, 1969.

STUDIO AND ARCHIVAL COLLECTIONS

University of Southern California (Los Angeles): Warner Bros. Archives.
Wisconsin Center for Film and Theater Research (Madison): United Artists Collection.

9. GEORGE RAFT IN CASABLANCA? (1943)

BOOKS

Anobile, Richard J., ed. *Casablanca*. New York: Universe Books, 1974.
Cameron, Evan William, ed. *Sound and the Cinema*. Pleasantville, N.Y.: Redgrave, 1980.
Francisco, Charles. *You Must Remember This . . . The Filming of Casablanca*. Englewood Cliffs, N.J.: Prentice-Hall, 1980.
Gassner, John, and Nichols, Dudley, eds. *Best Film Plays of 1943–1944*. New York: Crown, 1945.
Koch, Howard, compiler. *Casablanca: Script and Legend*. Woodstock, N.Y.: Overlook Press, 1973.
Wallis, Hal, and Higham, Charles. *Starmaker: The Autobiography of Hal Wallis*. New York: Macmillan, 1980.

PERIODICALS

Greenberg, Joel. "Writing for the Movies: Interview with Casey Robinson." *Focus on Film*, April 1979.
Haver, Ronald. "Finally, the Truth About *Casablanca*." *American Film*, June 1976 (also October 1976, "Letters").
Nolan, Jack Edmund. "Michael Curtiz." *Films in Review*, November 1970.

ORAL HISTORIES

Greenberg, Joel. *Casey Robinson*. Beverly Hills: An American Film Institute Oral History Project, 1974.
Sherman, Eric. *Howard Koch*. Beverly Hills: An American Film Institute Oral History Project, 1974.

STUDIO AND ARCHIVAL COLLECTIONS

University of Southern California (Los Angeles): Warner Bros. Archives.
Wisconsin Center for Film and Theater Research (Madison): United Artists Collection.

10. THE FACE IN THE MISTY LIGHT: LAURA (1944)

BOOKS

Caspary, Vera. *Laura*. Boston: Houghton Mifflin, 1943.
Caspary, Vera, and Sklar, George. *Laura* (Acting Edition). New York: Dramatists Play Service, 1948.

Preminger, Otto. *Preminger: An Autobiography.* Garden City, N.Y.: Doubleday, 1977.
Pratley, Gerald. *The Cinema of Otto Preminger.* New York: A. S. Barnes, 1971.
Tierney, Gene, with Herskowitz, Mickey. *Self-Portrait.* New York: Wyden Books, 1979.

PERIODICALS

Caspary, Vera. "My *Laura* and Otto's." *Saturday Review,* June 26, 1971.
Caspary, Vera. "Ring Twice for Laura." *Collier's,* October 17, 24, 31, 1942; November 7, 14, 21, 28, 1942.
Lourcelles, Jacques. "*Laura:* Scénario d'un Scénario." *L'Avant-Scene,* July–September 1978.
McVay, Doug. "Faithful in His Fashion: Otto Preminger's *Laura.*" *Bright Lights,* No. 8, 1979.
Preminger, Otto. "The Making of *Laura.*" *On Film,* Vol. 1, No. 0, 1970.
Tierney, Gene. "Farewell to the Orient." *The Hollywood Reporter,* November 5, 1945.

STUDIO AND ARCHIVAL COLLECTIONS

Twentieth Century-Fox Studios (Beverly Hills): Story Files.
University of Southern California (Los Angeles): Twentieth Century-Fox Script Collection.

11. WAVES OF LOVE OVER THE FOOTLIGHTS: ALL ABOUT EVE (1950)

BOOKS

Baxter, Anne. *Intermission, A True Story.* New York: Putnam's, 1976.
Carey, Gary, with Mankiewicz, Joseph L. *More about All About Eve* (includes screenplay). New York: Random House, 1972.
Geist, Kenneth L. *Pictures Will Talk.* New York: Scribners, 1978.
Mankiewicz, Joseph L. *All About Eve.* New York: Random House, 1951.
Stine, Whitney, and Davis, Bette. *Mother Goddam.* New York: Hawthorn, 1974.

PERIODICALS

Moore, Louis; Tait, Donald; and Johnson, Julian. "The Truth About *All About Eve.*" *Action* (Twentieth Century-Fox Studio Publication), December 1950.
Orr, Mary. "The Wisdom of Eve." *Cosmopolitan,* May 1946.

STUDIO AND ARCHIVAL COLLECTIONS

Twentieth Century-Fox Studios (Beverly Hills): Story Files.
University of Southern California (Los Angeles): Twentieth Century-Fox Script Collection.

12. THE RAVISHMENT OF THE TENDER: A STREETCAR NAMED DESIRE (1951)

BOOKS

Ciment, Michel. *Kazan on Kazan.* New York: Viking, 1974.

Garrett, George P.; Hardison, O. B., Jr.; and Gelfman, Jane R., eds. *Film Scripts One* (includes *A Streetcar Named Desire*). New York: Appleton-Century-Crofts, 1971.

Phillips, Gene D. *The Films of Tennessee Williams.* Philadelphia: Art Alliance Press, 1980.

Randall, Richard S. *Censorship of the Movies.* Madison: University of Wisconsin Press, 1968.

Schumach, Murray. *The Face on the Cutting Room Floor.* New York: William Morrow, 1964.

Vizzard, Jack. *See No Evil: Life Inside a Hollywood Censor.* New York: Simon & Schuster, 1970.

Williams, Tennessee. *27 Wagons Full of Cotton and Other One Act Plays.* (Includes *Portrait of a Madonna* and *The Lady of Larkspur Lotion.*) Norfolk: New Directions, 1953.

Williams, Tennessee. *A Streetcar Named Desire.* New York: New Directions, 1947.

Williams, Tennessee. *A Streetcar Named Desire.* New York: The New American Library, n.d. (paperback).

NEWSPAPER

Kazan, Elia. "Pressure Problem." *New York Times*, October 21, 1951, sec. 10, p. 5.

STUDIO AND ARCHIVAL COLLECTIONS

University of Southern California (Los Angeles): Warner Bros. Archives.

13. "REMEMBER ELEANOR ROOSEVELT'S SERENE SMILE": THE AFRICAN QUEEN (1951)

BOOKS

Agee, James. *Agee on Film, vol. 2.* (includes *The African Queen* screenplay.) New York: McDowell, Obolensky, 1960.

Bacall, Lauren. *Lauren Bacall by Myself.* New York: Knopf, 1979.

Forester, C. S. *The African Queen.* New York: The Modern Library (Random House), 1940.

Pratley, Gerald. *The Cinema of John Huston.* South Brunswick and New York: A. S. Barnes, 1977.

Viertel, Peter. *White Hunter, Black Heart.* Garden City: Doubleday, 1953.

PERIODICALS

Bacall, Lauren. "Hollywood vs. Africa." The Los Angeles *Mirror*, March 31, April 1, 2, 1952.

Huston, John. *"The African Queen." Theatre Arts,* February 1952.
Milne, Tom. "The Elusive John Collier." *Sight and Sound,* Spring 1976.

STUDIO AND ARCHIVAL COLLECTIONS

University of Southern California (Los Angeles): Warner Bros. Archives.
Twentieth Century-Fox Studios (Beverly Hills): Story Files.
Wisconsin Center for Film and Theater Research (Madison): United Artists Collection.

14. ALL TALKING! ALL SINGING! ALL DANCING!: SINGIN' IN THE RAIN (1952)

BOOKS

Comden, Betty, and Green, Adolph. *Singin' in the Rain* (includes screenplay). New York: Viking, 1972.
Fordin, Hugh. *The World of Entertainment.* Garden City: Doubleday, 1975.
Hirschhorn, Clive. *Gene Kelly.* Chicago: Henry Regnery, 1974.
Martin, Tony, and Charisse, Cyd. *The Two of Us.* New York: Mason/Charter, 1976.

PERIODICALS

Mariani, John. "Come on with the Rain." *Film Comment,* May–June 1978.

STUDIO AND ARCHIVAL COLLECTIONS

Metro-Goldwyn-Mayer Studios (Culver City): Legal and Script Files.
University of Southern California (Los Angeles): Arthur Freed Collection, Roger Edens Collection, MGM Script Collection.

15. DO NOT FORSAKE ME, OH MY DARLIN': HIGH NOON (1952)

BOOKS

Cawelti, John G. *The Six-Gun Mystique.* Bowling Green, Oh.: Bowling Green Popular Press, 1970.
Cogley, John. *Report on Blacklisting, Vol. 1.* The Fund for the Republic, 1956.
Garrett, George P.; Hardison, Jr., O. B.; and Gelfman, Jane R., eds. *Film Scripts Two* (includes *High Noon*). New York: Appleton-Century-Crofts, 1971.
Tiomkin, Dimitri, and Buranelli, Prosper. *Please Don't Hate Me.* Garden City, N.Y.: Doubleday, 1959.
Wald, Malvin, and Werner, Michael, eds. *Three Major Screenplays* (includes *High Noon*). New York: Globe, 1972.
Warshow, Robert. *The Immediate Experience.* Garden City, N.Y.: Doubleday, 1962.
Wister, Owen. *The Virginian.* New York: Macmillan, 1902.

PERIODICALS

Cooper, Texas Jim. "Tex Ritter." *Films in Review,* April 1970.
Cunningham, John. "The Tin Star." *Collier's,* December 6, 1947.

Giannetti, Louis. "Fred Zinnemann's *High Noon.*" *Film Criticism,* Winter 1976–1977.

Houston, Penelope, and Cavander, Kenneth. "Interview with Carl Foreman." *Sight and Sound,* Summer 1958.

Kramer, Stanley. "The Independent Producer." *Films in Review,* March 1951.

ORAL HISTORY

Pasquariello, Nicholas. *Floyd D. Crosby.* Beverly Hills: American Film Institute Oral History, 1973.

FILM CREDITS

FRANKENSTEIN   A Universal Picture

PRODUCER	Carl Laemmle, Jr.
ASSOCIATE PRODUCER	E. M. Asher
DIRECTOR	James Whale
BASED ON THE NOVEL BY	Mary Wollstonecraft Shelley
PLAY BY	Peggy Webling
ADAPTED BY	John L. Balderston
SCENARIO EDITOR	Richard Schayer
SCREENPLAY	Garrett Fort, Francis Edwards Faragoh
DIRECTOR OF PHOTOGRAPHY	Arthur Edeson
ART DIRECTOR	Charles D. Hall
SET DESIGN	Herman Rosse
MAKEUP	Jack Pierce
EDITOR	Clarence Kolster
71 MINUTES	

CAST

DR. HENRY FRANKENSTEIN	Colin Clive
ELIZABETH	Mae Clarke
VICTOR MORITZ	John Boles
THE MONSTER	Boris Karloff
DR. WALDMAN	Edward Van Sloan
FRITZ	Dwight Frye
BARON FRANKENSTEIN	Frederick Kerr
BURGOMASTER	Lionel Belmore
PEASANT FATHER	Michael Mark
MARIA	Marilyn Harris

LOST HORIZON   A Columbia Picture

PRODUCER-DIRECTOR	Frank Capra
BASED ON THE NOVEL BY	James Hilton

SCREENPLAY	Robert Riskin
DIRECTOR OF PHOTOGRAPHY	Joseph Walker
AERIAL PHOTOGRAPHY	Elmer Dyer
ART DIRECTOR	Stephen Goosson
COSTUMES	Ernst Dryden
EDITORS	Gene Havlick, Gene Milford
MUSIC	Dimitri Tiomkin
MUSIC DIRECTOR	Max Steiner
132 MINUTES	

CAST

ROBERT CONWAY	Ronald Colman
SONDRA	Jane Wyatt
GEORGE CONWAY	John Howard
MARIA	Margo
HENRY BARNARD	Thomas Mitchell
ALEXANDER P. LOVETT	Edward Everett Horton
GLORIA STONE	Isabel Jewell
CHANG	H. B. Warner
HIGH LAMA	Sam Jaffe
LORD GAINSFORD	Hugh Buckler
PRIME MINSTER	David Torrence
BANDIT LEADERS	Willie Fung, Victor Wong
LEADER OF PORTERS	Noble Johnson

SNOW WHITE AND THE SEVEN DWARFS   A Walt Disney Production

TECHNICOLOR

SUPERVISING DIRECTOR	David Hand
SEQUENCE DIRECTORS	Perce Pearce, Larry Morey, William Cottrell, Wilfred Jackson, Ben Sharpsteen
SUPERVISING ANIMATORS	Hamilton Luske, Vladimir Tytla, Fred Moore, Norman Ferguson
STORY ADAPTATION	Ted Sears, Otto Englander, Earl Hurd, Dorothy Ann Blank, Richard Creedon, Dick Rickard, Merrill De Maris, Webb Smith
CHARACTER DESIGNERS	Albert Hurter, Joe Grant
MUSIC	Frank Churchill, Leigh Harline, Paul Smith
LYRICS	Larry Morey
83 MINUTES	

VOICE CHARACTERIZATIONS

SNOW WHITE	Adriana Caselotti
PRINCE CHARMING	Harry Stockwell
THE QUEEN	Lucille LaVerne

MAGIC MIRROR	Moroni Olsen
SNEEZY	Billy Gilbert
SLEEPY AND GRUMPY	Pinto Colvig
HAPPY	Otis Harlan
BASHFUL	Scotty Mattraw
DOC	Roy Atwell
QUEEN'S HUNTSMAN	Stuart Buchanan
BIRD SOUNDS AND WARBLING	Marion Darlington
YODELING	The Fraunfelder Family

THE ADVENTURES OF ROBIN HOOD   A Warner Bros. A First National Picture

TECHNICOLOR

EXECUTIVE PRODUCER	Hal B. Wallis
ASSOCIATE PRODUCER	Henry Blanke
DIRECTORS	Michael Curtiz, William Keighley
SCREENPLAY	Norman Reilly Raine, Seton I. Miller
DIRECTORS OF PHOTOGRAPHY	Sol Polito, Tony Gaudio
TECHNICOLOR CONSULTANT	W. Howard Greene
ART DIRECTOR	Carl Jules Weyl
COSTUMES	Milo Anderson
EDITOR	Ralph Dawson
MUSIC	Erich Wolfgang Korngold
ARCHERY SUPERVISOR	Howard Hill
FENCING MASTER	Fred Cavens
102 MINUTES	

CAST

SIR ROBIN OF LOCKSLEY (ROBIN HOOD)	Errol Flynn
MAID MARIAN	Olivia de Havilland
SIR GUY OF GISBOURNE	Basil Rathbone
PRINCE JOHN	Claude Rains
WILL SCARLET	Patric Knowles
FRIAR TUCK	Eugene Pallette
LITTLE JOHN	Alan Hale
HIGH SHERIFF OF NOTTINGHAM	Melville Cooper
KING RICHARD	Ian Hunter
BESS	Una O'Connor
MUCH THE MILLER'S SON	Herbert Mundin
BISHOP OF THE BLACK CANONS	Montagu Love
SIR GEOFFREY	Robert Warwick
DICKON MALBETE	Harry Cording
CAPTAIN OF ARCHERS	Howard Hill
PROPRIETOR OF KENT ROAD TAVERN	Ivan Simpson

GUNGA DIN   An R.K.O. Radio Picture

EXECUTIVE PRODUCER	Pandro S. Berman
PRODUCER-DIRECTOR	George Stevens
SUGGESTED BY THE POEM BY	Rudyard Kipling
SCREENPLAY	Joel Sayre, Fred Guiol
STORY	Ben Hecht, Charles MacArthur
DIRECTOR OF PHOTOGRAPHY	Joseph H. August
ART DIRECTOR	Van Nest Polglase
ASSOCIATE	Perry Ferguson
SET DECORATOR	Darrell Silvera
EDITORS	Henry Berman, John Lockert
MUSIC	Alfred Newman
117 MINUTES	

CAST

CUTTER	Cary Grant
MACCHESNEY	Victor McLaglen
BALLANTINE	Douglas Fairbanks, Jr.
EMMY	Joan Fontaine
GUNGA DIN	Sam Jaffe
GURU	Eduardo Ciannelli
COLONEL	Montagu Love
MAJOR	Lumsden Hare
HIGGINBOTHAM	Robert Coote
GURU'S SON	Abner Biberman
STEBBINS	Cecil Kellaway
RUDYARD KIPLING	Reginald Sheffield

STAGECOACH   A Walter Wanger Production

PRODUCERS	John Ford, Walter Wanger
DIRECTOR	John Ford
BASED ON A SHORT STORY BY	Ernest Haycox
SCREENPLAY	Dudley Nichols
DIRECTOR OF PHOTOGRAPHY	Bert Glennon
SPECIAL PHOTOGRAPHY	Ray Binger
ART DIRECTOR	Alexander Toluboff
ASSOCIATE	Wiard B. Ihnen
COSTUMES	Walter Plunkett
EDITORIAL SUPERVISOR	Otho Lovering
EDITORS	Dorothy Spencer, Walter Reynolds
MUSIC ADAPTATION	Richard Hageman, W. Franke Harling, John Leipold, Leo Shuken, Gerard
96 MINUTES	Carbonara

CAST

THE RINGO KID	John Wayne
DALLAS	Claire Trevor
DOC BOONE	Thomas Mitchell
BUCK	Andy Devine
CURLY WILCOX	George Bancroft
MR. PEACOCK	Donald Meek
LUCY MALLORY	Louise Platt
HATFIELD	John Carradine
GATEWOOD	Berton Churchill
LT. BLANCHARD	Tim Holt
CHRIS	Chris Martin
YAKIMA	Elvira Rios
BILLY PICKETT	Francis Ford
LUKE PLUMMER	John Rickson
IKE PLUMMER	Vester Pegg
HANK PLUMMER	Tom Tyler
BARTENDER	Jack Pennick
CAPTAIN SIMMONS	Bryant Washburn
LUCY'S BABY	Mary Kathleen Walker
GERONIMO	Chief White Horse

THE GRAPES OF WRATH   A Twentieth Century-Fox Picture

PRODUCER	Darryl F. Zanuck
ASSOCIATE PRODUCER-SCREENPLAY	Nunnally Johnson
DIRECTOR	John Ford
BASED ON THE NOVEL BY	John Steinbeck
DIRECTOR OF PHOTOGRAPHY	Gregg Toland
ART DIRECTORS	Richard Day, Mark Lee Kirk
SET DECORATOR	Thomas Little
MUSIC	Alfred Newman
EDITOR	Robert Simpson
129 MINUTES	

CAST

TOM	Henry Fonda
MA	Jane Darwell
PA	Russell Simpson
GRAMPA	Charley Grapewin
GRANMA	Zeffie Tilbury
UNCLE JOHN	Frank Darien
CASY	John Carradine
MULEY	John Qualen
NOAH	Frank Sully

AL	O. Z. Whitehead
ROSE OF SHARON	Dorris Bowdon
CONNIE	Eddie Quillan
RUTHIE	Shirley Mills
WINFIELD	Darryl Hickman
CARETAKER	Grant Mitchell
POLICEMAN	Ward Bond

THE MALTESE FALCON   A Warner Bros.–First National Picture

EXECUTIVE PRODUCER	Hal B. Wallis
ASSOCIATE PRODUCER	Henry Blanke
DIRECTOR	John Huston
BASED ON THE NOVEL BY	Dashiell Hammett
SCREENPLAY	John Huston
DIRECTOR OF PHOTOGRAPHY	Arthur Edeson
ART DIRECTOR	Robert Haas
GOWNS	Orry-Kelly
EDITOR	Thomas Richards
MUSIC	Adolph Deutsch

100 MINUTES

CAST

SAM SPADE	Humphrey Bogart
BRIGID O'SHAUGHNESSY	Mary Astor
IVA ARCHER	Gladys George
JOEL CAIRO	Peter Lorre
LIEUTENANT DUNDY	Barton MacLane
EFFIE PERINE	Lee Patrick
CASPER GUTMAN	Sydney Greenstreet
DETECTIVE TOM POLHAUS	Ward Bond
MILES ARCHER	Jerome Cowan
WILMER COOK	Elisha Cook, Jr.
LUKE	James Burke
FRANK	Murray Alper
DISTRICT ATTORNEY BRYAN	John Hamilton
MATE OF THE *La Paloma*	Emory Parnell
CAPTAIN JACOBI	Walter Huston

CASABLANCA   A Warner Bros.–First National Picture

PRODUCER	Hal B. Wallis
DIRECTOR	Michael Curtiz
BASED ON A PLAY BY	Murray Burnett, Joan Alison
SCREENPLAY	Julius J. Epstein, Philip G. Epstein, Howard Koch

DIRECTOR OF PHOTOGRAPHY	Arthur Edeson
ART DIRECTOR	Carl Jules Weyl
SET DECORATOR	George James Hopkins
GOWNS	Orry-Kelly
EDITOR	Owen Marks
MUSIC	Max Steiner

SONGS: "As Time Goes By" by Herman Hupfeld
"Knock on Wood" by M. K. Jerome and Jack Scholl

102 MINUTES

CAST

RICK	Humphrey Bogart
ILSA	Ingrid Bergman
VICTOR LASZLO	Paul Henreid
CAPTAIN LOUIS RENAULT	Claude Rains
MAJOR STRASSER	Conrad Veidt
SENOR FARRARI	Sydney Greenstreet
UGARTE	Peter Lorre
CARL	S. Z. Sakall
YVONNE	Madeleine LeBeau
SAM	Dooley Wilson
ANNINA BRANDEL	Joy Page
BERGER	John Qualen
SASCHA	Leonid Kinsky
JAN BRANDEL	Helmut Dantine
PICKPOCKET	Curt Bois
CROUPIER	Marcel Dalio
SINGER	Corinna Mura
MR. LEUCHTAG	Ludwig Stossel
MRS. LEUCHTAG	Ilka Gruning
ITALIAN OFFICER TONELLI	Charles La Torre
ARAB VENDOR	Frank Puglia
ABDUL	Dan Seymour

LAURA   A Twentieth Century-Fox Picture

PRODUCER-DIRECTOR	Otto Preminger
BASED ON THE NOVEL BY	Vera Caspary
SCREENPLAY	Jay Dratler, Samuel Hoffenstein, Betty Reinhardt
DIRECTOR OF PHOTOGRAPHY	Joseph La Shelle
ART DIRECTORS	Lyle R. Wheeler, Leland Fuller
SET DECORATORS	Thomas Little, Fred S. Fox
WARDROBE DESIGNER	Bonnie Cashin
EDITOR	Louis R. Loeffler
MUSIC	David Raksin

88 MINUTES

CAST

LAURA HUNT	Gene Tierney
MARK McPHERSON	Dana Andrews
WALDO LYDECKER	Clifton Webb
SHELBY CARPENTER	Vincent Price
ANNE TREADWELL	Judith Anderson
BESSIE CLARY	Dorothy Adams
McAVITY	James Flavin
BULLITT	Clyde Fillmore

ALL ABOUT EVE   A Twentieth Century-Fox Picture

PRODUCER	Darryl F. Zanuck
DIRECTOR-SCREENPLAY	Joseph L. Mankiewicz
BASED ON A STORY BY	Mary Orr
DIRECTOR OF PHOTOGRAPHY	Milton Krasner
ART DIRECTORS	Lyle Wheeler, George W. Davis
SET DECORATORS	Thomas Little, Walter M. Scott
COSTUMES	Charles LeMaire; Edith Head (for Bette Davis)
EDITOR	Barbara McLean
MUSIC	Alfred Newman
138 MINUTES	

CAST

MARGO CHANNING	Bette Davis
EVE HARRINGTON	Anne Baxter
ADDISON De WITT	George Sanders
BILL SAMPSON	Gary Merrill
KAREN RICHARDS	Celeste Holm
LLOYD RICHARDS	Hugh Marlowe
MAX FABIAN	Gregory Ratoff
BIRDIE COONAN	Thelma Ritter
MISS CASWELL	Marilyn Monroe
PHOEBE	Barbara Bates
ELDERLY ACTOR	Walter Hampden
EVE'S FRIEND	Randy Stuart

A STREETCAR NAMED DESIRE A Charles K. Feldman Group Production

PRODUCER	Charles K. Feldman
DIRECTOR	Elia Kazan
BASED ON THE PLAY BY	Tennessee Williams
SCREENPLAY	Tennessee Williams

ADAPTATION	Oscar Saul
DIRECTOR OF PHOTOGRAPHY	Harry Stradling
ART DIRECTOR	Richard Day
SET DECORATOR	George James Hopkins
COSTUMES	Lucinda Ballard
EDITOR	David Weisbart
MUSIC	Alex North
122 MINUTES	

CAST

BLANCHE DUBOIS	Vivien Leigh
STANLEY KOWALSKI	Marlon Brando
STELLA KOWALSKI	Kim Hunter
MITCH	Karl Malden
STEVE	Rudy Bond
PABLO	Nick Dennis
EUNICE	Peg Hillias
COLLECTOR	Wright King
DOCTOR	Richard Garrick
MATRON	Ann Dere
MEXICAN WOMAN	Edna Thomas
SAILOR	Mickey Kuhn
STREET VENDOR	Chester Jones
NEGRO WOMAN	Marietta Canty

THE AFRICAN QUEEN   A Horizon-Romulus Production

TECHNICOLOR

PRODUCER	S. P. Eagle (Sam Spiegel)
DIRECTOR	John Huston
BASED ON THE NOVEL BY	C. S. Forester
SCREENPLAY	James Agee, John Huston
DIRECTOR OF PHOTOGRAPHY	Jack Cardiff
SECOND UNIT PHOTOGRAPHY	Ted Scaife
ART DIRECTOR	Wilfred Shingleton
ASSOCIATE	John Hoesli
COSTUMES	Connie De Pinna; Doris Langley Moore (for Katharine Hepburn)
SPECIAL EFFECTS	Cliff Richardson
EDITOR	Ralph Kemplen
MUSIC	Allan Gray
105 MINUTES	

CAST

CHARLIE ALLNUTT	Humphrey Bogart
ROSE SAYER	Katharine Hepburn

REV. SAMUEL SAYER	Robert Morely
CAPTAIN OF THE *Louisa*	Peter Bull
FIRST OFFICER (*Louisa*)	Theodore Bikel
SECOND OFFICER (*Louisa*)	Walter Gotell
PETTY OFFICER (*Louisa*)	Gerald Onn
FIRST OFFICER (*Shona*)	Peter Swanwick
SECOND OFFICER (*Shona*)	Richard Marner

SINGIN' IN THE RAIN   A Metro-Goldwyn-Mayer Picture

TECHNICOLOR

PRODUCER	Arthur Freed
ASSOCIATE PRODUCER	Roger Edens
DIRECTORS	Gene Kelly, Stanley Donen
CHOREOGRAPHY	Gene Kelly, Stanley Donen
SCREENPLAY	Betty Comden, Adolph Green
LYRICS	Arthur Freed
MUSIC	Nacio Herb Brown
MUSICAL DIRECTOR	Lennie Hayton
ORCHESTRATIONS	Conrad Salinger, Wally Heglin, Skip Martin
VOCAL ARRANGEMENTS	Jeff Alexander
DIRECTOR OF PHOTOGRAPHY	Harold Rosson
ART DIRECTORS	Cedric Gibbons, Randall Duell
SET DECORATION	Edwin B. Wallis, Jacques Mapes
COSTUMES	Walter Plunkett
HAIR STYLES	Sydney Guilaroff
EDITOR	Adrienne Fazan
103 MINUTES	

CAST

DON LOCKWOOD	Gene Kelly
COSMO BROWN	Donald O'Connor
KATHY SELDEN	Debbie Reynolds
LINA LAMONT	Jean Hagen
R. F. SIMPSON	Millard Mitchell
ZELDA ZANDERS	Rita Moreno
ROSCOE DEXTER	Douglas Fowley
DANCER	Cyd Charisse
DORA BAILEY	Madge Blake
ROD	King Donovan
PHOEBE DINSMORE	Kathleen Freeman
DICTION COACH	Bobby Watson
ASSISTANT DIRECTOR	Tommy Farrell
"BEAUTIFUL GIRL" SINGER	Jimmie Thompson

RUDY VALLEE IMPERSONATOR	Wilson Wood
VILLAIN, "DUELING CAVALIER" AND "BROADWAY RHYTHM"	Carl Milletaire
TALKING PICTURE DEMONSTRATOR	Julius Tannen

HIGH NOON   A Stanley Kramer Production

PRODUCER	Stanley Kramer
ASSOCIATE PRODUCER	Carl Foreman
DIRECTOR	Fred Zinnemann
BASED ON A STORY BY	John W. Cunningham
SCREENPLAY	Carl Foreman
DIRECTOR OF PHOTOGRAPHY	Floyd Crosby
PRODUCTION DESIGNER	Rudolph Sternad
SET DECORATOR	Emmett Emerson
EDITOR	Elmo Williams
MUSIC	Dimitri Tiomkin
LYRICS	Ned Washington
SINGER OF BALLAD	Tex Ritter
85 MINUTES	

CAST

WILL KANE	Gary Cooper
JONAS HENDERSON	Thomas Mitchell
HARVEY PELL	Lloyd Bridges
HELEN RAMIREZ	Katy Jurado
AMY KANE	Grace Kelly
PERCY METTRICK	Otto Kruger
MARTIN HOWE	Lon Chaney
WILLIAM FULLER	Harry Morgan
FRANK MILLER	Ian MacDonald
MILDRED FULLER	Eve McVeagh
COOPER	Harry Shannon
JACK COLBY	Lee Van Cleef
JAMES PIERCE	Bob Wilke
BEN MILLER	Sheb Wooley
BAKER	James Millican
MRS. SIMPSON	Virginia Christine
BARTENDER	Lucien Prival
HOTEL CLERK	Howland Chamberlin
CHARLIE	Jack Elam
TRUMBULL	John Doucette
KIBBEE	Dick Elliott
STATION MASTER	Ted Stanhope
BARBER	William Phillips
MINISTER	Morgan Farley

16MM FILM RENTAL SOURCES

Frankenstein: Twyman, Swank, Clem Williams
Lost Horizon: Audio Brandon, Kit Parker, Twyman, Swank, Clem Williams
Snow White and the Seven Dwarfs: not available
The Adventures of Robin Hood: United Artists Entertainment
Gunga Din: Films Inc.
Stagecoach: Audio Brandon, Budget, Kit Parker, Twyman, Films Inc., EmGee, Clem Williams
The Grapes of Wrath: Films Inc.
The Maltese Falcon: United Artists Entertainment
Casablanca: United Artists Entertainment
Laura: Films Inc.
All About Eve: Films Inc.
A Streetcar Named Desire: United Artists Entertainment
The African Queen: Audio Brandon, Budget, Twyman, Swank, Clem Williams
Singin' in the Rain: Films Inc.
High Noon: Audio Brandon, Budget, Kit Parker, Twyman, Clem Williams

Audio Brandon Films (multiple locations)
34 MacQuesten Parkway So.
Mount Vernon, NY 10550
outside N.Y.: 800/431-1994, in NY: 800/742-1889

Budget Films
4590 Santa Monica Blvd.
Los Angeles, CA 90029
213/660-0187

EmGee Film Library
6924 Canby Ave. Suite 103
Reseda, CA 91335
213/981-5506

Films Incorporated (multiple locations)
440 Park Ave. South
New York, New York 10016
outside N.Y.: 800/223-6246, in NY: 212/889-7910

Kit Parker Films
Carmel Valley, CA 93924
outside Ca.: 800/682-4841, in CA 800/682-4841

Swank Motion Pictures
201 S. Jefferson Ave.
St. Louis, MO 63166
(314) 534-6300

Twyman Films Inc.
4700 Wadsworth Road
Box 605
Dayton, OH 45401
outside Oh.: 800/543-9594, in OH: 513/276-5941

United Artists Entertainment
729 Seventh Ave.
New York, NY 10019
212/575-4715, outside N.Y.: 800/223-0933

Clem Williams Films Inc. (multiple locations)
5424 West North Ave.
Chicago, IL 60639
312/637-3322

Index